Genders and Sexualities in the Social Sciences

Series Editors
V. Robinson
Centre for Women's Studies
University of York
York, UK

D. Richardson
Department of Sociology
Newcastle University
Newcastle upon Tyne, UK

The study of gender and sexuality has developed dramatically over recent years, with a changing theoretical landscape that has seen innovative work emerge on identity, the body and embodiment, queer theory, technology, space, and the concept of gender itself. There has been an increasing focus on sexuality and new theorizing on masculinities. This exciting series will take account of these developments, emphasizing new, original work that engages both theoretically and empirically with the themes of gender, sexuality, and, crucially, their intersections, to set a new, vibrant and contemporary international agenda for research in this area.

Shuang Qiu

Gender and Family Practices

Living Apart Together Relationships in China

palgrave
macmillan

Shuang Qiu
School of Social, Political and Global Studies
Keele University
Keele, UK

ISSN 2947-8782　　　　　　　ISSN 2947-8790　(electronic)
Genders and Sexualities in the Social Sciences
ISBN 978-3-031-17249-6　　　ISBN 978-3-031-17250-2　(eBook)
https://doi.org/10.1007/978-3-031-17250-2

© The Editor(s) (if applicable) and The Author(s), under exclusive licence to Springer Nature Switzerland AG 2022
This work is subject to copyright. All rights are solely and exclusively licensed by the Publisher, whether the whole or part of the material is concerned, specifically the rights of translation, reprinting, reuse of illustrations, recitation, broadcasting, reproduction on microfilms or in any other physical way, and transmission or information storage and retrieval, electronic adaptation, computer software, or by similar or dissimilar methodology now known or hereafter developed.
The use of general descriptive names, registered names, trademarks, service marks, etc. in this publication does not imply, even in the absence of a specific statement, that such names are exempt from the relevant protective laws and regulations and therefore free for general use.
The publisher, the authors and the editors are safe to assume that the advice and information in this book are believed to be true and accurate at the date of publication. Neither the publisher nor the authors or the editors give a warranty, expressed or implied, with respect to the material contained herein or for any errors or omissions that may have been made. The publisher remains neutral with regard to jurisdictional claims in published maps and institutional affiliations.

Cover illustration: Danita Delimont Creative / Alamy Stock Photo

This Palgrave Macmillan imprint is published by the registered company Springer Nature Switzerland AG.
The registered company address is: Gewerbestrasse 11, 6330 Cham, Switzerland

This book is dedicated to my beloved parents.

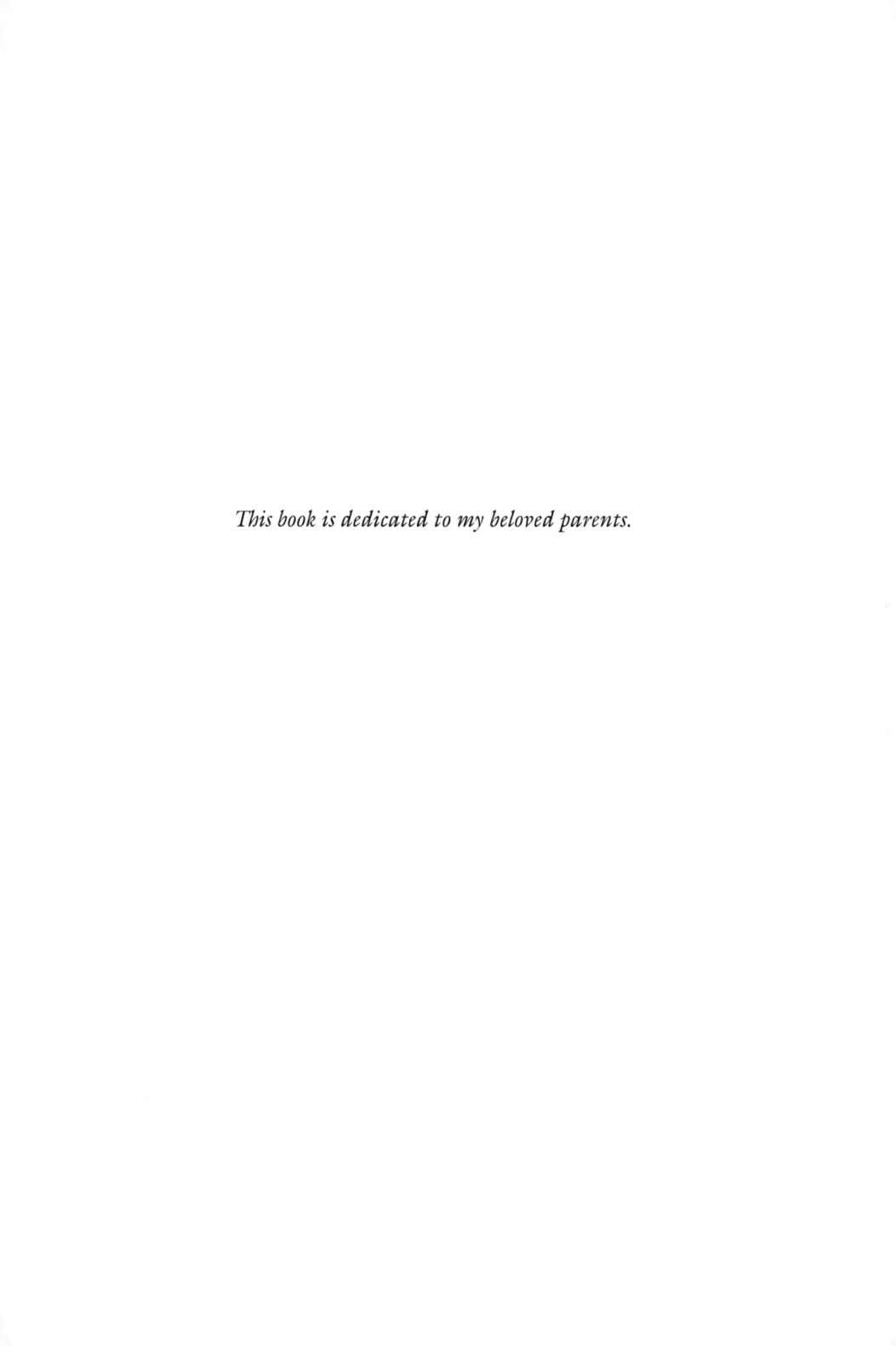

Acknowledgements

I am deeply grateful for many people who helped me in different ways at different times in completing this book. First of all, my thanks go to all the research participants who have genuinely shared their stories and experiences with me. We were strangers before but because of this research project, we sat together for hours and have crossed paths ever since. They made my fieldwork over the summer in China unforgettable and enjoyable.

I would like to particularly thank Professor Victoria Robinson for her continuous support, encouragement, and guidance at every stage of this project. Countless meetings and conversations about my research have inspired me to pursue an academic life. In my heart, she was not just my supervisor, as she went far beyond what was required. We went to Niagara Falls in Canada and spent a wonderful time together during the time I gave a presentation at a conference in Toronto. She came to my wedding in the UK, which made my big day become even more special and unforgettable. I also offer my sincere gratitude to my previous supervisor, Professor Stevi Jackson, for her intellectual inspiration, especially at the early stage of my research, and the excellent example she has set as a dedicated scholar, devoted researcher, and responsible professor. I also owe an enormous debt of gratitude to Dr Julia Carter, Dr Rachel Alsop, and Professor Vanessa May for their generous encouragement and constructive comments. My thanks also go to colleagues at the University of York who have supported me emotionally and made me feel not alone.

This research project has gained financial support from the Great Britain–China Educational Trust (GBCET), for which I am immensely thankful. I also acknowledge the patience and assistance of the Palgrave Macmillan editorial team for bringing this book to fruition.

Finally, I would like to give my heartfelt thanks to my beloved parents. Their endless love, selfless devotion, and unreserved support are the most important motivation that keeps me going. I am blessed to be their only daughter and have always felt loved although they were thousands of miles away. Dr Zeyu Fu is a good listener, reliable friend, and caring husband. He has witnessed the development of this book and I really appreciated his accompaniment and understanding.

It should be noted that some texts in this book have already been published in peer-reviewed journals and reused with permission by the following:

Qiu, S. (2020). Chinese 'study mothers' in living apart together (LAT) relationships: Educational migration, family practices, and gender roles. *Sociological Research Online*, 25(3), 405–420. https://doi.org/10.1177/1360780419871574

Qiu, S. (2022a). Family practices in non-cohabiting intimate relationships in China: Doing mobile intimacy, emotion and intergenerational caring practices. *Families, Relationships and Societies*, 11(2), 175–191. https://doi.org/10.1332/204674321X16468493162777

Qiu, S. (2022b). Negotiating intimacy and family at distance: Living apart together relationships in China. In S. Quaid, C. Hugman and A. Wilcock (Eds.), *Negotiating families and personal lives in the 21st century* (pp. 77–92). Routledge. https://doi.org/10.4324/9781003039433

Contents

1 Understanding 'Living Apart Together' (LAT) Relationships — 1

2 Detraditionalisation and Retraditionalisation of Family Lives: Gender, Marriage and Intimacy — 31

3 Reconsidered Agency: Why Do People Live Apart? — 65

4 Doing Family at a Distance: How Different Are LAT Relationships to 'Conventional' Partnerships? — 97

5 Doing Intimacy While Being Apart: Practices of Mobile Intimacy, Emotion and Filial Piety — 131

6 Conclusion — 169

Appendices — 177

Index — 181

About the Author

Shuang Qiu is a lecturer in Sociology based in the School of Social, Political and Global Studies at Keele University. She obtained her PhD in Women's Studies from the University of York and her research interests lie in the field of sociology of the family, intimacy, gender and sexualities, agency, emotion, migration, care, and East Asian studies. She has published several articles in peer-reviewed journals such as *Sociological Research Online* and *Families, Relationships, and Societies.*

List of Tables

Table 2.1	Marriage patterns in China, Hong Kong, Japan and South Korea	51
Table 4.1	Mini-biographies of six 'study mothers'	100
Table A.1	List of the socio-demographics of 39 participants	178

CHAPTER 1

Understanding 'Living Apart Together' (LAT) Relationships

INTRODUCTION

Understanding the impact of social change on personal relationships and family lives has become one of the key concerns of sociology. China's dramatic social and economic transformation over the past few decades has brought about diverse effects on different aspects of people's personal relationships and family lives. In contemporary Chinese society there is a growing diversity in family patterns accompanied by a marked decline in traditional pre-existing structures in relation to patriarchal and patrilocal family systems. Non-traditional partnerships and living arrangements, such as 'living apart together' (LAT) relationships (where committed couples live in separate households while maintaining their intimate relationships), are not uncommon in China. For example, the family pattern of out-migration of men and stay-behind married women with children (if any), as a result of rural-to-urban labour mobility under the process of urbanisation and modernisation, has been documented in migration literature (Fan, 2003). Due to increased educational attainment, young people stay for a longer time in education and college education can delay marriage for both men and women in China (Ji & Yeung, 2014). This leads to a considerable number of people living separately from their partner because of education and/or job locations.

© The Author(s), under exclusive license to Springer Nature Switzerland AG 2022
S. Qiu, *Gender and Family Practices*, Genders and Sexualities in the Social Sciences, https://doi.org/10.1007/978-3-031-17250-2_1

Couples in non-cohabiting intimate relationships have also gained scholarly attention in the West, such as commuter marriages (Gerstel & Gross, 1984), weekend couples (Kim, 2001) and long-distance relationships (Holmes, 2006). A considerable body of research has also shown a social tendency towards what has been termed the Second Demographic Transition, manifested in the growing rates of non-traditional family relationships globally over time. For example, previous Western studies have shown that around two-and-a-half million people in the United States are relating at a distance (Guldner, 2003). They live apart for a variety of reasons, such as work opportunities, care responsibilities and/or a desire for autonomy (Holmes, 2006; Levin, 2004). Existing literature suggests that this 'unusual' partnership challenges our taken-for-granted assumption that couples should live together, and that intimacy always entails physical proximity. Some theorists argue that these diverse forms of relationships have served to expedite the dissolution of the stability of conventional social bonds and disintegration of traditional notions of family, leading to a transformation of intimacy as a part of the de-traditionalisation of social life (Beck & Beck-Gernsheim, 2005; Giddens, 1992).

However, the circumstances of LAT vary with people's life stages and social circumstances. The Chinese cultural framework, combining an emerging emphasis on autonomy and personal choice as a response to the profound social transformations in relation to long-standing traditional values on gender roles and family obligations, provides a unique opportunity to explore how Chinese people construct family life and experience conjugal intimacy. Therefore, the focus of this book is to examine how gender and heterosexuality structure the lived experiences of people in non-conventional partnerships in present-day Chinese society. Through looking at LAT relationships (LATs), my hope is that this research makes a timely and valuable contribution to changing family practices and intimacy in contemporary China by giving a voice primarily to women's lived experiences in constructing their family lives and making sense of any subsequent changes in their personal relationships. Notably, though the focus in the study is on women participants, men's views will also be used to contradict and further explore women's perspectives, especially when it comes to gendered emotional work in a given context.

To this end, I start this chapter by demonstrating what an LAT relationship is and the rationale behind researching this 'unconventional' intimate partnership in China. This is then followed by a discussion of previous research on LAT mainly based on Western contexts. Given that there is a knowledge gap on what we know about LAT in China, these findings based on Western contexts play an important role in exploring, in my later data-led chapters in this book, whether and how much difference exists between LAT in the Western context and the Chinese context, as many scholars argue that the Western culture of individualism has transformed how Chinese people construct and understand their own family life and intimate relationships. I will then shift my focus to explain how I design this research in a feminist way as well as my own reflection on my epistemological and methodological engagement with Chinese LAT people. Finally, I conclude this chapter by outlining an overview of the book.

What Is an LAT Relationship and Why Does It Matter?

The phrase 'living apart together' and its acronym, 'LAT', was first used by a Dutch journalist, Michel Berkiel, who wrote an article about it in the *Haagse Post* in the Netherlands in 1978 (Levin, 2004). Since then, LAT has gained visibility in volume and become accepted in the field of social science study. Unfortunately, to date, it remains difficult to establish a standard definition for the term 'living apart together relationships' (LATs), given that scholars interpret and measure LATs differently. According to Levin and Trost (1999: 281), LAT refers to 'a couple which does not share the same household; both of them live in their own households, in which other persons might also live'. This relationship implies that people do not necessary live in the same household in order to be seen as couples (Levin, 2004). In addition, the term includes both married and non-married couples, and refers to both heterosexual and same-sex couples. However, some scholars exclude married people from LATs (Haskey, 2005; Strohm et al., 2009). In his research, Haskey (2005) stresses that LAT is a monogamous partnership in nature and reserved for non-married couples living in separate households. This research draws on the general agreement on the definition of LAT, which involves two heterosexual individuals living in separate households while maintaining an intimate and committed couple relationship (Duncan et al., 2014).

Literature shows that most studies on LATs have predominantly been carried out within in the context of Western Europe and North America, such as Sweden (Borell & Karlsson, 2003; Evertsson & Nyman, 2013; Levin, 2004), Britain (Carter et al., 2016; Coulter & Hu, 2017; Duncan,

2015; Ermisch & Seidler, 2009; Haskey, 2005; Haskey & Lewis, 2006), France (Régnier-Loilier et al., 2009), Canada (Kobayashi et al., 2017; Milan & Peters, 2003; Turcotte, 2013) and the USA (Strohm et al., 2009).[1] In Australia, research on LATs has also been observed (Reimondos et al., 2011; Upton-Davis, 2015). Sweden was one of the first European countries to study LATs (Levin & Trost, 1999). According to the 1993 Omnibus survey in Sweden, 4% of respondents considered themselves to be living in LATs. This increased to 14% of the respondents who were neither married nor cohabiting in 2001 (Levin, 2004). In Britain, there were no specific analyses of LATs until Haskey (2005), who drew on the 2002 Omnibus Survey to examine whether LATs really exist in Britain. The results show that the phenomenon of having a regular intimate partner who lives elsewhere does exist—around two million men and women aged 16–59 years were in LATs in Britain, the same number as were co-residentially cohabiting. More recent empirical research has been further developed by Simon Duncan and his colleagues, who point out that around 10% of the population live apart from their partner in Britain (Duncan & Phillips, 2010, 2011). In line with Duncan and Phillips' finding, Coulter and Hu (2017) provide a statistical analysis that 9% of adults were in LATs in the UK. Regarding the prevalence of LATs in Canada, in 2011, 7.4% of people aged 20 and over were single, widowed or divorced but were in an intimate relationship with someone living elsewhere, which are known as LATs (Turcotte, 2013). A recent study shows that nearly one-and-a-half million people aged 25–64 in Canada were reported to be in an LAT relationship in 2017.[2]

Although statistics show that the number of people who live apart from their partner is small in relative terms, the increasing body of research on LATs indicates that being a couple without sharing the same household has been a steadily growing phenomenon in many countries in recent years. With the attempts to explain the possible reasons for the emergence of new forms of relating and living arrangements, Levin (2004) suggests that several factors may help to make LATs more visible in many Western countries. The first factor is related to mortality rates. Previously, high rates of early mortality, to some extent, meant the dissolution of marriage.

---

[1] For an overview of LATs between European countries, see Ayuso (2019), Bawin-Legros and Gauthier (2001), Liefbroer et al. (2015) and Stoilova et al. (2014).

[2] Available at: https://www150.statcan.gc.ca/n1/daily-quotidien/190220/dq190220d-eng.htm.

However, the lower the mortality rate, the greater the likelihood for a person to live longer, experience separation from a marital cohabitation, and thus, the greater likelihood for the person to enter into an LAT relationship, or some other new relationship.

In addition, labour-market opportunities, along with women's participation in the workforce (Holmes, 2006), have also contributed to the increase in LATs. This is in contrast to the past, when women were more likely to follow their partners and find a new job where they relocated. It is now difficult to do so since labour markets have become less localised and more globalised. Economic independence and self-development also play a more important role than previously in women's lives. Due to the development of information and communication technologies (ICTs), people now find it easier to generate and maintain relationships with others at a distance. A central aspect of this research will provide a much-needed and previously lacking account regarding practices of mobile intimacy through ICT in LATs, specifically in the Chinese context, through analysis of my data in Chap. 5.

In the context of China, the first descriptive study on married couples living apart was conducted based on survey data to evaluate the effect of job-related marital separation on marital quality (Abbott et al., 1993). During the period of China's planned economy, jobs were once assigned by the government to guarantee people's right to work and to balance regional development.[3] It was estimated that about fifty million Chinese people had their spouse living somewhere else as a result of job allocation (Bonavia, 1982). However, to the best of my knowledge, little is known about how people arrange and experience their everyday family life and couple intimacy while being apart (Hare-Mustin & Hare, 1986). This is partly because people at that time were reluctant to talk about their intimate relationships publicly due to the sensitive nature of this topic. In addition, official figures often do not allow us to 'distinguish the different types of one-person households by demographic or socioeconomic characteristics' (Yeung and Cheung, 2015: 1102). Lacking a standard definition of LATs also makes it hard for social researchers and policymakers to collect statistical data in China, especially given its geographical size.

Since the 1980s, China has undergone dramatic social changes, leading to rapid economic growth, increased education attainment and completion of a demographic transition (Xie, 2011). These social transformations

---

[3] For more discussion about job assignments, see Bian (1994).

have diverse effects on different aspects of people's personal relationships and family lives. For example, there are a growing number of people living separately from their partner due to education and/or job locations and college education this can delay marriage for both men and women in China (Ji & Yeung, 2014). It is worth noting that China's economic decentralisation due to its transition from a socialist to a market-oriented economy has led to the replacement of job assignment by the government with the labour market (Hoffman, 2008; Tsui & Rich, 2002). This has given rise to an unprecedented rural-to-urban labour migration through the processes of urbanisation and modernisation (Peng, 2011), with about one in five being among a 'floating population'.[4] Statistics show that among the 0.29 billion migrant workers, 78% of them are married and over 65% of them are men.[5] Recent academic work shows that in most cases they are sole migrants who are separated from their spouse, children and parents in the countryside (Fan et al., 2011; Wu et al., 2020). This gendered family mobility pattern (out-migration of men and stay-behind married women with children, if any) has, in some respects, reinforced the prescribed social norms on gender roles, where women's contribution to family life is significantly shaped by their family roles (Chang et al., 2011; Chen, 2005; Fan, 2003; Fan & Li, 2020; He & Gober, 2003; Qiu, 2022).

Although previous quantitative studies draw our attention to split households in China, the changing meanings and practices of family life have not yet been systematically researched. This is partly because living together as a couple to establish a family remains the ideal and most socially accepted family arrangement in a contemporary Chinese context. As a result, non-conventional forms of family living have rarely been examined by 'family sociologists'. In addition, lacking a standard definition of what an LAT relationship is and the attendant difficulty in identifying LATs if they happen for short periods of time also cause the knowledge gap regarding this non-cohabiting partnership. Therefore, issues around why Chinese people end up living separately from their partner and how they negotiate their gender roles and identity still lack sufficient attention. More importantly, I am interested in exploring how practices of family and

---

[4] "Floating population" refers to migrants who stay in places different from their hukou (household registration) locations, the vast majority of whom are rural–urban migrants (NHFPC, 2012, 2016).
[5] Available at: http://www.stats.gov.cn/ztjc/ztfx/ggkf40n/201809/t20180918_1623598.html.

intimacy in non-conventional partnerships are worthy of sociology examination. In an effort to unpack these questions, this research represents one of the first in-depth qualitative examinations of LATs in a changing Chinese society. Before mapping out a feminist methodological framework for this study and the research process, I will provide a brief overview of existing literature on LATs in the Western context.

Who Lives Apart from Their Partner and Why?

Several Western studies have examined whether LATs are different demographically and socially to married, cohabiting and single people. Generally, people from all age groups and with varied socio-economic backgrounds can be found in LATs (Duncan & Phillips, 2010; Haskey & Lewis, 2006; Roseneil, 2006). In terms of age, LATs as a whole are over-represented among the younger age group. One plausible explanation for LATs in the younger age groups is that they are in the early stages of their relationship (Duncan et al., 2013). Drawing on the ONS Omnibus survey—the first survey to investigate LATs in Britain—the results show that 47% of people under 25 are reported to have a partner who lives elsewhere, accounting for the highest proportion in the overall age profile (Ermisch & Seidler, 2009; Haskey, 2005). Similarly, data from France reveal that the probability of being in an LAT decreases with age, as the highest prevalence of LATs for both men (72%) and women (68%) is in the age group of under 25s, followed by 38% of men and 33% women between the ages of 25 and 29 (Régnier-Loilier et al., 2009). For people aged over 60, only 4% are reported to have non-residential relationships. Although only a small proportion of elderly people engage in LATs after divorce or widowhood, a slight increase in couples living separately was observed. In Britain, 13% of respondents between the ages of 55 and 64 are in LATs (Duncan & Phillips, 2008). In Canada, the number of elderly people who live separately from their partner has increased slightly compared to 2001, although only 2% of those aged 60 years and over were involved in an LAT relationship in 2011 (Turcotte, 2013). Therefore, it could be generalised that the probability of being in an LAT relationship is closely associated with age and the different stages of the relationship.

Regarding education and socio-economic status, the UK data reveal little difference across socio-economic status as people with either professional or manual occupations can all be found in LATs (Duncan & Phillips, 2010). However, Haskey and Lewis' (Haskey & Lewis, 2006) analysis, based on both quantitative and qualitative data, indicate an interesting comparison between those who live apart from their partner and those who are in co-residential relationships. Again, it is a matter of degree. Compared to those who are currently living with their spouse in Britain, people in LATs aged 25–44 seem to be more likely to have high levels of education and relatively high-status occupations. The positive relation between the probability of being in an LAT relationship and educational background is also found in the US data (Strohm et al., 2009), with people in LATs, regardless of gender, having more schooling. This finding also applies to European countries, where people with higher education who have grown-up children or no children are more likely to be in LATs than in a marital or cohabiting union (Ermisch & Seidler, 2009; Liefbroer et al., 2015; Reimondos et al., 2011). An attempt to explain this was made by Holmes (2004a), who investigated dual-career, dual-household academic couples based on the assumption that, if individualisation processes are extending to women, this will be most obvious amongst elites. She argues that women's growing economic resources, with flexible working patterns, have freed them from fixed obligations, while the effects of individualisation for women on their intimate relationships are still limited.

With regards to ethnicity, there is no clear message about whether people in LATs are more heterogamous regarding this variable than those in other relationships. However, the US data indicate that women in LATs are more ethnically diverse than those in either marriage or cohabiting relationships (Strohm et al., 2009).

According to previous Western studies on LATs, the reasons for living apart from partners are diverse and are always subject to variations. Drawing on in-depth interviews with 100 people aged between 20 and 80 in Norway and Sweden, Levin (2004) summarises that people who live apart together can be divided into two subgroups. One subgroup consists of those who would not wish to live together even if they could do so, and still want to remain as a couple living apart together (Levin, 2004: 233). The 'preference' for LATs is evident in the group of divorced people because they believe that 'living together, in itself, will change the way each of them relates to the other and that those changes could threaten the relationship's survival' (Levin, 2004: 233). By living apart, however, they can have more control over their lives and gain more autonomy. In this way, LATs have been viewed as a strategy to avoid repeating and experiencing the same mistakes from a previous relationship (Duncan et al., 2013; Haskey & Lewis, 2006; Roseneil, 2006). Additionally, Levin (2004) also mentions that older people, such as retired couples, even though neither partner is working any more, do not need to worry about jobs and are likely to have sufficient financial resources to live apart in order to secure autonomy and facilitate contact with adult children (Haskey & Lewis, 2006; Karlsson & Borell, 2002).

The other group is people who would like to live together but cannot do so in practice due to external constraints. Caring reasons, the feeling of responsibility for significant others, such as children and elderly parents, can keep people from living together with their partner (Levin, 2004: 231; see also Duncan et al., 2013; Haskey & Lewis, 2006). Women, in particular, are expected to stay with and take care of children, while living apart from their partner. In this sense, LAT has been viewed as a strategy to prioritise and protect the well-being of children. Levin (2004) further points out that caring for elderly parents also serves as a driving factor for couples living separately, with the sense of 'repaying' parents for what they have done in raising them. In this way, LATs can be viewed as a solution that allows people to both maintain their already-existing relationships by caring for children or aged parents, and at the same time sustain an intimate relationship with their partner. Therefore, this 'both/and' solution to partnerships is appreciated, in particular, by those who have young children and/or older relations to care for.

Similar to the Western context, caring plays an important part in organising Chinese people's everyday life. The long-standing influence of traditional Confucian values in relation to filial piety, combined with the under-developed social welfare system, have transferred the caring responsibility from institutions to families (Zhu & Walker, 2018). Therefore, people (women in particular) are expected to provide primary care for their children and elderly parents.

In addition to caring for others, Levin (2004) also claims that working or studying in different places can cause couples to live in separate households. Because people do not want to choose one over the other, they have to live separately in order to maintain both their careers and intimacy with a partner (Holmes, 2004a, 2006; Lampard, 2016; Levin, 2004; Liefbroer et al., 2015). This is particularly evident among students, due to different educational locations. Taking myself as an example, I was in an LAT relationship during the time when my partner and I were pursuing PhD degrees in different UK academic institutions. However, we are not unusual in having this relationship. Based on my experience and that of others I know, some people in the same situation as me, both in the UK and China, often live on campus or at home with parents, while having a partner living elsewhere. In terms of future plans, many young people have high expectations of living together after graduation and finding jobs near their common home (Levin, 2004).

However, the above two groups (preference and constraint), regarding orientations towards cohabitation suggested by Levin, did not fit neatly into other available UK data. For example, Roseneil's (2006) data based on small qualitative interviews (22 participants) categorised LAT into three groups. She suggests that members of the small group (three participants in the cohort), in 'regretfully apart relationships', often give more emphasis to their individual careers, although still being committed to their heterosexual relationship. A larger group (eight participants) in 'gladly apart relationships' were on the opposite side of a willingness to cohabitate, as people were seen to express strong desires to protect their own time, space and relationships. The largest group (11 participants) in her study were the 'undecidedly apart group', with people being more ambivalent about their current relationship.

More recent research in the UK identifies five main reasons for couples to live apart, based on survey data and qualitative interviews (Duncan et al., 2013). These are: too early/not ready, financial constraints, situational constraints, obligated preference, and preference. Their research data show that the most prevalent reason for people (32%) to live apart from their partners is that it is too early in their relationship to live together, while 30% of respondents are constrained by external circumstances from desired cohabitation. Specifically, 18% of them are reported to live apart due to affordability, and the rest do so because of their partner's jobs location or the demands of employers. In addition, some (8%) are labelled as having an obligated preference for LAT due to obligations of care for others, such as children and aged parents. Only a minority (22%) choose LAT driven by personal 'preference' because they just want to keep their own homes. This left 8% who give other unclassified reasons for LAT.

Is LAT a New Family Form or a Temporary Stage?

The question of whether this kind of intimate relationship involving non-residential couples is a new family form or not has attracted a great deal of attention, at least in relation to Western LATs. For those who regard LAT as 'a historically new family norm', it provides a 'both/and' solution to partnership, in which people can keep their couple relationship and at the same time continue with their pre-existing commitments, such as responsibility and care for others (Levin, 2004). Interestingly, older people are most likely to see living apart as an alternative living arrangement, and many reported no plans regarding moving in together in the future (Duncan & Phillips, 2010; Reimondos et al., 2011). Similarly, Roseneil (2006) also views LAT as a new form of relationship through which people tend to de-prioritise sexual/love relationships and instead increase the importance of friendship, changing the meaning of coupledom itself. These findings demonstrate that LAT could be considered a new way of conducting democratic personal lives that is beginning to move beyond the dominant heteronormative framework, where life-long conjugal relationships have long been given prominence, which is in agreement with Giddens' (1992) notion of 'pure relationships', Beck and Beck-Gernsheim's (2005) emphasis on individualisation and Bauman's (2003) metaphor of 'liquid love'.[6]

In contrast to Levin (2004) and Roseneil (2006), who regard LAT as a new family form, others (Ermisch & Seidler, 2009; Haskey, 2005; Haskey & Lewis, 2006) hold a more 'continuist' perspective, asserting that LAT is just a temporary stage or a 'stepping stone' on the way to cohabitation and marriage. In Haskey and Lewis' (2006: 43) research, the respondents, especially those in LATs who are divorced, are conservative about their relationships and lives, and rarely express 'an explicit desire for an alternative form of partnership or even a rejection of marriage or cohabitation'. In addition, the never-married LATs, in particular, tend to have plans regarding living together in the future, if possible. From this continuist perspective, LAT couples in many respects are not radical pioneers, but may merely reflect a new mode of living in practice, which is characterised more by 'caution and conservatism than radicalism and individualism' (Haskey & Lewis, 2006: 46).

However, more recent studies on LATs support both 'new family form' and 'continuist' perspectives, although the latter are more evident in quantitative research. In this way, a 'qualified continuist' position emerges (Duncan et al., 2013). For example, based on the extensive range of attitudinal data from the 2006 BSAS survey, Duncan and Phillips (2010) explore whether LAT couples hold different attitudes towards families,

---

[6] According to Bauman (2003), people are now living in a world characterised as being one of precarious uncertainty, and traditional romantic relationships and communities that were seen to provide solidity and security have been liquefied by individualisation.

personal life and relationships, compared to married people, cohabitants and singles. Indeed, on some issues, LAT couples tend to be more liberal and permissive than other groups, as Roseneil (2006) describes. But only a minority expressed a positive preference for being apart or keeping their own home. However, in the view of Duncan and Phillips (2010: 131), this is a matter of degree rather than a radical departure from traditional married partnerships. As the British evidence shows, like cohabitants, LAT couples do emphasise friendship and often discuss personal problems with friends, whereas it is married people who pay relatively less attention to friends. As with attitudes towards partnering, again, it is married couples who stand out as disapproving of homosexual relations and, conversely, cohabitants are the least traditional about marriage. All this supports a continuist perspective, in which little in the way of a 'pioneer' attitudinal position about relationships and families is found among LATs.

Likewise, using survey data collected from 2004 to 2010 on LATs in ten European countries, Liefbroer et al. (2015) also suggest that for most people in their study LAT is mainly a temporary living arrangement driven by practical reasons and financial constraints, as the majority of respondents intended to live together within the following three years. Only specific groups, such as the highly educated and the divorced, may see LAT as an alternative to marriage or cohabitation.

Although the 'qualified continuist' perspective is easily found in statistical surveys, in later studies, Duncan et al. (2013: 326) question this position, arguing that various personal 'choices' and 'constraints' were often intertwined within an LAT relationship, which inevitably make them 'difficult to unpick from survey evidence alone'. To revise and reflect the range and diversity of LATs in Britain, they combined data from the 2011 national survey with 50 qualitative interviews and suggested that LATs should be better understood as a flexible pragmatism that combines elements of both 'new' and 'continuation' or 'tradition'. This combination stems from an assumption that 'people draw on existing practices, norms and understandings in order to adapt to changing circumstances' (Duncan et al., 2013: 337). Although some women in their study showed a certain degree of 'preference' for living apart (such as 'obligated preference' in caring for children and aged parents), in fact, an ambivalence about 'choices' and 'constraints' was often involved because people's choices were inevitably bounded by the social norms in which they were embedded. In other words, these constraints limit even those who appear to have considerable resources for the pursuit of autonomy (Holmes, 2004b).

In addition, caring and connections sometimes cannot be regarded as active choices because self-sacrifices are often involved at some point (Bauman, 2003). Therefore, an LAT relationship does not just carry on conventional relationship forms under a different name. It is not simply a temporary stage between singlehood and marital formations. Instead, it allows flexibility for individuals in conducting and maintaining their relationships. People can use the autonomy that LAT offers to manage different needs and desires around personal autonomy, job advancement, emotional closeness and other family commitments, or as a response to external circumstances.

To sum up, the existing research evidence described above is mainly based on the Western context, with many attempts being made to evaluate the prevalence of and motivations behind couples in LATs in Western societies. These pioneering studies are mostly based on data collected from surveys and qualitative interviews, although some research has employed both types of data. Specifically, the quantitative studies tend to provide demographic and social incidence information concerning who lives apart and how different they are, whereas the qualitative studies tend to reveal the diverse reasons underlying couples' living apart with the aim of understanding the meanings that people attach to LATs. In terms of those based on both forms of data (Duncan et al., 2013; Haskey & Lewis, 2006), there was still something missing in relation to how people at different life stages negotiate gender roles, experience conjugal intimacy and 'do' family across distance, which I will address by situating the empirical research in a non-Western context and by looking in more depth than many previous studies regarding the everyday practices, activities and experiences of those in LATs.

Researching People in LATs in China

A number of existing texts concerning intimate and personal relationships have focused on the theoretical grounds and research findings, while a few studies pay attention to the research process of these areas in particular (Gabb, 2008). Essentially, this is a feminist-driven piece of research. In contrast to traditional male-defined ways of knowledge production and viewing women as the 'other' and 'outsider', feminist ways of knowing give greater emphasis on the lives of women and other marginalised under-researched groups (Stanley & Wise, 1990, 1993). This feminist approach is particularly concerned with gender in a reflexive way with an emphasis on collaborative and participatory methodologies (Eichler, 1997; Letherby, 2003; Oakley, 1981).

While I acknowledge that there are no methods that can specifically be called 'feminist methods', what makes feminist research different from other types of research is the ways in which methods are used, questions are asked, and the sensitivity to the significance of gender within society (Hardling, 1987; Kelly, 1988; Letherby, 2015). My criteria for the choice of research methods were informed by Ann Oakley's (2004: 191) argument, suggesting that the use of research methods should 'fit with the question being asked in the research', and the theoretical position in which the researcher is located (see also Reinharz & Davidman, 1992). As I mentioned earlier, the central aim of this research is to investigate the ways in which people experience intimacy and construct their family lives when they are physically apart from their partner. One of the concerns is that people at different life stages in the life course with diverse social and economic backgrounds may have different experiences of LATs, and thereby understand the changes in their own personal lives differently in different contexts. This focus on experience and everyday lives fundamentally shaped the ways in which this research has been conducted. Given that people's experiences cannot be reduced to numbers (Scott, 2010; Stanley & Wise, 1993), I used qualitative in-depth interviews to gain knowledge of individuals' relational practices of family and intimacy in certain, specific settings from their own accounts (Kvale & Brinkmann, 2009; Mason, 2002; Maynard, 1994; Rubin & Rubin, 2005; Scott, 1998). In letting research participants 'tell their story', this approach has been considered crucial in studying relationships and everyday living (Gabb, 2008), especially for gaining in-depth insights into the complexities and dynamics of the lived experiences of people who have gone through social changes (Liu, 2007).

Inspired by feminist methodology, my research strategy is based on an inductive approach, with the aim of constructing knowledge from the interaction between the researcher and the individuals' accounts during interviews (Smith, 1990; Stanley & Wise, 1993). This approach, as Stanley and Wise (1990) maintained, specifies a model of research in which theory is systematically drawn from the actual experiences of individuals, and is often referred to as 'grounded theory' (Glaster & Strauss, 1967). I believe that there is no single 'truth' or 'fact' waiting to be discovered. The complexity of subjective experiences means that 'there are multiple realities and therefore multiple truths' (Taylor, 2001: 12; see also Stanley, 1993; Stanley & Wise, 1990). As a result, this requires the researcher to be aware of the responsibility of representing the voices of all participants, rather than one objective account (Brooks & Hesse-Biber, 2007; Stanley & Wise, 1993). Bearing in mind, this research has no intention of representing all the women in LATs in China, or applying research findings to all LAT people at different life stages in different social contexts, what I aim to achieve is to gather women's own voices and focus on activities and practices that are considered important to them. In doing so, this research attempts to address the knowledge gap regarding how the social construction of gender and sexual relations has shaped people's everyday practices of family, intimacy and agency in non-cohabiting partnerships.

Approaching LAT People

The fieldwork was conducted over the summer of 2016 in China. I situated my fieldwork in two places: Beijing and Liaoning Province. First, this is based on my personal familiarity with both places. I was born and grew up in a small town in Liaoning Province in northeast China, and later moved to Beijing for high-school study. I expected that the familiarity with the research sites would give me confidence in understanding the living environment and local culture in which people are embedded. Although it does not guarantee that I would be viewed as an insider by the potential participants, at least it was helpful in developing conversations and building rapport between myself and those I researched.

Second, I was aware of many differences between the two sites. Beijing is the nation's political, cultural and educational centre, with a per capita GDP (gross domestic product) in 2016 reaching RMB 118,198 (USD 17,795) (Beijing Municipal Bureau of Statistics, 2017). As the capital city of the People's Republic of China, Beijing has drawn much attention in contemporary sociological research due to rapid socio-economic development as well as greater cultural openness. As a result, it has attracted a large amount of people from different parts of China studying, working and living in Beijing. According to the Beijing Municipal Bureau of Statistics (2017), the total number of permanent residents of Beijing was 8.715 million in 1978, with a permanent migrant population of only 0.218 million. By 2016, however, the population had dramatically increased to 21.729 million permanent residents, including 8.075 million migrants, which means 38% of residents are from outside Beijing.

In contrast to the first-tier cities such as Beijing, very little attention has been paid to my hometown, which was classified as one of the fifth-tier cities. Liaoning Province, located in northeast China with a per capita GDP of RMB 50,791 (USD 7646) in 2016, is an out-migration province and the labour force outflow in this area has become increasingly severe due to fewer advantages in relation to geographical location, cultural development and economic growth (Liaoning Provincial Bureau of Statistics, 2017). Although I was aware that my purposive selection of research sites could not represent the diversity of forms of familial practices, these differences and regional inequalities in resource distribution enable me to investigate how people's lived experience of personal relationships and family lives are shaped by and, in turn, shape social structure.

By the end of September 2016, I interviewed 39 people (including four men) at different life stages living separately from their partner for whatever reasons. They were recruited through different methods in order to obtain a 'purposive' sample, rather than 'generalised and representative' data. At the initial stage, I used WeChat (in Chinese: Weixin; literally meaning 'micro message'), one of the most popular mobile-based instant-messaging apps in China, to find young prospective participants. The Weixin Impact Report in 2015 shows that the majority of WeChat users are relatively young—with an average age of 26—and almost 90% (86.2%) of users are less than 36 years old (see also Liu, 2007). To approach as wide a range of participants using this method as possible, I registered a subscription account (in Chinese, *gong zhong hao*) and publicly posted the 'looking for participants' call in Chinese on 25 April 2016 (two months ahead of the start of my fieldwork) while I was still in the UK. The more people knew about this research, the easier it would be for me to reach a wide variety of participants.

This led to twelve people (including two men) contacting me and joining my research project. Noticeably, this was the first time that I came across the male participants during the research process. Although I was initially looking for female participants, some valuable insights came out of my data by including male participants, especially when they recounted how they express intimacy and build closeness. I acknowledge that the small number of male participants means I cannot illustrate or represent LAT men in general, but they are used at some points in the following chapters to additionally supplement and/or construction women's practices of emotion. Therefore, the inclusion of male participants will also be examined later in this chapter, particularly when useful to methodological discussions of power dynamics.

Of these 12 people that were recruited via WeChat, the average age was 26.8, with the youngest being 23 years old and the oldest 34, which is in line with the general overall WeChat user age (26 years). In terms of their education, they all had received higher education, and therefore could be described as well-educated and work-oriented young people who are able to live alone and maintain their intimate couple relationships.

Although I benefited a lot from using WeChat when recruiting participants, this strategy only applied well to the younger generation, which I attribute to their heavy involvement in social media. Being aware of the unique social context where personal networks, or *guanxi*, often play an important role in everyday life in terms of meeting new people and building trust (Gold et al., 2002; Liu, 2007; Park & Lunt, 2015; Zarafonetis, 2017), I asked intermediaries (such as my friends, schoolmates and family members) to introduce anyone they knew in LATs. During the time of staying in Beijing, 12 people (two men included), whom I had never met before, were recruited via personal networks and snowball sampling, being referred by people who had participated in the study or my friends and older sister's introductions.

However, as the fieldwork progressed, I realised that the voices of middle-aged people were largely missing. I speculated that the social characteristics of both the researcher and the intermediaries may have an impact on the variety of the potential participants who are enlisted in the research project. Even though I have established my personal contacts since studying in Beijing, my social circle was largely based on my peer groups, and my connections with wider society in Beijing were limited to some extent. This inevitably led to the formation of group monotony in this sample, while I struggled to find a 'triangulation of subjects' (referred to specifically as older participants in this context) (Rubin & Rubin, 2005: 67).

In addition, due to the sensitivity of this research topic in a Chinese context, it became difficult to reach middle-aged and older people and ask them to share with me their private life, especially considering my identity at the time of the interviews, as a young unmarried woman who had spent years in a Western country studying for a higher-education degree. In order to hear more 'women's voices' in order to cover as diverse a sample as possible, I returned to my hometown halfway through my fieldwork because there were more (older) family members and relatives in Liaoning Province. Finally, 15 more women who had relatively low educational levels, with the oldest being aged 57, agreed to be interviewed.

It is clear that using informal personal networks was effective and successful, especially with respect to approaching participants who were not easily accessible (at least for me) and building up rapport. However, this method can also be problematic, as the intermediaries sometimes would use their autonomy and interpret my research in his/her own way. Additionally, the decisions about whom to include and exclude in the research were largely in the hands of intermediaries, and the snowballing method (my participants provided the contact details of further potential participants to me) had the potential to only attract participants who share similar characteristics (Mason, 2002). For example, my father's friend introduced me to five 'study mothers' who all accompanied their children to study during the course of interviews, while their husbands were working far away from home to provide financial support for the family. Interestingly, the commonalities in their LATs allowed me to design cases studies based on their everyday practices of family, which I will discuss in more detail in Chap. 4. Nevertheless, as soon as I realised that the diversity of data would be conditioned by the recruitment process, I addressed this during the course of fieldwork by using a purposive sampling strategy (Mason, 2002) and ensuring that I had wider social connections where possible, all in order to gain as much diversity in the sample as possible.

Although 'there are no rules for sample size in qualitative inquiry' (Patton, 2002: 244), the number in a sample is subject to external constraints, such as time and financial resources. I stopped recruiting, and later interviewing, on the grounds that I felt I had enough participants and subsequent data to allow me to answer my research questions in an informed manner (Bryman, 2016; Guest et al., 2006; Mason, 2010). Consequently, my overall samples include 39 people, who varied in terms of the length of their relationship and frequency in seeing each other due to geographic distance, the nature of their partner's occupation and stage of their relationship (see Table A.1 in the Appendix for details of participant profiles). Specifically, they varied in age from 23 to 57 and were from a variety of social backgrounds and occupations, ranging from graduate students to retired people, professionals and housewives. In terms of education, 24 people had university degrees with 8 of them having postgraduate degrees. I interviewed 24 of them in Beijing and the rest (15) in my hometown, Liaoning Province. In terms of marital status, 28 of them were married, 19 of whom had between one and two children aged between 1 and 32. None of them had experienced divorce.

However, as I have already commented on, I was aware that there was a lack of male voices in my sample, not only because of the scope of this research project, but also due to the fact that they were mostly working away from their partner during the course of my fieldwork. In this regard, my sample cannot represent all the people with different social characteristics who engage in an LAT relationship in China. Instead of providing a statistical analysis of the number of Chinese people relating at a distance, this qualitative research aims to provide in-depth insights into the ways in which couples experience intimacy and family and negotiate their gender roles. Therefore, these individuals' accounts were able to reveal the complexities and subtleties of subjective interpretations of LATs and their experiences of being heterosexual across various life stages of family life.

Reflexivity, Power Dynamics and Positionality

'Reflexivity is self-critical sympathetic introspection and the self-conscious analytical scrutiny of the self' (England, 1994: 82; see also Cotterill & Letherby, 1993). The practice of reflexivity is significant to the research process, and the researcher's own positionality and assumptions can affect the process of knowledge production (Chiseri-Strater, 1996; Hesse-Biber, 2012). Therefore, Stanley (1993: 49) argued that 'research is contextual, situational, and specific, and ... will differ systematically according to the social location (as gendered, raced, classed, sexualised person) of the particular knowledge-producer'. With that in mind, I will use this section to provide a reflexive examination of the research process through an autobiographical approach.

Reflections on power dynamics between the researcher and the researched in the research process have attracted increasing attention, especially in feminist research (Cotterill, 1992; Letherby, 2003; Taylor, 2011). Being aware of the power hierarchies and exploitative relationships that have often traditionally existed between researchers and the researched in practice, I am keen to develop equal research relationships by empowering research participants where possible (Cotterill, 1992; Millen, 1997; Ryan-Flood & Gill, 2009; Wolf, 1985). However, this ideal can become problematic when entering into fieldwork. During the course of fieldwork, I used my identity as a 20-something unmarried Chinese female doctoral student to build up rapport and develop a sense of trust, especially when interviewing those of the same gender (Oakley, 1981). To some extent, sharing some similarities with my participants enabled me to gain 'rich' data and pay continuous and reflexive attention to the significance of gender as an aspect of all social life and within research (Letherby, 2015: 78).

Having a specific consideration of gender does not obliterate other aspects of an individual's social identity, such as age, class, educational levels, marital status and geographical locations. These characteristics and the intersection of these differences are considered important in people's life experiences and thereby are relevant to the research process (Liamputtong, 2010). On many occasions, the boundary and relationship with my research participants are not fixed but subject to constant negotiation between all parties. For example, my insider identity was counteracted by other differentiations, such as age, religious belief and marital status, when I interviewed Rosy (46, married). As she stated,

> Because you're not a mother, so you might be unlikely to understand our age of people's minds. You might even not be able to understand the ways how I, as a Christian, view my family, work, and children. As a Christian, we see problems from a different perspective [compared to non-Christians].

In recognition of people's intimate life experiences being involved during the course of interviews, my personal experience of being in an LAT relationship was shared where appropriate, and some participants could relate and feel more comfortable to share their own stories. What surprised me is that my 'outsider within' identity (Collins, 1986), as someone with a higher education living and working in the UK, had facilitated them to openly express their feelings. On some occasions participants were emotional, especially when they evoked the hard times they had experienced. As I listened, I was also engaging and attending to their emotions while offering tissues and the option to stop recording. Instead of jumping to other topics, participants preferred to continue and reveal their innermost thoughts to me. This implies that my status as an 'outsider' and 'otherness' itself, in the sense of living far away from participants' immediate social networks and being unlikely to appear in their everyday lives in the future, helped people to be more open when talking about their lived LAT experiences.

Undoubtedly, an interview involves complex flows of power (Plummer, 1995). Although the researcher does have the ultimate control over both the participants and the research process (Hesse-Biber & Leavy, 2011; Letherby, 2003), the researched could exercise power in a number of ways at different stages of the research process. The unbalanced power dynamics occurred in different ways when interviewing some of the male participants. However, in some cases, my inferior position in terms of age, gender and life experience was somehow redressed by my educational attainment. In addition, I sometimes put myself in a vulnerable and powerless position by allowing the research participants' to decide where they would like to be interviewed and where they felt comfortable. Because of lack of control over the interview venue, the presence of other family members, noisy surrounding environments and unexpected occurrences would lead to the disruption of our interviews, especially if we were in public spaces such as a coffee shop, or even private spaces such as a participant's home. These encounters over the fieldwork site may constantly throw up issues that the researcher has to deal with on the spot, and it is only afterwards that they can reflect on how the methodological issues actually played out during the research process, and consider the ethical aspects potentially raised (Elwood & Martin, 2000; Leyshon, 2002).

Getting Familiar with the Data and Data Analysis

Reflexivity is an ongoing process and does not end when the researcher leaves the field. The first thing I did after each interview was to write down field notes as this offered me the opportunity to document my initial feelings and views on the whole interview process from the perspective of a researcher. This also enabled me to stand back to review my own performance and amend the interview questions if necessary (Arthur et al., 2014). In retrospect, I found this method especially useful in the data analysis stage, as it could bring my thoughts back to the field and ensure that my arguments were deeply rooted in the specific context in which each interview was conducted.

As soon as I finished my fieldwork in China, I started transcribing verbatim from audio-recordings to text formats in an attempt to present accurate accounts produced by participants at the research site (Patton, 1990). Although transcription is a time-consuming and labour-intensive process, it helped me get familiar with my data. When listening to the recorder and transcribing interview data, I also took notes and generated initial codes that appeared interesting and were relevant to my research questions. Through repeatedly reading my field notes and transcripts thoroughly, some recurrent themes around practices of agency, family practices and intimacy emerged.

I acknowledged that the researcher does have ultimate control over the research process as a whole, especially when it comes to presenting research findings in a language that is different from the one used to collect data. As a Chinese researcher who shares the same language with the research participants, our interviews were carried out in Mandarin Chinese. Therefore, translation of participants' accounts to (British) English was crucial for the purpose of data analysis and reporting. In this regard, my triple role as a researcher, transcriber and translator allowed me to reconsider the power relations between the researcher and the people being researched. This is because the decisions regarding how to translate and what to translate largely fall into the hands of the researcher (Chin, 2018; Temple & Young, 2004).

When I read the Mandarin transcripts, I was critically reflexive about how I translated a Chinese word into English. When some terms were difficult to translate, I decided to retain specific cultural implications by capturing 'conceptual equivalence', where the meanings of the text in my study in both Chinese and English are conceptually the same (Phillips, 1960; Mangen, 1999; see also Smith et al., 2008). To keep the nuances of the original data, literal equivalence was offered by carefully transliterating (transcribing a letter or word into corresponding letters of a different alphabet or language). For example, the Chinese term '*guo rizi*' is frequently used by participants in their accounts of everyday life. In this case, I directly used *pinyin* (romanised Chinese) in the text and then transliterated in English as 'to pass the days to live'. This is followed by a detailed explanation with the consideration of the context this word was given. The rationale of combining conceptual equivalence with text equivalence is to preserve both the reliability and the validity of the data so as to avoid linguistic difficulties in working with multiple languages (Smith et al., 2008; Temple & Young, 2004). When selected quotes were used to interpret meanings in this research, I used quotation marks to indicate that this is a direct quote from participants, with his/her pseudonyms being given in order to preserve anonymity.

Structure of the Book

This book contains six chapters. Chapter 1 introduces the research topic of LATs and reviews existing studies on LATs mainly in the Western context. I then reflexively examine my methodological standpoint and how this has informed the research process during this study, including the choice of research sites, recruitment strategies, power dynamics and data analysis. Chapter 2 is primarily concerned with key debates that this research has engaged in, such as those around individualisation, intimacy and family practices. I then shift the focus to explore the specific social context in which this research is situated and critically review the applicability of the Eurocentric concept of individualisation in the Chinese context.

Research findings around practices of agency, family and intimacy are discussed from Chaps. 3 to 5. In Chap. 3, I consider the motivations behind couples living apart and the interplay between agency and structure in their LATs. Inspired by Burkitt's (2016) idea of relational agency and Carter and Duncan's (2018) research on differential agency in LATs, the ways in which people's agency in living in a desired co-residential partnership intersect closely with practices of gender, social norms about family values and life stages as circumstances and contexts change. In the split households that are a result of structural constraints, family life is essentially shaped and constructed surrounding the gendered family roles and maintained through gender inequalities. Although there is evidence of the growth of individual reflexivity especially among the young generation in making individual choices, the interaction and contradiction between individualism and familism have significantly shaped the ways people negotiate and make sense of their personal lives.

In Chap. 4, I give special attention to the group of 'study mothers' as exemplars to examine how family practices are closely implicated with regard to gender and social norms. In addition, how people engage in family practices is also intertwined with their personal biographical experiences, as they often draw on their own family life in which they grew up in order to construct the meaning of family. Central to this case-study chapter is the premise that most of the women presented in this chapter are bound by their traditional feminine gendered habitus into a role that entails the employment of emotional skills to do relational emotion work, as they are (almost all) responsible for the emotional well-being of their relationships.

In Chap. 5, I turn the focus to 'doing' intimacy for couples in circumstances that prevent them from being able to meet each other on a regular basis. With the aid of mobile technologies, two aspects of communicating are examined: text-messaging and virtual activities. While distance often prevents practical care between couples, gift-giving and practices of filial piety are noted and considered as important to maintain intimate relationships across distance. The emotional aspect of intimacy is also discussed from both women's and men's perspectives.

In the Conclusion, I tie the findings together in response to the research questions that I indicated at the beginning of this research. This leads to my assessing the theoretical contribution that this research has made in relation to gender and family relationships in the context of LAT. The limitations of my research and suggestions for other, future studies in this area are also reviewed.

References

Abbott, D., Zhi, Z., & Meredith, W. (1993). Married but living apart: Chinese couples seeking a better life. *International Journal of Sociology of the Family, 23*(1), 1–10.

Arthur, S., Mitchell, M., Lewis, J., & Nicholls, C. (2014). Designing fieldwork. In J. Ritchie, J. Lewis, C. M. N. Nicholls, & R. Ormston (Eds.), *Qualitative research practice: A guide for social science students and researchers* (2nd ed., pp. 109–137). Sage.

Ayuso, L. (2019). What future awaits couples living apart together (LAT)? *The sociological review, 67*(1), 226–244.

Bauman, Z. (2003). *Liquid love: On the frailty of human bonds*. Polity Press.

Bawin-Legros, B., & Gauthier, A. (2001). Regulation of Intimacy and Love Semantics in Couples Living Apart Together. *International Review of Sociology, 11*(1), 39–46.

Beck, U., & Beck-Gernsheim, E. (2005). *Individualization: Institutionalized individualism and its social and political consequences*. Sage.

Beijing Municipal Bureau of Statistics. (2017). 北京统计年鉴—2017 [*Beijing statistical yearbook, 2017*] [Online]. Retrieved July 14, 2022, from http://nj.tjj.beijing.gov.cn/nj/main/2017-tjnj/zk/indexch.htm

Bian, Y. (1994). *Work and inequality in urban China*. State University of New York press.

Bonavia, D. (1982). *The Chinese*. Penguin Books.

Borell, K., & Karlsson, S. G. (2003). Reconceptualizing intimacy and ageing: Living apart together. In S. Arber, K. Davidson, & J. Ginn (Eds.), *Gender and ageing: Changing roles and relationships* (pp. 47–62). Open University Press.

Brooks, A., & Hesse-Biber, S. N. (2007). An invitation to feminist research. In S. N. HesseBiber & P. Leavy (Eds.), *Feminist research practice: A primer*. Sage Publications.

Bryman, A. (2016). *Social research methods* (5th ed.). Oxford University Press.

Burkitt, I. (2016). Relational agency: relational sociology, agency and interaction. *European journal of social theory, 19*(3), 322–339.

Carter, J., & Duncan, S. (2018). *Reinventing couples: tradition, agency and bricolage*. London: Palgrave Macmillan.

Carter, J., Duncan, S., Stoilova, M., & Phillips, M. (2016). Sex, love and security: Accounts of distance and commitment in living apart together relationships. *Sociology, 50*(3), 576–593.

Chang, H., Dong, X., & MacPhail, F. (2011). Labor migration and time use patterns of the left-behind children and elderly in rural China. *World Development, Pergamon, 39*(12), 2199–2210. https://doi.org/10.1016/J.WORLDDEV.2011.05.021

Chen, F. (2005). Employment transitions and the household division of labor in China. *Social Forces, 84*(2), 831–851. https://doi.org/10.1353/SOF.2006.0010

Chin, D. (2018). *Everyday gender at work in Taiwan*. Palgrave Macmillan.

Chiseri-Strater, E. (1996). Turning in upon ourselves: Positionality, subjectivity, and reflexivity in case study and ethnographic research. *Ethics and Representation in Qualitative Studies of Literacy, 1*, 115–133.

Collins, P. H. (1986). Learning from the outsider within: The sociological significance of black feminist thought. *Social Problems, 33*(6), 14–32. https://doi.org/10.2307/800672

Cotterill, P. (1992). Interviewing women: Issue of friendship, vulnerability, and power. *Women's Studies International Forum, 15*(5), 593–606.

Cotterill, P., & Letherby, G. (1993). Weaving stories: Personal auto/biographies in feminist research. *Sociology, 27*(1), 67–79.

Coulter, R., & Hu, Y. (2017). Living Apart Together and cohabitation intentions in Great Britain. *Journal of Family Issues, 38*(12), 1701–1729.

Duncan, S. (2015). Women's agency in living apart together: Constraint, strategy and vulnerability. *The Sociological Review, 63*, 589–607.

Duncan, S., & Phillips, M. (2008). New families? Tradition and change in partnering and relationships. In A. Park, J. Curtice, K. Thomson, M. Phillips, M. Johnson, & E. Clery (Eds.), *British social attitudes: The 24th report* (pp. 1–28). Sage.

Duncan, S., & Phillips, M. (2010). People who live apart together (LATs) – How different are they? *The Sociological Review, 58*(1), 112–134.

Duncan, S., & Phillips, M. (2011). People who live apart together (LATs): New family form or just a stage? *International Review of Sociology, 21*, 513–532.

Duncan, S., Carter, J., Phillips, M., Rosenil, S., & Stoilva, M. (2013). Why do people live apart together? *Families, Relationships and Societies, 2*(3), 323–338.

Duncan, S., Phillips, M., Carter, J., Rosenil, S., & Stoilva, M. (2014). Practices and perceptions of living apart together. *Family Science, 5*(1), 1–10.

Eichler, M. (1997). Feminist methodology. *Current Sociology, 45*(2), 9–36.

Elwood, S., & Martin, D. (2000). Placing interviews: Location and scales of power in qualitative research. *The Professional Geographer, 52*(4), 649–657.

England, K. (1994). Getting personal: Reflexivity, positionality, and feminist research. *The Professional Geographer, 46*(1), 80–89.

Ermisch, J., & Seidler, T. (2009). Living apart together. In M. Brynin & J. Ermisch (Eds.), *Changing relationships* (pp. 45–59). London.

Evertsson, L., & Nyman, C. (2013). On the other side of couplehood: Single women in Sweden exploring life without a partner. *Families, Relationships and Societies, 2*(1), 61–78.

Fan, C. C. (2003). Rural-urban migration and gender division of labor in transitional China. *International Journal of Urban and Regional Research, 27*(1), 24–47. https://doi.org/10.1111/1468-2427.00429

Fan, C. C., & Li, T. (2020). Split households, family migration and urban settlement: Findings from China's 2015 national floating population survey. *Social Inclusion, 8*(1), 252–263. https://doi.org/10.17645/si.v8i1.2402

Fan, C. C., Sun, M., & Zheng, S. (2011). Migration and split households: A comparison of sole, couple, and family migrants in Beijing, China. *Environment and Planning A, 43*(9), 2164–2185. https://doi.org/10.1068/a44128

Gabb, J. (2008). *Researching intimacy in families*. Palgrave Macmillan.

Gerstel, N., & Gross, H. (1984). *Commuter marriage: A study of work and family*. Guildford Press.

Giddens, A. (1992). *The transformation of intimacy*. Polity press.

Glaster, B., & Strauss, A. (1967). *The discovery of grounded theory: Strategies for qualitative research*. Aldine.

Gold, T., Guthrie, D., & Wank, D. (2002). *Social connections in China: Institutions, culture, and the changing nature of guanxi*. Cambridge University Press.

Guest, G., Bunce, A., & Johnson, L. (2006). How many interviews are enough? An experiment with data saturation and variability. *Field Methods, 18*, 59–82.

Guldner, G. T. (2003). *Long distance relationships: The complete guide*. J.F. Milne Publications.

Hardling, S. (1987). *Feminism and methodology*. Open University Press.

Hare-Mustin, R., & Hare, S. (1986). Family change and the concept of motherhood in China. *Journal of Family Issues, 7*, 67–82.

Haskey, J. (2005). Living arrangements in contemporary Britain: Having a partner who usually lives elsewhere and Living Apart Together (LAT). *Population Trends, 122*, 35–45.

Haskey, J., & Lewis, J. (2006). Living-Apart-Together in Britain: Context and meaning. *International Journal of Law in Context, 2*(1), 37–48.

He, C., & Gober, P. (2003). Gendering interprovincial migration in China. *International Migration Review, 37*(4), 1220–1251. https://doi.org/10.1111/j.1747-7379.2003.tb00176.x

Hesse-Biber, S. (2012). Feminist research: Exploring, interrogating, and transforming the interconnections of epistemology, methodology, and method. In

S. Hesse-Biber (Ed.), *Handbook of feminist research: Theory and praxis* (pp. 2–26). Sage Publications.

Hesse-Biber, S. N., & Leavy, P. (2011). *The practice of qualitative research*. Sage.

Hoffman, L. (2008). Post-Mao professionalism: Self-enterprise and patriotism. In L. Zhang & A. Ong (Eds.), *Privatizing China: Socialism from afar* (pp. 168–181). Cornell University Press.

Holmes, M. (2004a). An equal distance? Individualisation, gender and intimacy in distance relationships. *The Sociological Review, 52*(2), 180–200.

Holmes, M. (2004b). The precariousness of choice in the new sentimental order: A response to Bawin-Legros. *Current Sociology, 52*(2), 251–257.

Holmes, M. (2006). Love lives at a distance: Distance relationships over the life-course. *Sociological Research Online, 11*(3), 70–80. [Online]. Retrieved October 8, 2019, from http://www.socresonline.org.uk/11/3/holmes.html

Ji, Y., & Yeung, W. J. (2014). Heterogeneity in contemporary Chinese marriage. *Journal of Family Issues, 35*(12), 1662–1682.

Karlsson, S. G., & Borell, K. (2002). Intimacy and autonomy, gender and ageing: Living apart together. *Ageing International, 27*(4), 11–26.

Kelly, L. (1988). *Surviving sexual violence*. Policy Press.

Kim, S. (2001). "Weekend couples" among Korean professionals: An ethnography of living apart on weekdays. *Korea Journal, 41*(2000), 28–47.

Kobayashi, K., Funk, L., & Khan, M. (2017). Constructing a sense of commitment in 'Living Apart Together' (LAT) relationships: Interpretive agency and individualization. *Current Sociology, 65*(7), 991–1009.

Kvale, S., & Brinkmann, S. (2009). *Interviews: Learning the craft of qualitative research interviewing*. Sage.

Lampard, R. (2016). Living together in a sexually exclusive relationship: An enduring, pervasive ideal? *Families, Relationships and Societies, 5*(1), 23–41.

Letherby, G. (2003). *Feminist research in theory and practice*. Open University Press.

Letherby, G. (2015). Gender-sensitive method/ologies. In V. Robinson & D. Richardson (Eds.), *Introducing gender and women's studies* (4th ed., pp. 76–94). Palgrave Macmillan.

Levin, I. (2004). Living Apart Together: A new family form. *Current Sociology, 52*(2), 223–240.

Levin, I., & Trost, J. (1999). Living apart together. *Community, Work and Family, 2*(3), 279–294.

Leyshon, M. (2002). On being 'in the field': Practice, progress and problems in research with young people in rural areas. *Journal of Rural Studies, 18*(2), 179–191.

Liamputtong, P. (2010). *Performing qualitative cross-cultural research*. Cambridge University Press.

Liaoning Provincial Bureau of Statistics. (2017). 辽宁统计年鉴—2017 [*Liaoning statistical yearbook, 2017*] [Online]. Retrieved July 14, 2022, from at:http://tjj.ln.gov.cn/tjsj/sjcx/ndsj/otherpages/2017/indexch.htm

Liefbroer, A. C., Poortman, A., & Seltzer, J. A. (2015). Why do intimate partners live apart? Evidence on LAT relationships across Europe. *Demographic Research, 32*(8), 251–286.

Liu, J. (2007). *Gender and work in urban China: Women workers of the unlucky generation.* Routledge.

Mangen, S. (1999). Qualitative research methods in cross-national settings. *International Journal of Social Research Methodology, 2*(2), 109–124.

Mason, J. (2002). *Qualitative researching.* Sage.

Mason, M. (2010). Sample size and saturation in PhD studies using qualitative interviews. *Forum Qualitative Social Research, 11*(3) [Online]. Retrieved December 20, 2019, from http://www.qualitative-research.net/index.php/fqs/article/view/1428/3027

Maynard, M. (1994). Methods, practice and epistemology: The debate about feminism and research. In M. Maynard & J. Purvis (Eds.), *Researching women's lives from a feminist perspective* (pp. 10–26). Taylor & Francis.

Milan, A., & Peters, A. (2003). *Couples living apart. Canadian Social Trends.* No. 69. Summer. Statistics Canada Catalogue no. 11-008-X.

Millen, D. (1997). Some methodological and epistemological issues raised by doing feminist research on non-feminist women. *Sociological Research Online, 2*(3), 114–128. [Online]. Retrieved June 16, 2016, from http://socresonline.org.uk/2/3/3.html

National Health and Family Planning Commission of the People's Republic of China. (2012). 中国流动人口发展报告 —2012 [*Report on China's migrant population development 2012].* Zhongguo Renkou Chubanshe.

National Health and Family Planning Commission of the People's Republic of China. (2016). 中国流动人口发展报告 —2016 [*Report on China's migrant population development 2016].* Zhongguo Renkou Chubanshe.

Oakley, A. (1981). Interviewing women: A contradiction in terms. In H. Roberts (Ed.), *Doing feminist research* (pp. 30–61). Routledge.

Oakley, A. (2004). Response to 'Quoting and counting: An autobiographical response to Oakley'. *Sociology 38,* 191–192.

Park, S., & Lunt, N. (2015). Confucianism and qualitative interviewing: Working Seoul to soul. *Forum: Qualitative Social Research, 16*(2). https://doi.org/10.17169/fqs-16.2.2166

Patton, M. Q. (1990). *Qualitative evaluation and research methods.* Sage.

Patton, M. Q. (2002). *Qualitative research and evaluation methods.* 3rd ed. Thousand Oaks, CA: Sage.

Peng, X. (2011). China's demographic history and future challenges. *Science, 333*(6042), 581–587. https://doi.org/10.1126/science.1209396

Phillips, H. P. (1960). Problems of translation and meaning in field work. In R. N. Adams & J. J. Preiss (Eds.), *Human organisation research: Field relations and techniques* (pp. 184–192). Dorsey Press Inc.

Plummer, K. (1995). *Telling sexual stories: Power, change and social worlds.* Routledge.

Qiu, S. (2022). Family practices in non-cohabiting intimate relationships in China: Doing mobile intimacy, emotion and intergenerational caring practices. *Families, Relationships and Societies, 11*(2), 175–191. https://doi.org/10.1332/204674321X16468493162777

Régnier-Loilier, A., Beaujouan, E., & Villeneuve-Gokalp, C. (2009). Neither single, nor in a couple: A study of living apart together in France. *Demographic Research, 21*(4), 75–108.

Reimondos, A., Evans, E., & Gray, E. (2011). Living-apart-together (LAT) relationships in Australia. *Family Matters, 87*, 43–55.

Reinharz, S., & Davidman, L. (1992). *Feminist methods in social research.* Oxford University Press.

Roseneil, S. (2006). On not living with a partner: Unpicking coupledom and cohabitation. *Sociological Research Online, 11*(3), 111–124. [Online]. Retrieved April 5, 2019, from http://www.socresonline.org.uk/11/3/roseneil.html

Rubin, H. J., & Rubin, I. S. (2005). *Qualitative interviewing: The art of hearing data.* Sage.

Ryan-Flood, R., & Gill, R. (2009). *Secrecy and silence in the research process: Feminist reflections.* Routledge.

Scott, S. (1998). Here be dragons: Researching the unbelievable, hearing the unthinkable. A feminist sociologist in uncharted territory. *Sociological Research Online, 3*(3), 98–109. [Online]. Retrieved October 9, 2019, fromwww.socresonline.org.uk/socresonline/3/3/1.html

Scott, J. (2010). Quantitative methods and gender inequalities. *International Journal of Social Research Methodology, 13*(3), 223–236.

Smith, D. (1990). *The conceptual practices of power: A feminist sociology of knowledge.* University of Toronto Press.

Smith, H., Chen, J., & Liu, X. (2008). Language and rigour in qualitative research: Problems and principles in analyzing data collected in Mandarin. *BMC Medical Research Methodology, 8*(44), 1–8.

Stanley, L. (1993). On auto/biography in sociology. *Sociology, 27*(1), 41–52.

Stanley, L., & Wise, S. (1990). Method, methodology and epistemology in feminist research processes. In L. Stanley (Ed.), *Feminist praxis: Research, theory and epistemology in feminist sociology* (pp. 20–60). Routledge.

Stanley, L., & Wise, S. (1993). *Breaking out again: Feminist ontology and epistemology.* Routledge & Kegan Paul.

Stoilova, M., Roseneil, S., & Crowhurst, I. (2014). Living apart relationships in contemporary Europe: Accounts of togetherness and apartness. *Sociology, 48*(6), 1075–1091.

Strohm, C. Q., Seltzer, J. A., Cochran, S. D., & Mays, V. M. (2009). Living apart together relationships in the United States. *Demographic Research, 21,* 177–214.

Taylor, S. (2001). Locating and conducting discourse analytic research. In M. Wetherell, S. Taylor, & S. Yates (Eds.), *Discourse as data: A guide for analysis* (pp. 5–48). Sage.

Taylor, J. (2011). The intimate insider: Negotiating the ethics of friendship when doing insider research. *Qualitative Research, 11*(1), 3–22. https://doi.org/10.1177/1468794110384447

Temple, B., & Young, A. (2004). Qualitative research and translation dilemmas. *Qualitative Research, 4*(2), 161–178.

Tsui, M., & Rich, L. (2002). The only child and educational opportunity for girls in urban China. *Gender & Society, 16*(1), 74–92. https://doi.org/10.1177/0891243202016001005

Turcotte, M. (2013). *Living apart together.* [Online]. Statistics Canada. Retrieved May 19, 2019, from https://www150.statcan.gc.ca/n1/en/pub/75-006-x/2013001/article/11771-eng.pdf?st=ZoT2vOkH

Upton-Davis, K. (2015). Subverting gendered norms of cohabitation: Living Apart Together for women over 45. *Journal of Gender Studies, 24*(1), 104–116.

Wolf, M. (1985). *Revolution postponed: Women in contemporary China.* Stanford University Press.

Xie, Y. (2011). Evidence-based research on China: A historical imperative. *Chinese Sociological Review, 44*(1), 14–25. https://doi.org/10.2753/csa2162-0555440103

Yeung, W. J. J., & Cheung, A. K. L. (2015). Living alone: One-person households in Asia. *Demographic research, 32,* 1099–1112.

Zarafonetis, N. (2017). *Sexuality in a changing China: Young women, sex and intimate relations in the reform period.* Routledge.

Zhu, H., & Walker, A. (2018). The gap in social care provision for older people in China. *Asian Social Work and Policy Review, 12,* 17–28.

CHAPTER 2

Detraditionalisation and Retraditionalisation of Family Lives: Gender, Marriage and Intimacy

INTRODUCTION

The individualisation thesis, also known as 'detraditionlisation', formed by theorists within Western cultures with a long history of individualism, has been documented and used to explain the major changes in family life. In Western societies, recent decades have seen an increasing sociological concern with change and diversity in personal relationships accompanied by a marked decline in the popularity of marriage and the rise in heterosexual cohabitation (Chambers, 2012). In the meantime, same-sex marriage has grown significantly across an increasing number of Western countries (Heaphy et al., 2013; Trandafir, 2015). Such transformations of intimacy have been marked by the detraditionalisation of family life where the controlling influence of traditional values and social ties that once bound families together have now been lost (Beck, 2002; Giddens, 1992).

When it comes to intimate life and the broader social changes, globalisation is commonly understood as a complex set of processes with a global reach in economic, structural, cultural and political terms. Jamieson (2011) claimed that the changes in intimate relationships are closely implicated in the processes of globalisation that social integration and reproduction are often involved in. Global intersections with the development of communications and transportation technologies have profound

© The Author(s), under exclusive license to Springer Nature Switzerland AG 2022
S. Qiu, *Gender and Family Practices*, Genders and Sexualities in the Social Sciences, https://doi.org/10.1007/978-3-031-17250-2_2

implications for the expansion and the growth of economic capitals and cultural diffusion (Giddens, 2003). One consequence of globalisation is that 'distant events ... affect us more directly and immediately than ever before' (Giddens, 1998: 31).

The increasing prevalence of non-conventional family relationships in China provides an opportunity to critically engage in current sociological debates about the Eurocentric grand theories of modernity in relation to people's intimate lives. In order to understand whether and to what extent China has undergone individualisation and transformations of intimacy as described in Western societies, in the remainder of this chapter I will review the key theoretical discussions that this research has engaged with, such as those around Western notions of modernity, individualisation, intimacy and family practices. Following this, I move to review relevant literature that informs the context within which my participants are embedded. I particularly focus on the impact of China's dramatic societal and cultural transformation (including economic reform policies and the introduction of the one-child policy) on people's understandings and experiences of intimate lives and family relationships. This led me to the argument that China's changing patterns of individualisation are unique, in which individualism centred on personal choices is in tandem with traditional collective familism.

THE GRAND THEORIES: MODERNITY, GENDER AND TRANSFORMATIONS OF INTIMACY IN THE WEST

Since the 1990s, the sociological debate around modernity, gender and intimacy has emerged predominantly in the West and soon gained much attention across societies. In the Western context, Giddens (1991: 4) claimed that modernity is a 'post-traditional order' (Giddens, 1991: 4) or characterised as affected by 'detraditionalization' (Beck, 2002: 25–26), leading to significant changes to intimate lives. It is argued that under the processes of individualisation and detraditionlisation, pre-given life trajectories and the social ties of kinship, which once bound people together, have lost their control in guiding people's everyday lives. Instead, more emphasis has been placed on the rise of individual agency in constructing family lives and relationships according to their own wishes (Beck & Beck-Gernsheim, 1995; Beck-Gernsheim, 2002). From this perspective, people have been free from externally imposed structural constraints, cultural customs and moral ethics. This increasing reflexivity of the self has engendered a decreased value placed on romantic love and commitment, leading to relationships becoming unstable, fluid and temporary (Bauman, 2003; Beck & Beck-Gernsheim, 1995; Beck, 2002; Giddens, 1992). These changes have led some Western scholars to the argument that conventional heterosexual relationships, that is, a married, co-resident heterosexual couple with children, no longer occupy the centre position in society (Roseneil, 2006). The emergence of diverse forms of relationships, such as LATs, supports the notion that people are constructing a life of their own in response to emotional and economic opportunities and challenges.

Two different interpretations have taken shape when considering the changes to family life that have occurred under the process of individualisation within late, reflexive, second or liquid modernity. Giddens (1992) keeps an optimistic attitude towards the democratisation of personal life and suggests the idea of the 'transformation of intimacy'. This is evident in the separation of sexuality from reproduction, with 'plastic sexuality' being emphasised as a means of self-expression and self-actualisation. In place of older forms of romantic love with an emphasis on lifelong commitment ('till death do us apart'), Giddens (1992: 58) then proposes an idealised and democratic 'pure relationship':

> A social relation which is entered into for its own sake, for what can be derived by each person from a sustained association with another; and which is continued only in so far as it is thought by both parties to deliver enough satisfactions for each individual to stay within it.

In his view, 'confluent love', characterised as active, contingent and dependent, features the ideal of the 'pure relationship', which is based on sexual and emotional equality and sustained only as long as both parties are fulfilled. Trust and a form of intimacy is established through intensive mutual conversation and self-disclosure. Noticeably, Giddens (1992) located women and lesbians, as well as gay men, at the forefront of this transformation, seeking more egalitarian partnerships and enjoying increased autonomy and greater gender equality.

Under the context of a growing diversity of family forms and intimate relationships, the traditional notion of 'the family' as a social institution, which normally includes two people of the opposite sex—the breadwinning husband and homemaking wife with their dependent children—has conceivably been challenged somewhat in the face of the individualisation thesis. David Morgan (1996, 2011) shifts the focus from the family as an institution to a set of social practices. The idea of 'family practices' was then proposed with a greater emphasis on 'displaying' family (Finch, 2007). As defined by Morgan (1996: 11),

> the term 'family practices' refers to a set of practices which deal in some way with ideas of parenthood, kinship, marriage and the expectations and obligations which are associated with these practices.

With a focus on active 'doing' through everyday activities, rather than the 'being' of family, this 'practices' approach enables us to explore how families are constructed and experienced in a broader social context (Gabb, 2011). One related concept in researching the complexities and diversity of family and intimate relationships is intimacy, which refers to 'the quality of close connection between people and the process of building this quality' (Jamieson, 2011). According to Jamieson (1999, 2011), 'practices of intimacy' placed a greater emphasis on the 'doing' of intimacy, including not only a dialectic of mutual self-discourse (Giddens, 1992), but also the emotional sharing and performing of practical caring, which are also considered important in maintaining intimate relationships (Holmes, 2004; Jamieson, 2011).

Late modern theories, such as Giddens' (1992), as I discussed earlier, tend to view changes in family life and the transformation of intimacy in a positive way, arguing that people are entering a 'democratic' family situation. However, Beck (2002) are more pessimistic about the changes in family life, arguing that the future of the family is disintegration and fragmentation. Under globalisation, Beck and Beck-Gernsheim (1995) argued that lasting love is difficult to maintain because people may face more challenges to remain physically together while trying to meet the demands of the labour market (Bauman, 2003). Relatedly it is argued, many family members are forging experimental and creative associations out of the new challenges and opportunities with which they are presented (Gillies, 2003: 10). As a consequence, people's intimate relationships are becoming flimsier, fluid, fragile and contingent (Bauman, 2003; Beck-Gernsheim, 2002; Beck & Beck-Gernsheim, 1995; Beck, 2002). Modern social conditions will succeed in pulling families part (Smart, 2007: 19).

While the concept of individualisation and its consequences—a democratising notion of the 'transformation of intimacy' (Giddens, 1992)—have been used to explain the major changes in family life, the utopian vision of individual-driven and democratic relationships has been comprehensively and persistently criticised by feminists and other researchers (Heaphy, 2007; Jackson, 2015b; Jamieson, 1999, 2011; Smart, 2007). In fact, there is sparse empirical evidence to support Giddens' claim that people are entering into the democratisation of family life. Even in Euro-American family relationships, institutionalised family and marriage have not been erased, and the ways in which people live out their intimate lives are still modified by traditions and norms (Carter & Duncan, 2018; Jamieson, 1998). For example, Gross (2005: 286) makes a distinction regarding traditions between 'regulative' and 'meaning-constitutive', with the former involving the exclusion of an individual from various moral communities, and the latter involving 'patterns of sense making passed down from one generation to the next'. With this differentiation, Gross (2005) concludes that what may have declined in the process of detraditionalisation are only some certain regulative traditions around family life, through which external constraints are placed on social action. Meaning-constitutive traditions of romantic love and commitment, however, continue to play a crucial role in structuring contemporary intimacy. This argument has been further supported by other scholars who suggest that, in the UK, people still place greater emphasis on commitment (Carter, 2012) and value relationships with others, especially partners, parents and children, just as much as before (Thwaites, 2016; Twamley, 2019). If this is the case in the West then we should not be surprised that aspects of Confucian tradition continue to be 'meaning constitutive' in East Asia (Jackson & Ho, 2020: 27).

Whatever the changes in family structures, Giddens' (1992) transformation of intimacy and the supposed effects of individualisation and detraditionalisation on intimate lives stand accused of exaggerating individual agency and personal choice (Heaphy, 2007; Smart, 2007). In reality, the choices that people make regarding their intimate lives are still, to some extent, embedded in local culture and social context and bound by structural constraints such as social class, gender and ethnicity (Duncan & Irwin, 2004; Duncan & Smith, 2006; Jackson, 2015b; Jamieson, 1999; Smart & Shipman, 2004). Feminist literature has shown the continued importance of the interdependence of kin, gender and forms of collectivism in contemporary family practices (Heaphy, 2007; Morgan, 1996; Pahl & Spencer, 2004; Smart & Shipman, 2004). For example, in the specific context of China's rapid economic development and the rise of individualism, while on the one hand urban young people from the one-child generation embrace the Western idea of individualism in relation to choosing marriage partners and setting up their own homes, rather than living in extended families, on the other hand, they are still influenced by collectivism whereby filial piety, as central to traditional Confucian teachings, continues to organise people's everyday practices (Croll, 2006; Hansen & Pang, 2010; Jamieson, 2011; Yan, 2009;). Instead of considering alternatives to individualised 'free choice' marriage as a way of catching up with Western individualisation, the practices of intimacy in a non-Western context can be regarded as 'different ways of doing family' (Smart & Shipman, 2004: 496).

Giddens also suggested that mutual self-disclosure is the basis of intimacy in the 'pure relationship'. However, this statement ignores the significance of other forms of intimacy, such as caring and practical doing and giving, which are also 'as much the crux of their relationship, as a process of mutually discovering and enjoying each other' (Jamieson, 1999: 485). Furthermore, Jamieson (2011) points out that because of Giddens' failure in engaging with feminist work, the persistence of gender inequalities remains untouched. Although there is evidence of women's greater power within marriage, the continuing inequality between heterosexual relationships is still there (Holmes, 2004; Jamieson, 1999). In reality, most women have not fully benefited from the greater individual agency and choice that social change has brought about (Jamieson, 1999). This leads to the consideration that the consequences of the individualisation process may not be the same (Holmes, 2004; Jackson et al., 2013; Jamieson, 2011; Qi, 2015). Having said this, the applicability of individualisation in a non-Western context is worthy of critical examination (Smart & Shipman, 2004).

Contextualising Social Change in China

It is important to acknowledge that modernity is essentially framed and developed in post-industrial societies from a Eurocentric perspective. However, the hegemony of Western notions of modernity has overstated that Western societies are detraditionalised whereas other non-Western societies (such as Asian countries) are still burdened with traditions. Such rigid and binary opposition between modernity (of the West) and tradition (of the East) has been called into question for failing to account for changes to family lives and transformation of intimacy beyond the West (Jackson et al., 2013; Jamieson, 2011). Moving to the Chinese context, there is ample evidence showing that China is in the process of a major modernisation project (Yan, 2009). However, the Chinese path to detraditionalisation of personal life has its unique characteristics due to its specific social, cultural, economic and political environment. This has led some researchers to the argument that Western modernity is not everyone's modernity (Jackson, 2015b; Tanabe & Tokita-Tanabe, 2003). As such, we should take account of varied traditions and seek a balance between the ways in which tradition is constructed and 'recognising that particular histories and cultural ideals do create persistent differences between countries and regions of the world' (Jackson & Ho, 2020:16).

When considering whether and how far Chinese society has undergone individualisation and transformation of intimacy as described in Western societies, numerous previous studies have often concentrated on three developmental stages: The Mao Era (1949–1976), the Reform Era (1978–1991) and the Postreform Era (1992 onwards). It is important to understand the changes for intimate lives in the wider social, historical, economic and cultural context before examining the possible social implications for people's lives. In terms of the first stage, since the foundation of the People's Republic of China (PRC) under chairman Mao Zedong on 1 October 1949, Chinese family structures and women's status began to change. The First Marriage Law in 1950 legally replaced traditional arranged or forced marriage with free-choice monogamy marriage, which has played an important role in improving women's status. Under Mao's era, the Chinese Communist Party (CCP) controlled economic power through the socialist planned economy and its collective re-distribution system. With the central aim of constructing the wealth and power of the nation state under Maoist socialism, the CCP encouraged women to 'walk out of the house' (Jin, 2006; Wolf, 1985; Zuo & Bian, 2001) in order to participate in employment under the slogan 'women hold up half the sky'. Chinese women's contribution to productive work was socially recognised and their position relative to men also improved (Croll, 1981; Parish & White, 1978; Weeks, 1989). This can be seen from the discourses, throughout the Maoist period, about gender equality, such as 'the times have changed, men and women are the same' and 'women can do anything that men do'. It is argued that gender equality was promoted under the context of some collectivist programmes in the 1950s. At that time, women often dressed in the same androgynous way as men, cutting their hair short, wearing uniforms and having wide shoulders with strong arms, all in order to minimise gender differences and celebrate sexual equality

(Finnane, 1996). During the Cultural Revolution, the image of 'iron girls' was culturally created and referred to female model workers participating in productive labour and performing physically demanding jobs, such as working in the iron and steel industries.[1] Under this specific historical and social context, the de-sexualising movement as part of the socialist transformation project to some degree disembedded the individual from the constraints of the traditional gender roles and family values (Yan, 2010). Although people at that time had no freedom to choose where to work or to reside, their participation in 'party-state-sponsored political, economic, and social campaigns in public life' served to reconstruct individual self identity not merely as a member of the family (Yan, 2010: 493). Nevertheless, a great improvement was observed in many social and economic aspects of people's lives, unexpectedly leading to a partial individualisation of Chinese society in Mao's era (Yan, 2010).

During the reform era, China's economic transition to a market-oriented economy profoundly refashioned many areas of social life. This was manifested in people's greater freedom to take part in the labour market as a result of the disruption of state-allocated employment (Davis, 1999; Hoffman, 2008; Tsui & Rich, 2002) and the loosening of the *hukou* (household registration) system (Croll, 2006).[2] With the authoritarian state being challenged, the individual gained more power to create their own biography, which was no longer strictly fixed and conditioned by institutional constraints (Evans, 1997; Yan, 2009). In the 1980s, China launched the stringent one-child policy, which led to a sharp decline in the total fertility rate (Guo, 2012).[3] Data show that the fertility rate dropped sharply from 6.123 births per woman in 1965–1970 to below 1.5 from

---

[1] The Cultural Revolution (1966–1976) was a decade-long mass movement, during which universities were shut down entirely from 1966 to 1972. The propaganda of 'knowledge is useless' led a whole generation of Chinese youth to be less educated. For detailed accounts of the implications of the Chinese Cultural Revolution, see Bernstein (1977) and Lee (1978).

[2] The hukou system was first implemented in 1951 to require all households to be registered in the locale where they resided, with the aim of monitoring population migration and movements (for more details on the hukou system, see Chan & Zhang, 1999).

[3] Under the one-child policy, Chinese couples were only allowed to have one child (although some couples in which both partners were single children were exempted from this limitation). The governmental restriction has had particularly profound implications for controlling population growth. The national birth-rate declined rapidly from 23.33% in 1987 and 16.57% in 1997 to 8.52% in 2020. Furthermore, a substantial decline was also apparent in the national population growth rate, from 16.61% in 1987 and 10.06% in 1997 to 1.45% in 2020 (National Bureau of Statistics of China, 2021).

the 2000s (United Nations Population Division, 2017). China has shifted remarkably from a country with high fertility, high infant mortality and low life expectancy to a country with low fertility, low infant mortality and high life expectancy by the 1990s (Xie, 2011). This demographic transition is further reflected in the substantial decline in the average size of Chinese family households (persons per household), from 4.41 in 1982, 3.44 in 2000, 3.10 in 2010 to 2.62 in 2020 (NBS, 2021). Noticeably, the implementation of China's universal two-child policy in 2016 has arguably far-reaching implications in relation to fertility rate, the ageing population, gender equality and economic development (Qian & Jin, 2018; Zeng & Hesketh, 2016).

Deng Xiaoping's speech in 1992 marked China's economic reform entering a new era. The overarching goal was to achieve common prosperity through getting some people and some regions to become rich first. Despite the fact that this was at the cost of equality between people and across regions, this principle enabled China to experience rapid urbanisation and enormous economic growth. In conjunction with economic reform, education in China also experienced massive expansion in the 1980s. Previous studies have shown that enrolment in higher education rose from 1.15% in 1980 to 29.7% in 2013 (UNESO, 2015) and women now exceeded men in terms of the numbers of enrolment and competition rates in Chinese colleges and universities (Li, 1994; Wu & Zhang, 2010). Improving access to education for women, combined with a significantly rising rates of female labour-market participation, has resulted in women becoming more economically independent and in practice having more egalitarian attitudes concerning gender roles. More importantly, China's reconnecting to the world through joining the World Trade Organisation in 2001 has further enabled more and more people to access Western values and ideas of individualism. Empirical evidence shows that Chinese women's educational attainment and growing participation in the labour market since the economic reforms, along with the influence of Western ideas of individualisation, have empowered them to free themselves from prescribed gender roles and family obligations (Song & Ji, 2020). It is in this ever-changing social context that the discourse of the de-institutionalisation of family and marriage has started to appear in China (Davis & Friedman, 2014; Farrer, 2014).

Certainly, China's dramatic social and economic transformations have brought about many changes in personal lives in relation to attitudes towards and perceptions of intimacy and family life, which makes China a fruitful setting in which to examine the extent to which individualisation is applicable to societies beyond the Western world. Some scholars take Western individualisation and modernity as a benchmarks and predict that China will follow and 'imitate' family modernisation in Western industrial societies (Wu & Li, 2012). This is particular evident when the similarities in the changes in family life between West and East are observed, such as: later marriage, lower birth-rates, more divorce and higher female participation in the labour market (Jackson et al., 2013; Zeng & Wu, 2000). For example, Zheng et al. (2011) argue that the concept of 'detraditionalisation' applies well to the Chinese context, based on the changes in people's attitudes towards sexual behaviours. In the process of modernisation, familism, which has dominated most Confucian societies, has often been criticised as outdated and conservative. In contrast, individualism is seen as highly praised and, at the same time, the importance of marriage and family is seen to have declined, accompanied by weakened filial piety and familial collectivism (Davis & Friedman, 2014).

Others claim that it is not rational to assume that the consequences of individualisation and Western modernity have the same outcome for intimate life everywhere. Nevertheless, although we live in a globalised and late modern world, similarities in relation to the changes in family life are widely acknowledged (Jackson et al., 2013; Jamieson, 2011; Qi, 2015; Rofel, 1999; Tanabe & Tokita-Tanabe, 2003; Yan, 2008, 2009). Taking Britain and Hong Kong as examples, even if both do, to a large extent, share some similarities in aspects of family-related activities, the consequences of these features are variable in the light of cultural distinctiveness, socio-economic environment, political circumstances and material conditions (Jackson & Ho, 2020). In particular, non-marital sexual activity (except extra-marital or among those deemed 'too young') and single parenthood rarely attract opprobrium in countries such as the UK (Jackson & Ho, 2014). Whereas the situation in East Asia is rather different: the high value placed on women's virginity and Asian familialism, with its emphasis on family harmony and lineage continuity, does make it difficult to accommodate single mothers and same-sex relationships (Chang & Song, 2010; Jackson, 2015a; Jackson & Ho, 2014; Yan, 2009). As such, it has been argued that the consequences of Western modernity do not always fit neatly into East Asian countries due to differences in social conditions.

In contemporary China, people's lived experiences in intimate lives have also indicated a rather complex picture under the processes of individualisation and detraditionalisation (Chen, 2015; Wang & Nehring, 2014). While being exposed to Western ideas of individualism, traditional values on gender roles still have great purchase and continue to affect the ways people understand and construct their own family life (Yan, 2010). The 'family', as a social institution where two heterosexual married people with dependent children live in the same household, has been perceived as being an ideal and dominant living arrangement even in contemporary Chinese society (Xie, 2013). Within heterosexually, patriarchally ordered patterns of relating, women continue to undertake primary responsibility for caring for family members in their everyday lives (Ji, 2017; Raymo et al., 2015).

In addition, when linking the individualisation thesis to the Chinese context, it often neglects the 'process of reinterpretation and re-negotiation of filial obligation' (Qi, 2016: 39). Family bonds and the practice of family obligations remains crucial in Chinese society where adult children are, by law, obligated to care for their parents, given that the lack of a substantial social welfare system and the absence of cultural democracy or classic individualism has transferred the caring responsibility from the state to individual families (Yan, 2010). As a consequence, the traditionally patrilineal culture and discourse regarding filial norms reinforce the gendered patterns of parent care. Women still are expected to undertake primary responsibility for caring for family members in their everyday lives. In this light, researchers argue that family practices throughout China, and other Asian societies sharing a Confucian ideology of patrilineal family formation, remain heavily patterned (Jackson et al., 2008; Liu et al., 2019).

Transformations in intimacy and families during the social and economic development of China may have unique patterns and trajectories as 'grand social changes are mediated through local cultures' (Hareven, 2001: 35, see also Jackson, 2015b; Rofel, 1999; Yan, 2009). In order not to confine ourselves within the Western European perspective, the differences in social and cultural conditions between the West and East should be taken into account. With an attempt to unpack the coexistence of modernity and tradition in relation to gender and family dynamics, Ji (2017: 3) put forward the notion of 'mosaic familism' and argued that the contemporary Chinese family is 'characterised by a resurgence of Confucian patriarchal tradition' while being informed by the 'neoliberal rhetoric of individual responsibility'. This family system, on the one hand, has emphasised the traditional virtues of womanhood in the family, and on the other hand, constituted 'women's sacrifices as their own personal choice' (2017:

3). In a similar way, Yan (2021) documented the rise of 'neo-familism' where individual agency in family life has increased while China's modernity process intersects with the Confucian revival movement. This suggests that detraditionalisation of intimate lives may involve the process of retraditionalisation in that certain forms of traditions and norms are reinvented and reused to fit in the new social circumstance. In order to understand the transformation of intimacy and families during the social and economic development of China, we should attend to cultural specificity and local social contexts within which discourses and practices of gender and family are constructed. As Jackson (2013: 36) suggests, 'any aspect of human life is to be understood as constituted through and bounded by the social conditions of its existence'.

Gender Relations and Family Life in China

Women, Love and Family

There have been many discussions in the literature that attempt to examine the changing patterns in marriage and family life in China since the twentieth century, due to the spread of Western influences, particularly the process of individualisation and modernisation combined with internal campaigns (such as the founding of the People's Republic of China (PRC) in 1949, the implementation of the one-child policy and the 1978 economic reform) (Jankowiak & Moore, 2017; Jones & Yeung, 2014; Raymo et al., 2015). Historically, marriage and family in both China and other Asian societies shared a Confucian ideology of patrilineal family formation, which was seen as the bedrock of national development, facilitating social stability and harmony (Guo, 2010; To, 2013; Xu et al., 2015). The extended family with multiple generations living together has a long tradition in Chinese history and was seen as a typical and ideal Chinese family (Zeng & Xie, 2014). With a long history of the patriarchal and patrilineal family system in China, two sets of familial relations—conjugal (between husband and wife) and intergenerational (between parents and children)—have been considered to be the key organising principle of family relationships (Fei, 1939). Horizontally, conjugal relations were traditionally regulated by gender roles prescribing women as care providers and homemakers and men as primarily financial contributors (Evans, 1997; Hu & Scott, 2016). This division of labour in the domestic sphere contributes to the 'typical' practices of family: *nan zhu wai, nü zhu nei* (men are in charge of the outside and women take care of inside the home) (Shek, 2006). Vertically, the traditional Confucian practices of filial piety served as the foundational elements in maintaining the Chinese patriarchal family system that prescribed young adult children to provide old-age support for their parents (Jacka et al., 2013). In light of the strong tradition of patrilocal marital practices, the caring responsibility for elders has thus largely fallen on married women (Yan, 2003). In the context of the patriarchal, patrilineal and patrilocal organisation of Chinese extended families, Chinese women have historically been expected to become a *xian qi liang mu* (virtuous wife and good mother), taking good care of their husband and children, as well as the family elders (Smits & Park, 2009).

With respect to the formation of the marital union, marriage, especially in traditional China, was not ostensibly connected with love and mutual affection; rather, it was the union of two families (Pan, 2010). As a social institution, 'the marriage is arranged on the orders of the parents through the words of the matchmakers' (*fu mu zhi ming mei shuo zhi yan*) and was a common regulatory principle of mate selection in traditional China (Wang & Nehring, 2014: 585; see also Davis, 2014; Raymo et al., 2015; Thornton & Lin, 1994; Xu et al., 2000; Xu & Whyte, 1990). Only after a matchmaker's introduction, and when parents considered that the two families' status (such as wealth and social status) were similar and could be matched, would the marriage go forward (Croll, 1981; Yuen et al., 1998). This implies the importance of status-matching in the process of mate selection. In addition, young people, especially women, had little autonomy in relation to their own marriage in traditional Chinese society because the agreement about whom to marry and the timing was often made according to their parents' desires (Parish & White, 1978). Therefore, it has been argued that traditional marriage was often viewed as a way to maintain and improve family interests by connecting the political, social and economic resources between two families.

The founding of the People's Republic of China (PRC) on 1 October 1949, together with the effect of the First Marriage Law in 1950, played a fundamental role in changing the prospects for women and shaping marriage practices (Croll, 1981; Evans, 2002; Hannum, 2005; Jacka et al., 2013). The 1950 Marriage Law prohibited 'feudal' marriage based on exchange and calculations, and instead legislated free-choice monogamous marriage based on mutual affection and conjugal companionship among people (Yan, 2003). It has been argued that the First Marriage Law has shaped the family institution by empowering women in their marital relationships (Li, 1994; Lu, 2004; Whyte & Parish, 1984). In reality, however, traditional arranged marriages remained common (Dillon, 2009). Couples still relied on introductions from others (such as co-workers or relatives) to meet a potential spouse. In particular, parents often played a crucial role in their children's mate selection, especially in rural areas (Whyte & Parish, 1984; Yan, 2003). One plausible reason for the popularity of being introduced to a prospective partner is related to the 'transitional period' when young people were on the one hand deeply influenced by traditional arranged marriage and, on the other hand, had to 'adapt to the new values in marriage formation' (Yang, 2017: 119).

The anthropologist Yunxiang Yan carried out a ten-year-long fieldwork study in a village in Northeastern China (Yan, 2002). He observed that, during the 1960s and 1970s in rural China, the opportunities for young men and women to spend time together before marriage were still few. It was not a common practice to say *wo ai ni* (I love you), in a face-to-face situation, as a way of expressing love and mutual affection. Instead, other forms of expression, such as practical actions, sharing a political ideology, writing love letters or bodily gestures, were more acceptable and regarded as a signal of love. Mate selection and the meanings that people attached to 'love' were subject to various interpretations in accordance with the state's needs (Liu, 2004). For example, Chinese people often started a relationship with consideration of whether an individual had similar aspirations for their future (marital) life and if he/she had a determined motivation for 'working at it' (Hershatter, 2007). Due to political and social transformations in a particular social context, 'sharing the same political and ideological outlook was the most basic condition of love' (Evans, 1997: 91), and, for women, finding a politically 'promising' man became the top choice between the 1950s and early 1960s in China (Whyte & Parish, 1984). In other words, people in the Maoist era barely linked love and intimacy with marriage, even if a lifelong heterosexual monogamous marriage was greatly practised as the social norm and was considered the ideal type of intimate relationship in China. In this collectivist culture, love, which serves as the foundation of a marriage and marital stability in modern Western countries (Coontz, 2006; Lewis, 2001), at best was seen as a necessary but not sufficient prerequisite for a lasting relationship (Dion & Dion, 1988; Zang, 2011). In this regard, intimacy and personal happiness are less emphasised in non-Western marriage than in Western marriage (Dion & Dion, 1993). Instead, practical functioning in marriage was prioritised for having children, especially sons, in order to keep the family lineage alive (Chu & Yu, 2010). Due to expectations of women's virginity before marriage, pre-marital sex in Mao's era was very rare. In addition, married women were socially expected to follow the patrilocal arrangement—moving in with the groom's family. Divorce was very complicated and prohibited due to party–state interference (Ma et al., 2018).

Even though Chairman Mao's reform improved women's status relative to men, it is not fully true to suggest that Chinese women enjoyed gender equality, because little change in relation to women's roles has been found in the domestic sphere (Parish & White, 1978; Wolf, 1985). According to Evans (2002), women were, on the one hand, devoting themselves to socialist construction during Mao's era and, on the other hand, still needed to serve their own small families (see also, Yu & Xie, 2011). This view is also shared by Manning (2007: 144), who demonstrates that women were regarded as 'mothers at home and labourers with special needs'. Having said this, women's labour participation, driven by the socialist transformation project for economic construction, was seen as supplementary on the ground that once economic recovery was well under way, women were expected to return to the domestic sphere and make the family their priority. Therefore, some scholars have argued that Mao's remarks were simply justifying the exploitation of women's physical labour as well as men's, for the revolutionary cause (Jin, 2006; Zhang, 2003).

Moving to the 1980s, China has begun its economic reform shifting from a planned economy to a market-based economy. The 'open-door' policy initiated by Deng Xiaoping and subsequent social changes have brought about significant impacts on personal life as well as the overall structure of society (Ho et al., 2018). The influx of information and the romantic imagery of love from Western films, television and other mass media have enriched people's understanding of intimate relationships (Evans, 1997; Yan, 2002). With the dissolution of the *danwei* (work-unit) system in urban China, the government's intervention into individual private life has gradually weakened, with more autonomy and freedom in relation to marital experiences being exercised by people. For example, dating before marriage has become a common practice for young people in contemporary China, whereas this did not hold a central place during Mao's era (Whyte & Xu, 1990). Partner choices are also constantly subject to various socio-economic, historical, political and cultural influences in a specific context. With the influence of the Western idea of individualism coupled with less parental involvement in children's marriage-related activities, young people were shown a strong subjective desire to self-select a prospective partner based on freedom of choice (Blair & Madigan, 2016). In comparison with their parents' generation, when people often lived in a relatively closed sociocultural society and prioritised the practicality of love, younger generations who were born after the 1980s and established their dating relationships during the 2000s, are more open and vocal in expressing love and intimacy in more 'Western' ways. The importance of men's physical strength (to do farm work) has lessened, whereas the individual's compatibility with undertaking skilled work (such as non-agricultural jobs) and a strong educational background have greatly increased during the process of mate selection (Yan, 2002).

The generational differences in dating practices are particularly pertinent to the 'increased participation of women in the paid labour force and greater equality in educational opportunities' (Piotrowski & Tong, 2016: 130). These generational differences are also manifested in relation to attitudes towards premarital sex, cohabitation, divorce and extramarital love (Higgins & Sun, 2007; Woo, 2006; Yang, 2017). There was a subjective consciousness conveying that love is a personal thing, and should be decided by people's desires, not controlled by the state. In a similar way, as several studies on the sexual revolution have shown, premarital intercourse seems to be seen as a private affair and fairly acceptable behaviour among both engaged couples in rural areas (Pan et al., 2004; Whyte & Parish, 1984; Yan, 2002) and couples in urban areas (Farrer, 2002). The revision of the 1980 Marriage Law makes divorce easier when couple's emotional relationship (*ganqing*) has ruptured (Huang, 2005).

In the 1990s and early 2000s, growing consumer culture and rising living standards indicated a new sensibility among young Chinese citizens. This is evident in the increased expression of sexual love, pleasure and cosmopolitan desires among Chinese youth (Rofel, 2007; Yan, 2010). They were called 'desiring subjects' who operated through 'sexual, material, and affective self-interest' (Rofel, 2007: 3). In contrast with their mothers' generation in the Mao era when sexual desire was repressed and marriage often formed out of kinship obligations, young people see themselves 'as having within their grasp the possibility of becoming free from all constraints' (Rofel, 2007: 118). The changing pattern of love and sexual desire has initially emerged in urban cities, such as Shanghai during the 1990s (Farrer, 2002, 2011) and has apparently since become widespread (Farrer, 2014; Jeffreys & Yu, 2015; Zarafonetis, 2017). The rise of sexualised forms of love indicates a transformation towards intimacy in couple relationships in China (Yan, 2002) and supports Jackson's (2013: 36) argument that love is 'produced and reproduced through socially located interactions and practices, through the "doing" of love in given relationships'.

Since the housing market opened up as a result of rapid economic development, people's living expenses have significantly increased, generating pressures for both the younger generation and their parents (Wu et al., 2012). Therefore, people have become more materialistic, with more attention being paid to a prospective partner's financial resources in the formation of marriage (Cai & Feng, 2014; Mu & Xie, 2014; Osburg, 2013; Yu & Xie, 2015). There is clear evidence that an abundance of choices exist in relation to conducting family arrangements (Yan, 2009). For example, traditional three-generation extended families have greatly declined in numbers, while smaller, independent and more mobile family units are experiencing rapid growth leading to a nuclear family form. Being exposed to Western ideas of individualism and increasing peer connections outside family networks, young people, in particular, demand privacy and intimacy, and tend to form a conjugal family in urban areas after marriage, instead of living with the husband's parents (Yan, 2009). In addition, a continuing tendency towards an increase in one-person households over the past three decades was noted, rising from 4.9% in 1990 to 14.5% in 2010 (Cheung & Yeung, 2015). Under these circumstances, some researchers have demonstrated that the traditional Chinese patrilineal extended family has been gradually replaced by the nuclear family—two-generational households—under the process of socio-economic changes and rising individualism (Xu & Xia, 2014).

However, recently researchers have documented a 'revival' of the intergenerational co-residence living arrangement in spite of modernisation in contemporary China. First, high living costs and housing problems in urban areas resulting from rapid economic development over the past few decades have led to the persistence of the extended family in contemporary China (Xu et al., 2014). In addition, in the context of insufficient state welfare support, caring for the elderly, as informed by the culture of reciprocity (Yang, 1994), has greatly increased the likelihood of living in an extended family (Chen et al., 2017; Lei et al., 2015; Xu, 2013). In the case of couples living apart together, it becomes difficult in practical terms for only one parent, who may still have a paid job to do, to raise young children. China has a cultural tradition of emphasis on paternal and maternal grandparents, rather than the state and institution, for providing childcare on a regular basis. Especially in the circumstance where there are young children at home and the wife or husband is absent due to work commitments, married people often seek practical help from their elderly parents. Under this circumstance, there is frequently a family consisting of elderly parent(s), grandchildren and one parent (normally the mother, not the father, who may usually be working away from home). The formation of intergenerational co-residence is seen to be facilitated by the absence of the father from a family for providing access for children's care (Chen et al., 2011; Lei et al., 2015; Settles et al., 2013).

Changing Marital Practices

Situated in the broader context of rapid socio-economic development and globalisation, the social institution of marriage in China has been confronted with challenges. One example of this can be seen from the declining rate of marriage and a modest increase in the average age at first marriage for both Chinese women and men in the past decade (Cai & Feng, 2014; Gao & Wu, 2012; Jones & Yeung, 2014; Raymo et al., 2015; Yu & Xie, 2015). Some argued that Chinese families have become more similar to Western families, leading to the decline in the institution of marriage as manifested in greater tolerance to premarital sex and cohabitation, increasing divorce rate, rising age at first marriage, and declining rate of marriage (Ji & Yeung, 2014; Zheng et al., 2011).

However, without looking into reasons underlying the changes in marriage patterns, we cannot fully engage in the debates about whether the institution of marriage in China is in decline. The rise in age at first marriage as one key aspect of the changing patterns of marriage can be taken as an example of this. Studies suggest a clear link between the timing of marriage and an individual's socio-economic characteristics, such as gender, educational attainment and employment (Cai & Feng, 2014). As a result of China's rapid economic expansion, economic prospects (such as employment status) have increasingly played an important role in marriage formation, which simultaneously brings pressures on young people to survive in the competitive labour and marriage market (Mu & Xie, 2014; Yu & Xie, 2015). In conjunction with market-oriented reform, education is also found to have direct effects on the timing of marriage (Cai & Feng, 2014; Thornton & Lin, 1994). This is mainly because of the expansion of China's higher education since the 1980s, which results in people spending more time in school. In addition, the one-child policy has empowered (urban) daughters to have access to education as they do not have to compete with their brothers for educational resources (Fong, 2002). Consequently, Chinese women's educational attainment and growing participation in the labour market since the reform era have significantly empowered them with economic independence (Ji, 2015a). For some urban professional women, career development is reported to be more attractive at a certain stage in their lives than getting married, as a way to seek financial resources. This is despite the fact that women may still face challenges, both from the 'gender double standard of aging' and increasing discrimination in the labour market (Ji & Yeung, 2014).

From the perspective of economic independence theory (Willis, 1987), building upon family exchange theory, an increase in women's labour-force participation and earning potential can reduce their financial dependence upon their husbands, thus deprioritising the importance of marriage for women (Qian & Qian, 2014). In addition, the place of origin can also lead to delaying marriage, with cities such as Shanghai and Beijing clearly seeing a rise in the age of marriage in recent years due to housing problems, financial pressures and competitive work environments (Ji, 2015b; Ji & Yeung, 2014). More importantly, limited changes in family obligations and gender roles have also given rise to delayed marriage. The 'marriage package', in the traditional Chinese marriage system, includes multiple expectations placed on women, such as intensive mothering for raising children and responsibility for taking care of two sets of parents, alongside an asymmetric division of housework (Bumpass et al., 2009; Parish & Farrer, 2000). Although lessening over time, the traditional gender roles regarding obedient daughters, virtuous wives and kind mothers remain central in practical and cultural terms (Hu & Scott, 2016). In this way, women's increasing demands for individual choice and autonomy, facilitated by higher educational attainment and greater financial independence, may coexist with the socially defined familial expectations for gender roles (Raymo et al., 2015; Xie, 2013). The intricate transformation of marriage patterns that China has been undergoing makes it distinct from those in Western societies.

Admittedly, Chinese young people's agency and power in deciding when and whom to marry is significantly greater than it was for earlier generations. Meanwhile, young generations also experience greater sexual freedom due to China's 'sexual revolution' (Pan, 2006). However, same-sex marriage and non-heterosexual relationships are still stigmatised and not legally recognised in China (Kong, 2012, 2016). The state control and censorship of the media has significantly increased since Xi Jining came to power in 2012 (Ringen, 2016). Diversity and alternative sexualities are potentially subversive if framed positively. On 30 June 2017, the *wangluo shiting jiemu neirong shenhe tongze* (Network Audio-visual Program Content Audit General Rules) were passed, which immediately caused great controversy. The problem is mainly concentrated in Section 6 of the general rules, which prohibits the promotion and representation of pornography and 'bad taste'. These include images and scenes of prostitution, promiscuity, rape and masturbation; the representation of abnormal sexual relationships and practices, including incest, homosexuality, sexual perversion, sexual assault, sexual torture and sexual violence; and the promotion of unhealthy values on marriage, extra-marital relationships, one-night stands and sexual liberation. The promulgation of the general rules is arguably flawed as the constitutional right to creative freedom will be affected and the rights of sexual minorities are threatened (Li, 2017).[4]

The family in contemporary China is constructed as the cell of society and monogamous marriage is crucial to sustaining social stability (Sigley, 2006; To, 2015). Recent statistics on marital status reveal that marriage is still unwavering in China. As shown in the Table 2.1, about 95.5% of Chinese women aged between 30 and 34 were married in 2013, whereas the same proportion dropped sharply to 65.4% and 62.5% for Japanese and South Korean women, respectively, in 2015 (United Nations, 2017). Even though the 1980 Marriage Law has increased the legal minimum age of marriage to 22 for men and 20 for women, the mean age of entry into marriage remains earlier in China in comparison with other East Asian societies (Ji & Yeung, 2014).[5]

The younger 'marriageable ages' reflect that marriage continues to be a strong social institution, one deeply rooted in kinship systems to favour the practices of patriarchal and patrilineal families (Cai & Feng, 2014). This universality of marriage undoubtedly poses particular challenges, especially for those not following the trend. For example, in China, women unmarried in their late 20s, and especially after 30 years old, are negatively

[4] The Chinese sexuality scholar and social activist Li Yinhe posted comments on her Weibo page and only five hours later, her blog post was deleted. https://freedomhouse.org/country/china/freedom-net/2018.

[5] In 2010, the mean age of a first marriage in Japan was 29.7 for women and 31.2 for men; it was 30.1 for women and 32.9 for men in South Korea, and 30.4 for women and 32.7 for men in Taiwan (Jones & Yeung, 2014).

Table 2.1 Marriage patterns in China, Hong Kong, Japan and South Korea

% Ever married	Aged 25–29	Aged 30–34	Aged 35–39
PRC men	63.7 (2010)	87.4 (2010)	93.6 (2010)
	64.5 (2013)	89.6 (2013)	95.2 (2013)
PRC women	78.4 (2010)	94.7 (2010)	98.2 (2010)
	78.5 (2013)	95.5 (2013)	98.7 (2013)
HK men (2011)	17.4	50	71.2
HK women (2011)	32.3	65	77.4
Japanese men	28.2 (2010)	52.7 (2010)	64.4 (2010)
	27.3 (2015)	52.9 (2015)	65 (2015)
Japanese women	39.7 (2010)	65.5 (2010)	76.9 (2010)
	38.7 (2015)	65.4 (2015)	76.1 (2015)
South Korean men (2005)	18.3	58.7	81.6
South Korean women	40.9 (2005)	81.0 (2005)	92.4 (2005)
	22.7 (2015)	62.5 (2015)	80.8 (2015)

Source: United Nations, Department of Economic and Social Affairs, Population Division (2017). World Marriage Data 2017. All the above figures derive from census data

labelled by the public and officials as *sheng nü* (leftover women), including those well-educated women with successful careers (Fincher, 2014; Gui, 2020; To, 2015).[6] Given that the persistence of traditional-status hypergamy practices remain common in contemporary China,[7] Chinese women with 'three highs' (high education, high income and advancing age) are placed at a very disadvantaged position in the marriage market to find a 'capable' partner, because some women are reluctant to experience downward mobility (Cai & Feng, 2014; To, 2013; Zarafonetis, 2017). As such, anxious Chinese parents, again, get involved in their children's love relationship through gathering together at the 'marriage market' to trade information on their adult unmarried children (Wong, 2014). Men also feel intense familial pressure to marry as China's patrilineal kinship system placed on men the duty to carry on the family line (Evans, 1997; Song,

---

[6] The term *sheng nü* is propagated by the Chinese Ministry of Education (2007) to stigmatise unmarried women. Sheng nü specifically refers to urban professional women aged over 27 years old with high educational levels, high salaries, high intelligence and attractive appearance, but also overly high expectations for marriage partners. As such, they are 'left behind' in the marriage market.

[7] 'Status hypergamy' refers to the tendency of young women to marry up with regard to education and higher social status. This indigenous practice has long been a prevalent cultural norm in China, while it may have been eroded along with women's improved social stuts (Croll, 1981; Mu & Xie, 2014; Xu et al., 2000).

2008). Those unmarried and childless men are commonly known as 'bare branches'. Ho et al. (2018) claim that by marrying and having at least one child, people are seen as ideal sexual citizens fulfilling their duty to their families and nation. For both Chinese men and women, 'childless is not read as choice, but as pathology: either she or her husband is too sick, too old or just "too weak"' (Evans, 2002: 348).

Furthermore, marital pressure has also had a non-negligible impact on sexual minorities. It is no doubt that China's opening up has facilitated sexual freedom, and the emergence of *gay*, *tongzhi* and *lala* communities since the 1990s has received considerable attention (Kam, 2013; Kong, 2016; Rofel, 2007, 2012). The term *tongzhi* literally means 'comrade', has political connotations and was often used between the Republic of China and Mao eras. It is now widely used in China, Hong Kong and Taiwan to refer to lesbian, gay, bisexual, transgender, queer (LGBTQ) communities as it is seen as less stigmatising than the alternative, *tongxinglian* (homosexuality) (Lau et al., 2017). While previous studies on homosexuality tended to draw on a biomedical framework, positioning homosexuals as 'other' to the 'normative' sexuality (Li & Wang, 1992), this has changed since the 1990s. Researchers have shifted their focus to examine homosexuality at the individual level and explored the everyday life experience of lesbians and gay men in Shanghai (Kam, 2013), Beijing (Engebretsen, 2014), Hainan (Cummings, 2022) and Hong Kong (Kong, 2016; Tang, 2011). Despite the fact that sexual desires and practices are experienced, their lifestyles are under surveillance. As a result, members of LGBTQ communities need to manage their relationships with both lovers and wider families.

As Chinese culture places great emphasis on conformity and fitting in, it is estimated that among male homosexuals and bisexuals living in urban areas, 70–80% are married or are engaged to be married to a woman, compared to 90% for those living in rural areas (Zhang & Chu, 2005). As a means of conforming to the hegemonic heteronormative family system, recent years have seen a growing number of gay men and *lalas* entering a 'cooperative marriage' to accommodate their parents' demands, whilst carving out time and space for same-sex relationships (Wang, 2019, see also Choi & Luo, 2016; Kam, 2013; Liu, 2013).[8] This form of relationship is often referred to as a 'contract marriage' or 'marriage of conve-

---

[8] The term *lala* refers to same-sex desiring women in the Chinese context, including lesbian, bisexual and trans women.

nience' (*xinghun*; see Choi & Luo, 2016; Liu, 2013). While cooperative marriage, on the one hand, embodies the agency of sexual minorities in the construction of alternative support networks and 'families of choice', on the other hand, it reaffirms 'the dominance of the heteronormative family' (Engebretsen, 2017: 164). Cummings' (2022) research on gay men in Hainan provides empirical evidence of the enduring importance of family and marriage in shaping the choices and lives of non-heterosexual individuals in present-day China. The Confucian value of filial piety has been found to be a major cause of minority stigmas used to force Chinese people with same-sex attraction into heterosexual marriage (Hu & Wang, 2013; Wei et al., 2021). Having said this, alternative ways of being and living to heterosexual marriage and family are largely silenced and suppressed by China's family-centred morality and Confucianism (Ho et al., 2018).

Conclusion

In this chapter, a general theoretical context on the discussion of individualisation for understanding the changes in people's family life has been outlined. Under the individualisation thesis, personal lives are becoming more fluid and unstable, characterised as the disembedding of the individual from traditional personal and relationship ties. I acknowledged that China has undergone dramatic changes in relation to marital and family practices. These changes are closely associated with China's major social and economic transformations in the post-reform era, alongside the influence of Western individualisation, which together have facilitated a detraditionalisation of the long-standing patriarchal familial system that positioned women at the bottom of the family hierarchy in traditional Chinese society. Consequently, younger cohorts, due to their greater exposure to Western culture and individualism, may develop preferences for marriage and family in a different manner from the previous generations. These shifts in attitudes, behaviours and lifestyles towards new marital norms present challenges for the institution of marriage in China.

However, some scholars argue that the detraditionalisation of marriage has not been fully seen in contemporary China, due to the long-standing traditional family values shaped by Confucian ideology (Chen & Li, 2014). For example, in a collectivist society like China, the traditional familial culture places strong emphasis on extended family, in which couples living together with dependent children to establish a 'family' is a socially accepted practice. Far less emphasis is given to the individual, and especially for women who were traditionally ascribed as subordinate to men. Although the improved social status of women may affect preferences for marriage and spousal choice, as well as changed family practices, it is also necessary to recognise that these preferences develop within a cultural context in which Confucian patriarchal tradition remains strong. Empirical research shows that marriage still serves as an almost universal practice for Chinese people (at least until very recently; see also, Davis, 2014; Ji & Yeung, 2014; Xu, 2010; Yu & Xie, 2015; Zarafonetis, 2017). This has profound implications for non-heterosexual relations in the hegemonic, heteronormative social environment. In addition, long-standing norms such as filial obligation are still a salient element of Chinese culture (Chu & Yu, 2010) and may also influence preferences for marriage and family patterns. That is to say, researchers need to be cautious when considering the applicability of individualisation beyond the Western context, due to the differences in social, political, cultural and economic aspects from the West.

Drawing on Western ideas of individualisation and transformation of intimacy in particular, my central concern in this research is to examine whether and to what extent the Western theorising of the transformation of intimate relationships applies to and can be used to interpret the incidence of LAT in contemporary China. Given that there is a lack of research on LATs relationships (LATs) in China, when it comes to why Chinese people live apart and their perceptions of LATs, careful consideration should be given to the specific historical, social and cultural settings, as well as gender differences within Chinese society generally, and within LATs specifically, because without it the complexity of marriage and family life cannot be fully understood. In so doing, my research will not only fill a gap by providing empirical data on the lived experience of LAT in Chinese society, but also add a much-needed global perspective to Western theorising on the key debates around intimacy, individualisation, family practices and gender relations.

References

Bauman, Z. (2003). *Liquid love: On the frailty of human bonds*. Polity Press.
Beck, U. (2002). *Individualization: Institutionalized individualism and its social and political consequences* (Vol. 13). Sage.
Beck, U., & Beck-Gernsheim, E. (1995). *The normal chaos of love*. Polity Press.
Beck-Gernsheim, E. (2002). *Reinventing the family: In search of new lifestyles*. Polity.

Bernstein, T. (1977). *Up to the mountains and down to the villages: The transfer of youth from urban to rural China.* New Haven, Conn: Yale University Press.

Blair, S., & Madigan, T. (2016). Dating attitudes and expectations among young Chinese adults: An examination of gender differences. *Journal of Chinese Sociology, 3*(12), 1–19.

Bumpass, L. L., Rindfuss, R. R., Choe, M. J., & Tsuya, N. O. (2009). The institutional context of low fertility: The case of Japan. *Asian Population Studies, 5*(3), 215–235.

Cai, Y., & Feng, W. (2014). (re) emergence of late marriage in Shanghai: From collective synchronization to individual liberalization. In D. Davis & S. Freedman (Eds.), *Sexuality and marriage in cosmopolitan China* (pp. 97–117). Stanford University Press.

Carter, J. (2012). What is commitment? Women's accounts of intimate attachment. *Families, Relationships and Societies, 1*(2), 137–153.

Carter, J., & Duncan, S. (2018). *Reinventing couples: Tradition, agency and bricolage.* Palgrave Macmillan.

Chambers, D. (2012). *A sociology of family life.* Policy.

Chang, K. S., & Song, M. Y. (2010). The stranded individualizer under compressed modernity: South Korean women in individualization without individualism. *British Journal of Sociology, 61*(3), 540–565.

Chan, K. W. and Zhang, L. (1999). The hukou system and rural-urban migration in China: Processes and changes. *The China Quarterly, 160,* 818–855.

Chen, R. (2015). Weaving individualism into collectivism: Chinese adults' evolving relationship and family values. *Journal of Comparative Family Studies, 46*(2), 167–179.

Chen, Y. C., & Li, J. A. (2014). Family change in East Asia. In J. Treas, J. Scott, & M. Richards (Eds.), *The Wiley Blackwell companion to the sociology of families* (pp. 61–82). John Wiley & Sons.

Chen, F., Liu, G., & Mair, C. A. (2011). Inter-generational ties in context: Grandparents caring for grandchildren in China. *Social Forces, 90*(2), 571–594.

Chen, T., Leeson, G., & Liu, C. (2017). Living arrangements and intergenerational monetary transfers of older Chinese. *Ageing and Society, 37,* 1798–1823.

Cheung, A. K., & Yeung, W. J. (2015). Temporal-spatial patterns of one-person households in China, 1982–2005. *Demographic Research, 32*(44), 1209–1238.

Choi, S. Y. P., & Luo, M. (2016). Performative family: Homosexuality, marriage, and intergenerational dynamics in China. *British Journal of Sociology, 67*(2), 260–280.

Chu, C. Y., & Yu, R. R. (2010). *Understanding Chinese families: A comparative study of Taiwan and Southeast China.* Oxford University Press.

Coontz, S. (2006). *Marriage, a history: How love conquered marriage.* Penguin.

Croll, E. J. (1981). *The politics of marriage in contemporary China.* Cambridge University Press.

Croll, E. J. (2006). The intergenerational contract in the changing Asian family. *Oxford Development Studies, 34*, 473–491.

Cummings, J. (2022). *The everyday lives of gay men in Hainan sociality, space and time*. Springer Nature.

Davis, D. (1999). Self-employment in Shanghai. *China Quarterly, 157*, 22–43.

Davis, D. (2014). Privatization of marriage in post-socialist China. *Modern China, 40*(6), 551–557.

Davis, D. S., & Friedman, S. (2014). *Wives, husbands, and lovers: Marriage and sexuality in Hong Kong, Taiwan and urban China*. Hong Kong University Press.

Dillon, M. (2009). *Contemporary China: an introduction*. London: Routledge.

Dion, K., & Dion, K. (1988). Romantic love: Individual and cultural perspectives. In R. J. Sternberg & M. L. Barnes (Eds.), *The psychology of love* (pp. 264–289). Yale University Press.

Dion, K. K., & Dion, K. L. (1993). Individualistic and collectivistic perspectives on gender and the cultural context of love and intimacy. *Journal of Social Science, 49*(3), 53–69.

Duncan, S., & Irwin, S. (2004). The social patterning of values and rationalities: Mothers' choices in combining caring and employment. *Social Policy and Society, 3*(4), 391–399.

Duncan, S., & Smith, D. (2006). Individualisation versus the geography of 'new' families. *21st Century Society, 1*(2), 167–189.

Engebretsen, E. (2014). *Queer women in urban China: An ethnography*. Routledge.

Engebretsen, E. (2017). Under Pressure: Lesbian–Gay Contract Marriages and their Patriarchal Bargains. In G. Santos & S. Harrell (Eds.), *Transforming Patriarchy: Chinese Families in the 21st Century* (pp. 163–181). Washington University Press.

Evans, H. (1997). *Women and sexuality in China: Dominant discourses of female sexuality and gender since 1949*. Polity Press.

Evans, E. (2002). Past, perfect or imperfect: Changing images of the ideal wife. In I. S. Brownell & J. N. Wasserstrom (Eds.), *Chinese femininities/Chinese masculinities: A reader* (pp. 335–360). University of California press.

Farrer, J. (2002). *Opening up: Youth sex culture and market reform in Shanghai*. University of Chicago Press.

Farrer, J. (2011). Global nightscapes in Shanghai as ethnosexual contact zones. *Journal of Ethnic and Migration Studies, 37*(5), 747–764. https://doi.org/10.1080/1369183X.2011.559716

Farrer, J. (2014). Love, sex and commitment: Rethinking premarital intimacy from marriage in urban China. In D. Davis & S. Friedman (Eds.), *Wives, husbands, and lovers: Marriage and sexuality in Hong Kong, Taiwan, and Urban China* (pp. 62–96). Stanford University Press.

Fei, H. T. (1939). *Peasant life in China*. Routledge.

Finch, J. (2007). Displaying families. *Sociology, 41*(1), 65-81.

Fincher, L. (2014). *Leftover women: The resurgence of gender inequality in China*. Zed Books.

Finnane, A. (1996). What should Chinese women wear? A national problem. *Morden China, 22*(2), 99–131.

Fong, V. L. (2002). China's one-child policy and the empowerment of urban daughters. *American Anthropologist, 104*(4), 1098–1109.

Gabb, J. (2011). Family lives and relational living: Taking account of otherness. *Sociological Research Online, 16*(4), 10. [Online]. Retrieved March 19, 2016, from http://www.socresonline.org.uk/16/4/10.html

Gao, Y. (高颖), & Wu, H. (吴昊). (2012). 人口流迁对北京市 平均初婚年龄的影响. [Impact of migration on average age at first marriage in Beijing]. *Population Research, 36*(5), 58–68.

Giddens, A. (1991). *Modernity and self-identity*. Polity Press.

Giddens, A. (1992). *The transformation of intimacy*. Polity press.

Giddens, A. (1998). *The third way: The renewal of social democracy*. Blackwell.

Giddens, A. (2003). *Runaway world: How globalisation is reshaping our lives*. Routledge.

Gillies, V. (2003). *Family and intimate relationships: A review of the sociological research*. Families & Social Capital ESRC Research Group Working Paper No. 2. London South Bank University.

Gross, N. (2005). The detraditionalization of intimacy reconsidered. *Sociological Theory, 23*(3), 286–311.

Gui, T. (2020). Leftover women or single by choice: Gender role negotiation of single professional women in contemporary China. *Journal of Family Issues, 41*(11), 1956–1978. https://doi.org/10.1177/0192513X20943919

Guo, Y. (2010). China's celebrity mothers: Female virtues, patriotism, and social harmony. In L. Edwards & E. Jeffreys (Eds.), *Celebrity in China* (pp. 45–66). HKU Press.

Guo, Z. (2012). *China's low fertility level and the neglected population risk*. Social Sciences Academic Press. (in Chinese).

Hannum, E. (2005). Market transition, educational disparities, and family strategies in rural China: New evidence on gender stratification and development. *Demography, 24*, 275–299.

Hansen, M. H., & Pang, C. (2010). Idealizing individual choice: Work, love and family in the eyes of young rural Chinese. In M. H. Hansen & R. Svarverud (Eds.), *iChina: The rise of the individual in modern Chinese society* (pp. 1–38). NIAS.

Hareven, T. K. (2001). The impact of family history and the life course on social history. In R. Wall, T. K. Hareven, & J. Ehmer (Eds.), *Family history revisited: Comparative perspectives* (pp. 21–39). Associated University Press.

Heaphy, B. (2007). *Late modernity and social change: Reconstructing social and personal life*. Routledge.

Heaphy, B., Smart, C., & Einarsdottir, A. (2013). *Same sex marriages: New generations, new relationships*. Palgrave Macmillan.

Hershatter, G. (2007). *Women in China's long twentieth century*. University of California press.

Higgins, L., & Sun, C. (2007). Gender, social background and sexual attitudes among Chinese students. *Culture, Health and Sexuality: An International Journal for Research, Intervention and Care, 9*(1), 31–42.

Ho, P. S. Y., Jackson, S., Cao, S., & Kwok, C. (2018). Sex with Chinese characteristics: Sexuality research in/on 21st-century China. *Journal of Sex Research, 55*(4–5), 486–521. https://doi.org/10.1080/00224499.2018.1437593

Hoffman, L. (2008). Post-Mao professionalism: Self-enterprise and patriotism. In L. Zhang & A. Ong (Eds.), *Privatizing China: Socialism from Afar* (pp. 168–181). Cornell University Press.

Holmes, M. (2004). An equal distance? Individualisation, gender and intimacy in distance relationships. *The Sociological Review, 52*(2), 180–200.

Hu, Y., & Scott, J. (2016). Family and gender values in China. *Journal of Family Issues, 37*(9), 1267–1293.

Hu, X., & Wang, Y. (2013). LGB identity among young Chinese: The influence of traditional culture. *Journal of Homosexuality, 60*, 667–684. https://doi.org/10.1080/00918369.2013.773815

Huang, P. (2005). Divorce law practices and the origins, myths, and realities of judicial "mediation" in China. *Modern China, 31*(2), 151–203.

Jacka, T., Kipnis, A. B., & Sargeson, S. (2013). *Contemporary China: Society and social change*. Cambridge University Press. https://doi.org/10.1017/CBO9781139196178

Jackson, S. (2013). Love, social change, and everyday heterosexuality. In A. Jonasdottir & A. Ferguson (Eds.), *Love: A question for feminism in the twenty-first century* (pp. 33–47). Routledge.

Jackson, S. (2015a). Families, domesticity and intimacy: Changing relationships in changing times. In V. Robinson & D. Richardson (Eds.), *Introducing gender and women's studies* (4th ed., pp. 169–187). Palgrave Macmillan.

Jackson, S. (2015b). Modernity/modernities and personal life: Reflections on some theoretical lacunae. *Korean Journal of Sociology, 49*(3), 1–20.

Jackson, S., & Ho, S. Y. (2014). Mothers, daughters and sex: The negotiation of young women's sexuality in Britain and Hong Kong. *Families, Relationships and Societies, 3*(3), 387–403.

Jackson, S., & Ho, P. S. Y. (2020). *Women doing intimacy: Gender, family and modernity in Britain and Hong Kong*. Palgrave Macmillan.

Jackson, S., Liu, J., & Woo, J. S. (2008). *East Asian sexualities: Modernity, gender and new social cultures*. Zed Books.

Jackson, S., Ho, S. Y., & Na, J. N. (2013). Reshaping tradition? Women negotiating the boundaries of tradition and modernity in Hong Kong and British families. *The Sociological Review, 61*, 667–687.

Jamieson, L. (1998). *Intimacy: Personal relationships in modern society*. Polity Press.

Jamieson, L. (1999). Intimacy transformed? *Sociology, 33*(10), 477–494. https://doi.org/10.1080/08858190209528804

Jamieson, L. (2011). Intimacy as a concept: Explaining social change in the context of globalisation or another form of ethnocentricism? *Sociological Research Online, 16*(4), 151–163.

Jankowiak, W., & Moore, R. (2017). *Family life in China*. Polity press.

Jeffreys, E., & Yu, H. (2015). *Sex in China*. Polity.

Ji, Y. (2015a). Asian families at the crossroads: A meeting of east, west, tradition, modernity and gender. *Journal of Marriage and Family, 77*(5), 1031–1038.

Ji, Y. (2015b). Between tradition and modernity: 'Leftover' women in Shanghai. *Journal of Marriage and Family, 77*(5), 1057–1073.

Ji, Y. (2017). A mosaic temporality: New dynamics of the gender and marriage system in contemporary urban China. *Temporalités, 26*. https://doi.org/10.4000/temporalites.3773

Ji, Y., & Yeung, W. J. J. (2014). Heterogeneity in contemporary Chinese marriage. *Journal of Family Issues, 35*(12), 1662–1682. https://doi.org/10.1177/0192513X14538030

Jin, Y. (2006). Rethinking the 'iron girls': Gender and labour during the Chinese cultural revolution. *Gender and History, 18*(3), 613–634.

Jones, G., & Yeung, W. J. (2014). Marriage in Asia. *Journal of Family Issues, 35*(2), 1567–1583.

Kam, L. Y. L. (2013). *Shanghai lalas: Female tongzhi communities and politics in urban China*. Hong Kong University Press. https://doi.org/10.5790/hongkong/9789888139453.001.0001

Kong, T. S. K. (2012). Reinventing the self under socialism: The case of migrant male sex workers ("money boys") in China. *Critical Asian Studies, 44*(2), 283–308. https://doi.org/10.1080/14672715.2012.672829

Kong, T. S. K. (2016). The sexual in Chinese sociology: Homosexuality studies in contemporary China. *The Sociological Review, 64*(3), 495–514. https://doi.org/10.1111/1467-954X.12372

Lau, H., Yeung, G., Stotzer, R. L., Lau, C. Q., & Loper, K. (2017). Assessing the tongzhi laber: Self-identification and public opinion. *Journal of Homosexuality, 64*(4), 509–522. https://doi.org/10.1080/00918369.2016.1191241

Lee, H. Y. (1978). *The politics of the Chinese cultural revolution*. Berkeley: University of California Press.

Lei, X., Strauss, J., Tian, M., & Zhao, Y. (2015). Living arrangements of the elderly in China: Evidence from the CHARLS national baseline. *Chinese Economic Journal, 8*(3), 191–214.

Lewis, J. (2001). *The end of marriage? Individualism and intimate relations*. Edward Elgar.

Li, E. (1994). Modernization: Its impact on families in China. In P. L. Lin, K. Mei, & H. Peng (Eds.), *Marriage and the family in Chinese societies: Selected readings* (pp. 39–44). University of Indianapolis Press.

Li, Y. (李银河) (2017, July 9). 我们为什么应该彻底取消言论审查制度？*[Why should we completely abolish censorship?]* [blog post]. Weibo. Retrieved from https://ia800606.us.archive.org/15/items/WeChatImage20170715111116/WeChat%20Image_20170715111116.jpg

Li, Y. H. & Wang, X. B. (1992). 他们的世界：中国男同性恋群落透视 [Their World: China's Homosexual Male Community]. Shanxi: Shanxi Peoples Publishing House.

Liu, J. (2004). Holding up the sky? Reflections on marriage in contemporary China. *Feminism and Psychology, 14*(1), 195–202.

Liu, M. (2013). Two gay men seeking two lesbians: An analysis of Xinghun (formality marriage) ads on China's Tianya.cn. *Sexuality and Culture, 17*, 494–511. https://doi.org/10.1007/s12119-012-9164-z

Liu, J., Bell, E., & Zhang, J. (2019). Conjugal intimacy, gender and modernity in contemporary China. *The British Journal of Sociology, 70*(1), 283–305.

Lu, M. (2004). The awakening of Chinese women and the women's movement in the early twentieth century. In J. Tao, B. Zheng, & L. M. Shirley (Eds.), *Holding up half the sky* (pp. 55–70). Feminist Press.

Manning, K. (2007). Making a great leap forward? The politics of women's liberation in Maoist China. In D. Ko and Z. Wang, (Eds.). Translating feminisms in China pp. (138–163). Oxford: Blackwell Publishing.

Ma, L., Turunen, J., and Rizzi, E. (2018). Divorce Chinese style. *Journal of marriage and family, 80*, 1287–1297.

Ministry of Education of the People's Republic of China. (2007). *New terms in the Country's official lexicon in 2006*. Ministry of Education of the People's Republic of China. Retrieved June 18, 2022, http://www.moe.gov.cn/publicfiles/business/htmlfiles/moe/moe_1551/200708/25472.html

Morgan, D. (1996). *Family connections: An introduction to family studies*. Cambridge Polity.

Morgan, D. (2011). *Rethinking family practices*. Palgrave Macmillan.

Mu, Z. and Xie, Y. (2014). Marital age homogamy in China: A reversal of trend in the reform era? *Social Science Research, 44*, 141–157.

National Bureau of Statistics. (2021). 中国统计年鉴—2017 *[China statistical yearbook, 2021]* [Online]. Retrieved July 14, 2022, from at: http://www.stats.gov.cn/tjsj/ndsj/2021/indexch.htm

Osburg, J. (2013). *Anxious wealth: Money and morality among China's new rich*. Stanford University Press.

Pahl, R., & Spencer, L. (2004). Personal communities: Not simply families of 'fate' or 'choice'. *Current Sociology, 52*(2), 199–221.

Pan, S. (2006). Transformations in the primary life cycle: The origins and nature of China's sexual revolution. In E. Jeffreys (Ed.), *Sex and sexuality in China* (pp. 21–42). Routledge.

Pan, Y. (潘允康). (2010). 中国婚姻家庭的社会管理 [Chinese marriage and family social management]. *Acta Gansu Administration Institute, 1*, 56–64.

Pan, S. (潘绥铭)., Parish, W. L., Wang, A. L., & Laumann, E. O. (2004). 中国人的相关关系与性行为 *[Chinese peoples' sexual relationships and sexual behaviours]*. Social Science Document Publishing House.

Parish, W. L., & Farrer, J. (2000). Gender and family. In W. Tang & P. William (Eds.), *Chinese urban life under reform* (pp. 209–231). Cambridge University Press.

Parish, W. L., & White, M. K. (1978). *Village and family in contemporary China*. University of Chicago Press.

Piotrowski, M., & Tong, Y. (2016). Education and fertility decline in China during transitional times: A cohort approach. *Social Science Research, 55*, 94–110.

Qi, X. (2015). Filial obligations in contemporary China: Evolution of the culture-system. *Journal for the Theory of Social Behaviour, 45*(1), 141–161.

Qi, X. (2016). Family bond and family obligation: Continuity and transformation. *Journal of Sociology, 52*(1), 39–52.

Qian, Y., & Jin, Y. (2018). Women's fertility autonomy in urban China: The role of couple dynamics under the universal two-child policy. *Chinese Sociological Review, 50*(3), 275–309.

Qian, Y., & Qian, Z. (2014). Gender divide in urban China: Singlehood and assortative mating by age and education. *Demographic Research, 31*, 1337–1364.

Raymo, J. M., Park, H., Xie, Y., & Yeung, W. J. (2015). Marriage and family in East Asia: Continuity and change. *Annual Review of Sociology, 41*(1), 471–492. https://doi.org/10.1146/annurev-soc-073014-112428

Ringen, S. (2016). *The perfect dictatorship: China in the 21st century*. Hong Kong University Press.

Rofel, L. (1999). *Other modernities: Gendered yearnings in China after socialism*. University of California Press.

Rofel, L. (2007). *Desiring China: Experiments in neoliberalism, sexuality, and public culture*. Duke University Press.

Rofel, L. (2012). Queer positions, queering Asian studies. *Positions, 20*(1), 183–193. https://doi.org/10.1215/10679847-1471438

Roseneil, S. (2006). On not living with a partner: Unpicking coupledom and cohabitation. *Sociological Research Online, 11*(3), 111–124.

Settles, B. H., Sheng, X., Zang, Y., & Zhao, J. (2013). The one-child policy and its impact on Chinese families. In K. Chan (Ed.), *International handbook of Chinese families* (pp. 627–646). Springer.

Shek, D. T. L. (2006). Chinese family research: Puzzles, progress, paradigms, and policy implications. *Journal of Family Issues, 27*(3), 275–284. https://doi.org/10.1177/0192513x05283508

Sigley, G. (2006). Sex, politics, and the policing of virtue in the People's Republic of China. In E. Jeffreys (Ed.), *Sex and sexuality in China* (pp. 43–61). Routledge.

Smart, C. (2007). *Personal life: New directions in sociological thinking*. Polity.

Smart, C., & Shipman, B. (2004). Visions in monochrome: Families, marriage and the individualization thesis. *The British Journal of Sociology, 55*(4), 491–509.

Smits, J., & Park, H. (2009). Five decades of educational assortative mating in 10 East Asian societies. *Social Forces, 88*(1), 227–255.

Song, Z. (2008). *Flow into eternity: Patriarchy, marriage and socialism in a North China village*. ProQuest.

Song, J., & Ji, Y. (2020). Complexity of Chinese family life: Individualism, familism, and gender. *The China Review, 20*(2), 1–18.

Tanabe, A., & Tokita-Tanabe, Y. (2003). Introduction: Gender and modernity in Asia and the Pacific. In Y. Hayami, A. Tanabe, & Y. Tokita-Tanabe (Eds.), *Gender and modernity: Perspectives from Asia and the Pacific* (pp. 1–16). Kyoto University Press.

Tang, D. T.-S. (2011). *Conditional spaces: Hong Kong lesbian desires and everyday life*. Hong Kong University Press.

Thornton, A., & Lin, H. S. (1994). *Social change and the family in Taiwan*. University of Chicago Press.

Thwaites, R. (2016). *Changing names and gendering identity: Social organisation in contemporary Britain*. Routledge.

To, S. (2015). *China's leftover women: Late marriage among professional women and its consequences*. Routledge Publications.

To, S. (2013). Understanding Sheng Nu (Leftover women): the phenomenon of late marriage among Chinese professional women. *Symbolic interaction, 36*(1), 1–20.

Trandafir, M. (2015). Legal recognition of same-sex couples and family formation. *Demography, 52*(1), 113–151.

Tsui, M., & Rich, L. (2002). The only child and educational opportunity for girls in urban China. *Gender & Society, 16*(1), 74–92. https://doi.org/10.1177/0891243202016001005

Twamley, K. (2019). "Cold intimacies" in parents; negotiations of work-family practices and parental leave? *The Sociological Review, 67*(5), 1137–1153. https://doi.org/10.1177/0038026118815427

UNESO. (2015). Institute for Statistics. Retrieved May 14, 2022, from http://data.uis.unesco.org/

United Nations Population Division. (2017). World population prospects: The 2017 revision [Online]. Retrieved July 14, 2022, from https://www.un.org/development/desa/publications/world-population-prospects-the-2017-revision.html

Wang, S. Y. (2019). When tongzhi marry: Experiments of cooperative marriage between lalas and gay men in urban China. *Feminist Studies, 45*(1), 13–35.

Wang, X., & Nehring, D. (2014). Individualisation as an ambition: Mapping the dating landscape in Beijing. *Modern China, 40*(6), 578–604.

Weeks, M. R. (1989). Virtuous wives and kind mothers: Concepts of women in urban China. *Women's Studies International Forum, 12*(5), 505–518.

Wei, T. H., Jervis, L. L., Jiang, Y., et al. (2021). Cultural unintelligibility and marital pressure: A grounded theory of minority stigma against women with same-sex attraction in mainland China. *Archives of Sexual Behavior, 50*, 3137–3154. https://doi.org/10.1007/s10508-021-02050-4

Whyte, M. K., & Parish, W. L. (1984). *Urban life in contemporary China*. University of Chicago Press.
Whyte, M. K., & Xu, X. (1990). Love matches and arranged marriages: A Chinese replication. *Journal of Marriage and Family, 52*(3), 709–722.
Willis, R. (1987). What have we learned from the economics of the family? *American Economic Review, 77*, 68–81.
Wolf, M. (1985). *Revolution postponed: Women in contemporary China*. Stanford University Press.
Wong, W. M. (2014). Finding 'love' in China: An overview of Chinese marriage markets (BaiFaXiangQin). *Inquiries Journal, 6*(12) [Online]. Retrieved March 2, 2022, from http://www.inquiriesjournal.com/articles/946/finding-love-in-china-an-overview-of-chinese-marriage-markets-baifaxiangqin
Woo, M. Y. K. (2006). Contesting citizenship: Marriage and divorce in the People's Republic of China. In E. Jeffreys (Ed.), *Sex and sexuality in China* (pp. 62–71). Routledge.
Wu, X., & Li, L. (2012). Family size and maternal health: Evidence from the one-child policy in China. *Journal of Population Economics, 25*, 1–24.
Wu, X., & Zhang, Z. (2010). Changes in educational inequality in China, 1990–2005: Evidence from the population census data. *Research in Sociology of Education, 17*, 123–152.
Wu, J., Gyourko, J., & Deng, Y. (2012). Evaluating conditions in major Chinese housing markets. *Regional Science and Urban Economics, 42*(3), 531–543.
Xie, Y. (2011). Evidence-based research on China. *Chinese Sociological Review, 44*(1), 14–25.
Xie, Y. (2013). *Gender and family in contemporary China*. Population studies center research report, 13, 808.
Xu, A. (徐安琪). (2010). 白头偕老:新世纪的神话?——终身婚姻态度的代际比较研究 [Husband and wife living together forever: a fairy-tale in the new century? A comparative research on attitudes towards lifelong marriage in generation]. *Youth Research, 4*, 1–13.
Xu, Q. (许琪). (2013). 探索从妻居———现代化、人口转变和现实需求的影响 [An exploring matrilocal coresidence: The influence of modernization, population transition and practical needs]. *Population and Economics, 6*(201), 47–55.
Xu, X., & Whyte, M. K. (1990). Love matches and arranged marriages: A Chinese replication. *Journal of Marriage and Family, 52*, 709–722.
Xu, A., & Xia, Y. (2014). The changes in mainland Chinese families during the social transition: A critical analysis. *Journal of Comparative Family Studies, XLV*(1), 31–53.
Xu, X., Ji, J., & Tung, Y. K. (2000). Social and political assortative mating in urban China. *Journal of Family Issues, 21*(1), 47–77.
Xu, Q., Li, J., & Yu, X. (2014). Continuity and change in Chinese marriage and the family. *Chinese Sociological Review, 47*(1), 30–56.

Yang, M. (1994). Gifts, favours and banquets: the art of social relationships in China. NY: Cornell University press.

Yan, Y. (2002). Courtship, love and premarital sex in a North China village. *The China Journal, 48*, 29–53.

Yan, Y. (2003). *Private life under socialism: Love, intimacy, and family change in a Chinese village, 1949–1999*. Stanford University Press.

Yan, Y. (2008). Introduction: Understanding the rise of the individual in China. *European Journal of East Asian Studies, 7*(1), 1–9.

Yan, Y. (2009). *The individualization of Chinese society*. Bloomsbury Academic.

Yan, Y. (2010). The Chinese path to individualization. *British Journal of Sociology, 61*(3), 489–512.

Yan, Y. (2021). *Chinese families upside down: Intergenerational dynamics and neofamilism in the early 21st century*. Brill.

Yang, C. (2017). *Television and dating in contemporary China*. Springer.

Yu, J., & Xie, Y. (2011). The varying display of "gender display". *Chinese Sociological Review, 44*(2), 5–30.

Yu, J., & Xie, Y. (2015). Changes in the determinants of marriage entry in post-reform urban China. *Demography, 52*(6), 1869–1892.

Yuen, S., Law, P., & Ho, Y. (1998). *Marriage, gender, and sex in a contemporary Chinese village*. M. E. Sharpe.

Zang, X. (2011). Family and marriage. In X. Zhang (Ed.), *Understanding Chinese society* (pp. 35–48). Sage.

Zarafonetis, N. (2017). *Sexuality in a changing China: Young women, sex and intimate relations in the reform period*. Routledge.

Zeng, Y., & Hesketh, T. (2016). The effects of China's universal two-child policy. *Lancet, 388*, 1930–1938.

Zeng, Y., & Wu, D. (2000). Regional analysis of divorce in China since 1980. *Demography, 37*(2), 215–219.

Zeng, Z., & Xie, Y. (2014). The effects of grandparents on children's schooling: Evidence from rural China. *Demography, 51*(2), 599–617.

Zhang, J. (2003). Gender in post-Mao China. *European Review, 11*(2), 209–224.

Zhang, B. C., & Chu, Q. S. (2005). MSM and HIV/AIDS in China. *Cell Research, 15*, 858–864. https://doi.org/10.1038/sj.cr.7290359

Zuo, L., & Bian, Y. (2001). Gendered resources, division of housework, and perceived fairness – A case in urban China. *Journal of Marriage and Family, 63*, 1122–1133.

CHAPTER 3

Reconsidered Agency: Why Do People Live Apart?

Introduction

Due to the transformative nature of the everyday (Robinson, 2015) and the importance of experience in the account of agency (McNay, 2004), this chapter attempts to draw out the reasons underlying the phenomena of Chinese people living apart together (LAT), and provides a possible explanation for how LAT has come about in heterosexual intimate relationships. Therefore, the centrality of agency needs to be examined and conceptualised in terms of people's everyday life and experience (Hockey et al., 2007: 36). In reviewing previous research on LAT relationships (LATs) in the Western context, there seems to be a close association between how people perceive LAT and how far people can be seen to exercise individual agency within such a partnership. As I demonstrated in Chap. 1, when LAT was seen as a 'new family form' (Levin, 2004) that allowed people not only to gain freedom but also to retain a sense of intimacy, an individualistic and agentic view of social action was emphasised. For example, Upton-Davis' (2015) research with women over 45 years old in Australia showed that people use LAT to purposely or reflexively subvert and transform the traditional taken-for-granted patterns regarding couplehood and family form. In this sense, these women's agentic power in emphasising individualism and securing personal autonomy was evidenced.

© The Author(s), under exclusive license to Springer Nature Switzerland AG 2022
S. Qiu, *Gender and Family Practices*, Genders and Sexualities in the Social Sciences, https://doi.org/10.1007/978-3-031-17250-2_3

In contrast, the continuist perspective tends to see LAT as a continuing stage, in which people's desire to live together as a 'normal' couple is somewhat constrained by wider social structures and power institutions. In this regard, agency was often considered within a deterministic and structured view as people may feel different degrees of constraints and vulnerabilities in this LAT relationship. Nevertheless, this strict dualist view on agency and structure had failed to capture the flexibility and relationality involved in making sense of the changes in people's everyday family life depending on contexts and life stages.

The Chinese cultural framework provides a unique opportunity to explore the relational practices of agency in family lives. This is attributed to the tension arising from the continued importance of traditions associated with values of familism in China coexisting with the rise of Western notions of individualism that value autonomy and personal choice (Jackson, 2010; Ji, 2017). On the one hand, people's engagement in a non-conventional partnership signifies a new form of relating and living (Levin, 2004). On the other hand, the long-standing traditional values on gender roles and family obligations remain robust, especially in a social context that lacks culturally embedded ideas of individualism (Qiu, 2020). As such, the ways in which people construct their family lives cannot be simply understood as a matter of personal choice. Informed by Morgan's (1996) 'practice' approach and Smart's (2007) idea of relationality, this chapter examines how agency is practised and exercised in practical terms and how relationality plays out when making a decision in intimate life. In so doing, my analysis reveals a more nuanced and inclusive account of how agency is seen through a relational lens through which the dynamics of social structure, gender and life stages are constituted.

Conceptualising Agency and Relationality

The concept of agency has been central to understand people's action-making processes. Ortner (2001: 78) suggests that 'agency is virtually synonymous with the forms of power people have at their disposal, their ability to act on their own behalf, influence other people and events, and maintain some kind of control in their own lives'. McNay (2004: 177–179) advocated a perspective that emphasised social relations, suggesting that

> the idea of agency is a key mediating category but it cannot be deduced from abstract social structures. Instead, agency mediates the inter-connection

between cultural and economic forces, identity formations and social structures ... Agency refers to the individual's capacity for self-reflection and self-evaluation and is thus related to subjects' experience of the world ... and cannot be simply understood as a property of unstable discursive structures.

Although it remains inconsistent by definition, one commonality is the emphasis on the agentic individual to reflect upon and make conscious actions (Rahman & Jackson, 2010). The individualisation thesis has provided a frame of reference to understand the interplay between individuals and society from the standpoint of individuals. In this theory, agency was often understood in a way that is related to purposive and conscious action in that individuals can monitor themselves and reflexively conduct a life of their own (Beck & Beck-Gernsheim, 1995, 2002; Giddens, 1991, 1992). From Giddens' perspective (1984), the individuals are considered as agents of change with the capacity and power to influence social events in a conscious way and make a difference to a pre-existing state of affairs (also see Giddens, 1992). In this way, agency implies doing and can overcome structural constraints. Consequently, the significance of social structures and given expectations that once constrained people's everyday lives were downplayed, as Giddens (2000, vii) claimed that 'we can no longer learn from history'. This one-sided view of agency as either enabled or constrained has also been supported by Bauman (2003), who holds a more pessimistic view, arguing that traditions may have lost their control over people's lives.

However, this positive understanding of individual agency has been strikingly challenged by scholars for ignoring the continuity and persistence of traditions and taken-for-granted social norms. Although some regulatory traditions concerning intimate practices are in decline, Gross (2005) argued that social actions are deeply informed by meaning-constitutive traditions, ones associated with culture, meaning-making and interpretation, which are passed down through generations. Even in Western culture with its established traditions of individual autonomy and democratising practices in relationships, socialised expectations for gender roles are still prevalent (Holmes, 2004b; Jamieson, 1999). Duncan's (2015) research on agency in heterosexual LATs in the UK showed that LAT was not simply a matter of personal choice. In fact, it has been associated with the reaffirmation of 'redoing' gender to construct the conventional family, as people often 'do' family drawing on pre-existing practices, and their agency in doing so is closely bound with intimate others. Arguing in a similar way, Carter (2017) noticed that young women in the UK, despite encountering new social customs, such as cohabitation, still adhere strongly to the social institution of marriage. That is to say, certain ideas, customs, and practices that are part of taken-for-granted aspects continue to shape the ways people negotiate and construct their personal lives (Brannen & Nilsen, 2005).

Furthermore, to see agency as merely a reflexive and unbounded individualistic action is problematic as it leaves out the consideration of relational contexts, within which people live their lives and make connections with others (Mason, 2004; May, 2011; Smart, 2007). A similar viewpoint was noted by Holmes (2010), who argued that reflexivity, which is often conceived of by individualisation theorists as an integral part of agency, is only one possible facet of agency. Agency can be unconscious, habitual, and is often relational and demonstrates emotional relatedness to others. We never confront social structures as a single individual. Such a view with an emphasis on relationality and connectedness moves beyond the dualist conceptualisation of agency as either enabled or constrained (Burkitt, 2016; Smart, 2007). As Burkitt (2016: 326) argued, the wider social relationships in which people are located form contexts in which agency should be understood as constituted within relationships. In defining agency in the wider sense of action, an individual's constraints in cohabitation are rooted not only in external powerful agencies or institutions, but also in relational connections with intimate others. Taking Duncan's (2015) research on people's choices about LATs as an example, Burkitt (2016: 334) interpreted agency as relational, arguing that

> The women's agency was informed by the past in terms of previous experiences, habit, and hegemonic ideas about coupledom; it was also oriented to the future in terms of plans to cohabit or by piecing together different traditions and alternative ideas about intimacy in an imaginative process of 'bricolage'; yet the contingencies of the moment also played a role in agency.

Similar to Morgan's (1996) practice approach, the term 'bricolage' enables us to understand agency as something individuals 'do' and negotiate in a given context of relations. It describes the process in which people piece together, assemble and draw on multifarious resources, such as tradition and relationality, in making decisions about relationships in response to new circumstances and changes (Carter & Duncan, 2018). People, therefore, are not isolated individuals, but rather 'relational, connected, and embedded' in and imbued by their sociocultural contexts within which they make pragmatic responses relationally (Mason, 2004: 163; see also, Burkitt, 2016; Roseneil & Ketokivi, 2016; Smart, 2007, 2011). To some extent, my data support this view, as people usually make decisions regarding personal relationships pragmatically with reference to their material, social, cultural and institutional circumstances, while being reflexively critical of traditions and asserting their desires for living their own life.

While there are different approaches to investigate people's practice of agency, little attention has been paid to the relationship and interplay between the idea of agencies people had developed. They seemed to presume that each aspect of agency remains static as things change. In fact, people may exercise different forms of agency in a given context and, as circumstances change, the extent to which they can exercise their agency is subject to variations. With the focus on 'doing', I would argue that agency should not be seen as a discrete entity but as fluid, dynamic and interrelated. Taking a relational approach, this chapter explores how different forms of agency are practised and developed as peoples' lives change over the life course. In an effort to elucidate the complexity and ambivalence in people's experience in their family life, I am particularly interested in understanding how gender, social structures, relational connections and the intersection among them have shaped the ways in which people exercise their agency.

STRUCTURAL CONSTRAINTS

Many factors can influence people's choice and experience in living their family lives, and structural constraints and scripted gender roles, in particular, have led some women in this study to engage in a non-cohabiting conjugal partnership. With the hope of making their lives better, those in LATs are characteristically often less well educated with poor family backgrounds, with one partner working away from the family home. This finding is in contrast with Holmes' (2004a, 2010) research based on the data of the dual-career, dual-household couple in the West. Because she targeted well-educated people who had the possibility of living their lives based on personal choice, she argued that professionals who gained financial dependence from their work are more likely to be in LATs. Thus, this section pays special attention to those participants who are explicitly in LATs, but who often do not have the financial means that those in Holmes' research did. I will examine why people (especially with less well-educated and poor family backgrounds) live apart and how their agency in cohabiting was constrained by labour mobility and external institutions.

Labour Mobility: Out-Migration of Men and Left-Behind Women

In my data, financial constraints were reported as one of the most common reasons preventing couples from living together in China. As such, people often ended up living apart in an unfavourable way. For example, Shanrui (28, married, Liaoning), a full-time housewife with secondary school education, had been living with her husband since marriage until they got into debt and lost their self-operated restaurant. Under such painful circumstances, her husband worked away as a long-haul truck driver who came back home about once every two or three months. A strong sense emerged from her narrative that she wanted to live together with her husband but could not as they needed money to survive and 'raise two kids'.

In a similar way, financial constraints also prevented Jieyu (45, married, Liaoning), with a primary-school education level, from living together with her husband. Following the patrilocal living arrangement after marriage, she had been taking care of her two children and parents-in-law. Her husband, as the household's sole financial provider, has been working as a construction worker in Beijing for over 16 years and normally comes back home at Chinese New Year and during the autumn harvest season. In her village in Hebei Province with limited job opportunities, people live by farming. Some married couples lived separately to make a better life, with men being absent and working in economically developed regions (Wu et al., 2020). Under such circumstances, sending remittance by migrant workers to people being left behind at home to meet the financial needs of the family is seen as a common practice of sustaining a stable family relationship in China (Fan et al., 2011). This was also substantiated by other participants in their mid-life, who said that for the well-being of the family, their husband would often remit their wages to them to control the finances, save and spend, as necessary. In Jieyu's understanding, couples physically living separately to have a better life seem to be seen as having common and acceptable family living arrangements. As she put it, 'What else could we do? How could we survive if he [her husband] didn't go away to earn money?' The 2010 census data reveal that more and more rural young people migrated to urban areas for a better life. Over 30% of rural families had seen one or more family members moving out, compared to only 10% of urban families (Wang, 2013). Both Shanrui and Jieyu's accounts explicitly indicate how limited financial resources can place people in a vulnerable position and considerably influence how they respond to problematic situations they confronted in their married life. In this sense, living apart is perceived as a way to merely 'live their lives' as it were, rather than as a result of active choices.

In the split households that are a result of economic constraints, family life is essentially shaped and constructed surrounding the gendered family roles and maintained through gender inequalities. From this perspective, women are bound to domestic duties as they are often seen as less capable of taking on challenges and financially feeding a family but better at providing daily care for family members. In this study, rural, less-educated married women, especially with dependent children, were all left at home to bear the burden of caring and, if necessary, sacrifice their individual desires. Shanrui's account is a good illustration of this, as she complained,

> Both my natal and my husband's family said that they don't need me to earn money, it's fine as long as I take good care of my children. But I don't agree, because [in this way] I have to ask him [her husband] for money. It would be better if he actively gave me some, but in fact, I have to phone him every month for money … I very much want to go out to find a paid job. No one always likes to stay at home looking after children.

As a mother with young children to be cared for, Shanrui's desire to achieve a sense of autonomy and financial independence was devalued by both sides of her family. This is in contrast to her male partner whose primary responsibility is not necessarily related to everyday housework but closely associated with outside roles as breadwinners. This kind of taken-for-granted gendered family practice, informed by habitual or societal expectations on gender roles, remains highly prevalent today, especially when taking women's identity as the mother and their 'feminine' role as caregiver into account (Luo et al., 2017; Roseneil, 2006). Under the context of lacking well-developed social protection against the burdens of childcare, the tension between work and childcare provision has become a barrier for some women to access paid work (Xie, 2013). As a result, financial vulnerability and prescribed gender roles intersect to shape women's practices of their agency in living a desired lifestyle, if characterised by a co-residential conjugal partnership in the Chinese context. This demonstrates that the willingness and capacity to construct a specific desired family life is class-related and subject to gender role expectations.

As our interview continued, a shift from vulnerability to agency occurred in Jieyu's account. This transition has seemed to relate to people's life stage. As a 45-year-old mother, Jieyu had temporarily 'freed' herself from caring obligations on a daily basis (her older daughter was in college and her younger daughter had reached middle school age and could now go to school by herself). In light of this, she decided to go to Beijing and found a job in a hotel as a cleaner. In fact, this was the first time she left her village to work and considered the idea of finding paid employment, entirely dependent on herself. As she said,

> It's up to me. If I don't like it, I'll not go out [to work]. It's me, and he didn't ask me to find a waged work. But I think he felt the same way as me; our life may become easier if I could earn some money. Otherwise, you don't have [more] money to spend. We still need it to afford two children. It's good if I can earn some money.

What underlines this narrative is the recognition that the practice of agency is not fixed but flexible and dynamic depending on circumstances and different contexts. Meadows' (1997) research on women's experience of agency in heterosexual relationships indicates how women's age and time increased their ability to secure what they wanted while being clearer to define what they did not want. While both Jieyu and her husband were in Beijing, they continued living apart (Jieyu shared a room with six other female workers in the hotel she worked for, and her husband lived in a dormitory provided by his contractor). The shifting relationship between conformity (to the traditional gendered division of labour) and reinvention (of gender roles) across Jieyu's heterosexual life serves to challenge the dualist understandings of a structure–agency framework.

Hongli (40, married, Liaoning) is one of the six study mothers in this research, who I will consider in more depth in the next chapter. Her experience provides another illustration of the relational practice of agency. The existing caring obligations to her children have caused her family to split geographically. During the time of our interviews, she and her school-aged son moved to town, while her husband, an electrician, worked in a different city. Every time that her husband had to go back to work, she was left with no choice, as she claimed:

I felt lonely emotionally, you know, a sense of powerlessness. But this is life, nothing can be done about it. The jobs in [our] hometown don't fit him. This [situation of the husband working away] is for our family and children.

To an extent, accompanying her children for his studies placed her in a 'disadvantaged' position when there were emotional costs identified, largely experienced as the loss of contact with her partner. However, she seemed to take LAT for granted, as she said, 'it was indeed quite a common phenomenon having a man working outside the home and a woman taking care of the inside'. Her identity as a mother and wife does not shatter her desire for pursuing a more autonomous and individual identity. This can be seen from her eagerness to 'find something to do' during the time of accompanying her only son for his studies. She managed to find a part-time job with flexible working hours as a cleaner, working from 7:30 to 10:30 a.m. in the morning and then going back home to prepare her son's lunch. This was followed by three consecutive working hours starting from 1:30 p.m. in the afternoon. Her insistence on working for money is articulated as follows:

From my deep heart, I feel like [financially] depending on men will lose my autonomy. It feels bad when I have to ask him for money when I want to buy something. If I can earn money, I'm free to buy my favourite things [without his permission].

Hockey et al. (2007) use a life-course approach to examine how people growing up as heterosexual exercise their agency and how heterosexuality as an institution shapes people's everyday life. They found complexity and subtleties in people's experiences of being heterosexual across life stages, as people negotiate their agency when constructing their lives in a 'fluid, negotiable and changeable' way (Hockey et al., 2007: 63). Here, within the mundane experiences relating to heterosexual couple relationships in the Chinese context, caring responsibilities constrained women's capacity for migrating together with their male partners, and to some degree further limited their opportunities to be financially independent. However, Jieyu and Hongli's decision to join or re-join the labour market in later life illustrates that agency is not static, but rather evolves and develops in a complex way in terms of an overall life strategy. Constraints and some degree of choice could both be seen to be involved. Yet, it is important to note that these choices are not always a consequence of an individual's 'free will', as the work schedule of Hongli, a study mother at the time of the interviews, revealed, which was 'tailored' in line with her family members' demands (see also Holmes, 2004b).

External Authoritative Forces

LAT can happen under the condition of people's understanding of their powerlessness against external institutions and authorities. For example, Beibei (28, married, Beijing) secured a permanent position in an institutional organisation in Beijing, where she was born and educated. She would continue living alone because her husband had been assigned to serve as a military officer in Urumqi, in the northwest of the country. Likewise, Bingyu (29, married, Beijing) did not want to give up her career in Beijing, so, she had to wait for her husband's army service to end.

In addition, male partners' work demands can sometimes put women in a passive position and prevent the formation of a co-residential partnership. This is apparent in the case of Nan (24, unmarried, Liaoning), who worked as a civil servant in her hometown in North China. She explicitly expressed a desire for having a stable couple relationship but could not because of her boyfriend's unstable career plans as a pilot in South China. Mei (34, married, Beijing) also lived alone due to her husband's one-year overseas training in the USA. Because people under such circumstances often had little capacity to challenge or change the perceived vulnerability of their partnership, a strong sense of emotional loss arose. Mei vividly recounted,

> Loneliness is a description of psychological state, but for me, it's like a material and tangible object which can send out a sound when it falls to the ground ... When I got up [in the morning], I would ask myself where I was, what I was supposed to do. Such rhetorical questions reflect my loneliness ... it has become a physical and tangible thing.

This sense of emotional loss was also strongly echoed by Hua (31, married, Beijing), a high school teacher in Beijing. According to Hua's account, her husband served in the military in Guangzhou and was required to stay five more years due to his demanding work. The following excerpt describes her most inner feelings when her partner was far away:

> Very soon after his departure, what I was most afraid of was weekends. Because that was my most lonely time while exactly the happiest time for

others. So, I loved working very much, at least I have colleagues and students around me ... Sometimes I was in a deep trance and wondered whether I really was married. Those kinds of feelings didn't go away until my little boy was born. He is my [emotional] sustenance and makes me feel homely [due to his existence].

The above excerpt highlights that the practice of relational agency sometimes requires the work of managing feelings, so that, in this case, Hua could distract herself from the sensation of sadness associated with being physically apart from her partner. The relational context and webs of relations that direct people's practice of agency are closely implicated with showing emotion, which will be discussed in Chap. 5. However, being in an LAT relationship does not always place women in a vulnerable position, as almost all participants noted some benefits to a varying extent. For example, as Hua continued,

Living together means that we have to make changes to fit in with each other, whereas [if we are] living apart there's no need to do this. I can do whatever I like. He won't bother me, and I won't be mad like if he was at home and messed it up.

In addition to the benefits of allowing individuals to retain their individual autonomy and pursue personal identity (Borell & Karlsson, 2003; Holmes, 2006; Liefbroer et al., 2015; Roseneil, 2006; Upton-Davis, 2015), LAT also offers people room to restore and pursue their own friendships (Duncan & Phillips, 2011; Roseneil & Budgeon, 2004). Thus, Beibei (28, married) would often 'go shopping, hang out with friends and watch movies' when her husband was not around. However, she then commented on people's ambivalent attitude towards these benefits offered by LATs:

Sometimes you really want to enjoy being on your own when you're together [with your partner]; whereas having been alone for a long time you'll [have a] desire for living together. These are human beings—they always want something which they actually can't easily get.

The practice of agency can certainly influence the ways in which people understand their own personal relationship. For those who viewed these benefits as 'incidental and temporary' (Carter & Duncan, 2018), LATs could be seen as a temporary separation for couples (Ermisch & Seidler,

2009; Haskey, 2005) and serve as a practical response to having only limited financial resources and feeling vulnerable in the face of the power of institutions. In this regard, LATs are not conceptualised as the 'ideal' family form (if characterised by a co-residential heterosexual partnership). Once circumstances allowed, it was both anticipated and preferred by participants that they would move into traditional coupledom, which entails a co-residential partnership. As Beibei envisaged regarding her partner, 'he would come back [to Beijing] as soon as possible as I am here, and our future kid will be coming three years later'. While acknowledging that women's agency was variously constrained, people can develop and exercise a degree of agency across the life course in relation to their mundane, everyday experiences.

Negotiated Agency: Family Values and Hegemonic Ideas About Marriage

Our personal life is relational and it is often these relations with others and the social contexts in which these interactions are developed that influence people's decisions, actions and choices (Carter & Duncan, 2018; Smart, 2007). Corroborating previous studies, many discussions with the women participants in this research regarding the reasons for LAT are relational in the sense that they often reflexively took into account connectivity with intimate others. Thus, this section is primarily concerned with the importance of relational others (such as partners and parents) and, in particular, perceived obligations to their children in affecting family living arrangements. I will also investigate how this further affects the construction and maintenance of relations beyond the heterosexual couple relationship—friendship.

Relational Bonds with Family Members

Being embedded in a web of relationships that include people who were once seen as intimate others, agency can be informed by past relationships. Linjuan (32, unmarried, Beijing) showed a level of self-reflexivity about how the idea of the de-institutionalisation of marriage has been relationally informed by her growing up and previous (unsuccessful) love relationships:

> When I was young, my parents had a poor relationship. I often saw them fighting. My mum didn't divorce because of me and my sister. I felt very sorry for her. Also, I don't think it's really necessary [for women] to devote themselves to children, revolving around them since they were born … Marriage is not an imperative thing for me. This is also probably related to my past love relationship. We often had quarrels when I lived with my ex-boyfriend. Personally, I also knew people who were married with children and gave all their attention to their children and two sets of families, leaving their personal lives aside. I am particularly not willing to live a life like that. I would think the same way if I hadn't met my Mr Right. I like living in my way—two individuals don't have to get married if they want to be together or have offspring.

Based on these relational considerations, it seems that LAT provided Linjuan the opportunity for the reflexive and strategic undoing of gender in which taken-for-granted patterns regarding couplehood are undermined and destabilised (Evertsson & Nyman, 2013). Therefore, a sense of resistance to traditional couplehood and family form was articulated in Linjuan's account, which can be seen from her hesitation about developing a stable couple relationship with a man she knew at the time of being dispatched by her company to work in Tianjin, a coastal city near Beijing. As she explained,

> I'd like to go back to Dalian [her hometown] where both my sister and parents were living [after her work in Tianjin is done]. If I said yes [to marry him], I probably wouldn't be able to go back. Because he is a native Beijinger and wouldn't move away.

Having grown up in a rural family in Dalian with a university education, Linjuan assumed that her partner, who was born and raised in Beijing with overseas studying experience, would not move to her hometown to live. Her sense of vulnerability was developed within a social context implicitly organised in line with hegemonic heterosexual relations. Under such circumstance, she had to negotiate and balance the tension between the couple's living arrangements and her own desire to be close to her family members. This means that the decision where to settle down is not simply based on her own specific desires and needs but involves the considerations of power balances and relational contexts in which each of them was embedded (Burkitt, 2016; Mason, 2004). In emphasising the significance of contexts and connectivity with others, LAT was seemingly an indication of a compromised solution in that she can avoid choosing between her partner and the caring obligations to her parents.

Although Linjuan's narratives showed some resistance to traditional family values, she has no intention to permanently view LAT as an alternative to marriage or a new-life option. As a thirty-something unmarried woman, Linjuan later in the interview told me that she thought her current partner is her Mr. Right and wanted to get married as soon as possible. This indicates that greater commitment to individualism with an emphasis on independence and autonomy seems to have little impact on the existing social institution of marriage in contemporary Chinese society. As empirical research shows, people still highly value and desire to have a stable marital relationship (Ji & Yeung, 2014; Kam, 2015; Xu et al., 2015). It is plausible to argue that the paradox of lingering traditional cultures of familism and changes in coupledom and marriage create increasing instability in Chinese family life, leading to people's new family practices.

In addition, my data with married women with children show that the perceived needs of their children can also make LAT occur, which further complicates the dualism framework of 'preference/constraint'. This was particularly manifested in the group of 'study mothers', who physically accompanied their children so as to provide them with optimal living and study conditions. For example, Rosy (46, married, Beijing) had quit her promising job in Beijing in order to accompany her high school-aged son to study in the USA, considering her husband could not give up his business in China and her son was too young to take care of himself in a foreign country. Another study mother, Guanya (37, married, Liaoning), rented an apartment near her twin sons' high school to provide them with a better learning environment. Similar to Guanya, Xutong (40, married, Liaoning), who was born into a peasant family in a rural area, also moved to town for her son's study while her husband was working in their hometown as the sole breadwinner in the family.

In these examples, children's well-being was prioritised over women themselves and other family members, especially when there were tensions between childcare provision and personal career development. This was labelled by Carter and Duncan (2018) as an 'obligated preference', given that these women's agency in cohabiting was conditioned by their prior responsibilities to others, in particular, their children. In the split household driven by children's education, it is often mothers who physically accompany their children. This decision often seems to have been made 'by instinct' and is informed by habitual or unconscious calculation, especially when taking women's identity as a mother and their 'feminine' role as a caregiver into account (Roseneil, 2006). Although it has been noted earlier in this book, that the long-standing traditional Confucian family values regarding gendered norms have recently been considered less influential under the influences of individualism and modernisation, the literature on changing patterns of family practices in China shows that women are still considered as being very family-centred (Inoguchi & Shin, 2009; Lim & Skinner, 2012; Qiu, 2020). This is strongly echoed by Guanya, who states that 'women must be family-centred. In my understanding, family is the most important thing for women.'

It should be noted that none of the study mothers in this research complained about heavy household chores being left behind by their absent male partner. In fact, women saw shopping, cooking, doing laundry and washing as their 'duty'. What they most complained about, during the times of living separately from their partner, was the work often seen as 'men's tasks', and thereby women found hard to do, such as harvesting the corn, dealing with tricky contractors, fixing a broken radiator or pipes. In terms of future family planning when their children go to university, all study mothers expressed a strong desire for 'reuniting' and living together with their partner when it allows. The idea of married couples living together is so normative that Xutong (40, married) said, 'it would be abnormal if a woman does not expect her husband to go home'. Compared to 'ordinary' couples who co-reside, being in an LAT relationship in my sample is still very much grounded in the most socially acceptable familial living arrangement that I have previously defined.

In these instances, women's LAT experiences are highly relational and gendered in that their identity as 'study mothers' is contextually constructed and practised through daily care for their children imposed by social norms relating to gendered parenting practices. In doing so, a sense of 'motherhood' was increasingly prioritised over 'wifehood' and/or 'selfhood'. These accounts are indicative of how agency is negotiated and bounded by family practices and the relationships of others. As the research continued, I found that some key issues arose through study mothers' accounts regarding family practices, gender roles and identity construction. In order to better understand the gendered experiences of women who are involved in LATs due to their children's education, I undertake an in-depth examination in a case study of 'study mothers' in the next chapter of this book.

However, married women with children, in this study, do not always share the same 'obligated preference' as the study mothers often have, albeit their agency in living together is also conditioned by the obligation of caring for children. Some young mothers with pre-school children reported that taking care of young children on a daily basis was more about constraint than 'preference', especially when the tension between the desire to achieve independence and caring obligations for children was taking place. For example, at the time of interview, Shanrui (28, married, Liaoning), a mother of two, lived at a more substantial distance from both her sets of parents. She was often alone at home as her husband took on the sole breadwinner role as a long-haul truck driver, who came back home about once every two or three months, depending on his workload. As she explains,

> I think being independent is good for women. Not only living independently but being independent in all aspects of life. But I'm now financially dependent [on my husband] and feel like I'm not being highly valued. If I had a monthly salary of 3,000 RMB [about 350 GBP], he [her husband] would at least consider my [emotional] feelings and pay more attention to me ... Both my natal family and my husband's family said that the family doesn't need me to earn money, as long as I take good care of my children. But I don't agree, because I have to ask them for money. It would be better if they actively gave me some, but in fact I have to phone them every month for money.

Obviously, Shanrui was not satisfied with her current life and status as a full-time housewife and felt vulnerable during those times, because the obligations of caring for children were seen as a barrier for her to access paid work and be independent, especially when both her husband and parents were largely absent from her daily life. As she said, 'I desperately hoped that my mum could come to take care of my children ... I very much want to go out to find a paid job.' Situated in the web of relationships, a sense of relational constraint emerges in that people can hardly make individual decisions about and formulate a project of the self (Mason, 2004). Instead, they may easily articulate a sense of powerlessness or lack of control due to the tension between paid work and childcare provision, as illustrated in the research by Wang and Dong (2010). They draw on data from 592 households in low-income rural villages in China and provide strong evidence that having children to care for places constraints on women's access to employment in China. Likewise, Yu and Xie (2011) also hold this view and further argue that the traditional gender-based division of domestic labour may impede women's participation in the labour market. Under this ideology, women are constantly expected to sacrifice their own interests in order to satisfy other family members' needs and to maintain familial and social harmony (Delphy & Leonard, 1992; Weeks, 1989; Wolf, 1985). In this regard, women's agency was very practically related to the perceived needs of their children, with more negative consequences being noted by young women in particular, but agency was also related to and impinged on by the economic constraints I have noted.

People often construct and constitute self-identify in relation to others (Mason, 2004; Roseneil & Ketokivi, 2016). Similarly, Jackson (1999) argued that women's identity is often constructed in light of their heterosexual relations, such as being mothers, wives and daughters-in-law. As people organise their lives according to a gendered division of labour, the identity of mothers is commonly practised through providing daily care for their children. Due to the bodily needs of the baby, Shanrui identified her primary family responsibility as childcare, as her daily life has fundamentally revolved around her children. Consequently, her sense of vulnerability in an LAT relationship is informed by her dominant identity as a mother, as she maintained:

> I feel like I'm a housemaid, taking care of *chi* (food), *he* (drink), *la* (poop), *sa* (piss) and *shui* (sleep). I'm just like a single parent, or housemaid who gets paid every month. [The difference is that] the housemaids can spend it on themselves, while all my money went on the household expenses.

This sense of vulnerability was more evident in situations when people's expectations of practical and mundane aspects of caring or help are failed to be delivered, which may undermine intimacy hitherto successfully sustained through other practices' (Jamieson, 2013: 19; see also Jamieson, 1999). Shanrui recalled her feeling of total and utter helplessness when her husband left her alone to take care of their six-year-old daughter and a toddler:

There was a time when my baby always cried at midnight, it made no difference whether cuddling or singing to her. I was dead tired and sleepy. At that time, he was not at home. Sometimes when the baby cried, I didn't cuddle and sing to her, but cried with her. Actually, I have thought of divorce. [I'm] just so tired.

However, Shanrui was not the only woman in this research who spoke of her identity in terms of being a single parent. Wangyang (38, married, Liaoning) also very much viewed herself in this manner, given that her husband was away from home and paid little (or even no) attention to their marital relationship or their family. Due to the nature of his job, Wangyang's husband worked away for half a month and then came back home to rest for the other half. Sometimes he returned home once every two months, depending on his work schedules. According to Wangyang, her husband's annual salary is three times higher than hers. In fact, she preferred living separately from her husband because he would break her daily routine and did not help in doing housework and caring for the children when he was home. By implication, Wangyang thought he had failed to do what he, as her husband, her children's father, and son in his own family, should do. She claimed,

> You [the husband] made your wife become very independent, then you will be totally useless. What else I can expect from you as I'm so independent and strong? ... Yes, my mum did help me a lot, but it was my mum helping me to take care of our children. As my husband, why don't you help me?

Therefore, she said stoutly and defiantly, 'I don't want him to come back [home].' However, she still kept her marital relationship going, under the circumstances of having 'no communication' with her husband. It might therefore be deduced from this example that the meaning of an LAT relationship encompasses a sense of protection for other family members in unfavourable circumstances, even at the expense of their own happiness and their emotional needs not being met by their partners. Therefore, I would argue that the decisions that individuals make as to their personal relationship are not simply individual choices but are more often tightly related to various relationships, which in turn, for my participants, are informed by the traditional gender roles and the responsibilities that are attached to them (see also Stoilova et al., 2016). As Wangyang said, 'I sacrifice my whole life for my children. But I have no choice.'

As Twamley (2012) and Faircloth (2015) suggest, the concepts of gender and notions of intimacy and care stand in contrast to the notions of 'gender equality'. The unequal burden of domestic care, alongside women's economic dependence, which is often practised in traditional models of marriage and the family, remains prominent, even in non-conventional family forms. In this sense, the endurance of heterosexuality as an institution is still apparent in LATs (Hockey et al., 2007) when seen in the context of China and the traditional patriarchal family system in particular. This finding, however, is in sharp contrast to Upton-Davis' (2015) argument that women use LAT to undo gender and transform traditional gendered norms—both practically and emotionally. Within the context of institutionalised heterosexuality, the Chinese women from the study that I have identified here are embedded in the wider contexts of relations that can be characterised as lingering patriarchal and familial gender norms. Wangyang's agency was largely compromised in the face of overwhelmingly dependent children within this relational network, leading her to identify herself as a single parent. In my other examples, the adoption of LAT for study mothers and young care providers, like Shanrui and Wangyang, was inseparable from the perceived caring duties imposed by social norms relating to gender roles and parenting practices. From their perspective, LAT was not a new way of doing intimacy, nor some subversion of the gendered norms of coupledom. I would argue, with my data presented in this chapter so far, that there is little evidence of the existence of detraditionalisation in relation to the practices of family life. On the contrary, at times, the non-conventional partnership of an LAT in some ways has strengthened the gendered division of labour and reaffirmed gendered norms in favour of traditional coupledom.

Friendship

In the Western context, sociological studies note that patterns of family practices and personal relationships may be shifting (Smart, 2007), and that there may be more flexibility now for individuals to organise, and perhaps prioritise, relationships such as friendships (Allan, 2008). Roseneil and Budgeon's (2004) study found that some individuals who are not in co-resident partnerships in reality actively decentred their sexual/love relationships but highly valued friendships. By implication, there is an alternative way of ordering and organising their intimate lives (Roseneil, 2006), resonating with Giddens' (1992) notion of the 'pure relationship'. Likewise, Ketokivi (2012: 482) found that heterosexuals who were not in a co-resident couple relationship had 'a more inclusive definition of closeness' and more diverse patterns of intimate life, including more friends.

It is argued that when people engage in an LAT relationship, they are more likely to consider intimacy and care beyond 'the family' (Roseneil & Budgeon, 2004). In my data, my participants often echoed the benefits that LAT offered in terms of having free time and space to develop their own friendship circles. This is evident in the story of Hua (31, married), a high school teacher in Beijing who lived with her parents-in-law, caring for her two-year-old son. She commented,

> [The relationships between] family and my personal life are not a *quanji* [universe]. It's just an intersection relation, and we need to give each other some personal space. I always told my husband that 'you'd better not intervene in my personal life when you come back. I'll not stay with you all the time.' Of course, I certainly wouldn't do things against moral principles. Yes, the reunion time for us is indeed short, as he has only just over a month's holiday a year. But I also need to network with my friends occasionally. I need to have my own life. I can't stand you [her husband] asking me [to always keep you company] once you're back.

Clearly, Hua appreciated the reunion with her partner, but meanwhile was expecting to retain autonomy to maintain her own friendship circles outside of the heterosexual intimate relationship. However, by saying 'occasionally', this implies that her partnership remains of importance within the coupled nature of social life (Cronin, 2015; Ketokivi, 2012), even if she lives in a non-conventional family arrangement. This appears to be the case at least for LAT people in my sample, as shown in the following extract from Yuqing (30, engaged, Liaoning):

> Four months ago, I received two movie tickets which would expire soon, but I didn't get an opportunity to find people to go together with. If we two [her and her husband] can go and have dinner together, that would be my first choice. Those people with families or partners being around can't keep me company every day. In that case, I would have *zi ji wan* (have fun alone).

Furthermore, she frankly said,

> You know, I'm already 30. How many women [of my age] haven't formed a family or found a boyfriend? Who would accompany me every day? I can meet and talk with my friends, but, basically, they're all busy with their own stuff.

In line with the dominance of 'the couple' as a norm within a heterosexual context, my data confirmed the centrality of the heterosexual partnership in an individual's heterosexual life (Budgeon, 2008; Cronin,

2015; Gabb et al., 2013; Ketokivi, 2012). In this sense, the hegemonic idea of couplehood directly and indirectly limits people's agency in developing the wider social ties and connections, even in the case of their male partners being absent from their daily lives. Although Yuqing would like to spend more time with her (female) friends, following the traditional coupledom route was emphasised, as she said 'that would be my first choice'. This was with the understanding that people in her age cohort are often either married or in a dating relationship with their intimate others based around them. Thus, few opportunities are available for married people to maintain wider social ties and practice intimacy such as that seen between friends (Roseneil & Budgeon, 2004). This arguably suggests that, in the Chinese context, the extent to which women can exercise their power and autonomy in developing friendship circles is relationally constrained by the primary gender roles attached to them as a wife and mother in the family.

RELATIONAL INDIVIDUALISM: REFLEXIVITY AND LIFE STAGES

In this study, there are some young people who could have more easily moved in together with their partners but chose to (temporarily) live alone. As such, they ended up in an LAT relationship as an active choice in general and tended to express positive attitudes towards this living arrangement. For example, Yuqing (30, unmarried, Liaoning) explicitly maintained that LAT released her from the gendered division of domestic labour by 'just cleaning myself up', and others appreciated the extra time LAT offered to 'devote themselves to their careers' (as witnessed by the views of Hua, 31, married, Beijing; Zhonglan, 24, unmarried, Liaoning). The subjective awareness of wanting to prioritise personal career development was also echoed and exemplified by Xiaobo (26, married, Beijing). After graduating with a postgraduate degree in the UK, she didn't go back to China but remained only to keep her husband company during the course of his PhD study. In this regard, her married life seemed to mesh seamlessly with the requirements of hegemonic ideas about family, in the sense that 'married couples should be living together', as she put it.

However, six months later, Xiaobo took the initiative to move to an LAT relationship, leaving her husband alone in the UK. She explained,

> I feel like it wasn't saying that women have to have a big career, at least [she should be] financially independent. In other words, you should be able to

live alone when you're separated from your husband. If I stay in the UK for two or three more years simply for him, I will be 27, 28 years old without any work experience. By then, I won't be eligible to apply for on-campus recruitment [as I won't be a recent graduate], and also, I won't be qualified to apply via society recruitment due to lacking work experience, which all placed me in a dilemma. In this sense, I think I would have sacrificed too much if I couldn't get a job that I really wanted to do, couldn't go to the company that I dreamed of, and couldn't get paid what I'd hoped for. If we were both unemployed, it would also generate more pressure on our parents. After weighing both sides, it might be better to temporarily separate. [By doing so,] I will be able to gain some work experience and reduce my parent's burden. If he wants to buy something but doesn't want to put pressure on his parents, then I can help him. I think it's not a bad thing [if we live apart].

It is clear that Xiaobo herself took the initiative here to detach from 'conventional' family practices through moving to an LAT relationship and leaving her husband alone in the UK to complete his higher education. At the time of the interview, Xiaobo has been working as an auditor since she was back to Beijing. Thus, being in an LAT relationship strategically allowed her to fulfil her plan to be employed. For her, LAT is a win-win situation and 'both/and' solution (Levin, 2004) by which her career path was strategically secured with a sense of fulfilment, whilst maintaining her intimate relationship and making a financial contribution to their family.

Furthermore, she continued to exercise her agency by living in her favourite city rather than following the traditional post-marital patrilocal living arrangement. As she stated, 'The only prerequisite for our marriage is that we have to be settled in Beijing, as I'm used to living here. I grew up here where all my family members and friends are based. I don't want to go somewhere else.' Xiaobo further explained to me that her husband had originally planned to immigrate to the UK after completing his PhD. As a result of their marriage, he gave up this idea of immigration and went back to China as she wished. Obviously, Xiaobo actively sought to gain control of her own life in terms of when and whom she should marry, whether or not she should accompany her husband to a foreign country, when she should return to her home to work and where she would like to settle down in the longer term.

Similarly, Xinyi (27, married, Beijing), a primary school teacher, is a good illustration of how the demands for independence and freedom from a patriarchal family life are achieved through LAT. Xinyi and her husband were born, educated and worked in Xiamen, South China. She encouraged her husband—a medical practitioner—to enrich himself by attending avocational training in Beijing, even though they had only just got married. When I asked her if she experienced any difficulties during the time they were working in different cities and living separately, she recounted that

> I was actually looking forward to it [chuckles]. Because I really wanted to live alone, and this was the opportunity. The training was not mandatory. It was me who encouraged him to attend.

Although Xinyi is the only child in her family, she is not emotionally close to her father because he was seen as a dominating figure. When she was young, she had not spoken to him for a year after a quarrel. Therefore, 'living alone and having my own time' was always part of her dream. During the time of the interview, Xinyi came to Beijing visiting her husband over summer holidays, while enjoying freedom and autonomy when they were apart. It is clear that there are some elements of reflexive and self-conscious narratives in each of these accounts. The practice of relatively strategical and purposeful agency in living a desired lifestyle is more apparent in the younger generation than in the old one. This is arguably related to their higher-educational achievements, increased employment opportunities, greater economic independence and rising individualism, all as a response to the profound (and uneven) effects of the social, economic and cultural landscape in contemporary China (Jackson & Ho, 2020). Some scholars even suggest that China appears to be experiencing the 'deinstitutioinalisation' of family life characterised by a higher acceptance of premarital sex, cohabitation and same-gender sex (Davis & Friedman, 2014; Yeung & Hu, 2016), and that woman in particular have benefited from this decline in traditional structures (Giddens, 1992).

However, Mason (2004) reminds us of the importance of keeping 'the processes of relating in focus just as much as, if not more than, the individual or the self' (p. 177). This is because people can hardly make sense of their relationships without taking into account their relations to social norms (May, 2011; Smart, 2011). From the accounts from young people, a significant adherence to more traditional cultural expectations was evident especially when it comes to future plans for family life. Therefore, I used the term 'relational individualism' to identify people experiencing relatively unconstrained agentic power in relation to their family life, while being informed by the wider contexts in which culturally prescribed ideas about family and marital relationships are constructed. For example, although Xiaobo was able to make individual choices about relational practice, at the same time, she expressed hopes to live an 'ordinary person's life':

> I told him [her husband] that I'd like to give birth in the next three years. We should have stable jobs by then and will consider whether or not to move to a bigger house. Just having an ordinary person's life that he takes charge of the outside and I take care of inside the home.

It is plausible to argue that different stages of the life course play roles in influencing the extent to which people can exercise their agency. In Chinese culture, it is still a dominant family pattern that the birth of a baby comes after marriage and married couples are expected to live together with their dependent children to establish a nuclear family. As a married woman in her late 20s, Xiaobo had no intention of using LAT to question gender roles or challenge the long-standing conventional family. Instead, she organised her marital life in a conventional way—living together as a couple with a baby envisaged at some point in life. The marital institution and attendant norms have directly and indirectly affected how people live their family lives in a given social and cultural context. In this context, agency does not exist as some given absolute (Carter & Duncan, 2018: 148). LAT for Xiaobo also incorporates traditional forms of family life because her agency was bound up with 'the availability of ideas about family and relationships' (Duncan, 2015: 600).

This mixture of traditional and modern values in family relationships is even more evident when it comes to conflicts between work and family life. In line with prescribed gender roles and the traditional family practice that *nan zhu wai nu zhu nei* (men are in charge of the outside and women take care of inside the home), Xiaobo explained her career development plan: some adjustments will have to be made. In this regard, having a decent but low-stress job has become her favoured occupational choice. As she claimed,

> I'll not stop working. But I won't find a busy job like my current one. [I hope I can find] a cushy nine-to-five job where I don't need to overwork and will be free at weekends, so I can have more time to focus on our children. I don't want to be a full-time housewife, [because] I'll be disconnected from society as time goes by, and we two may have contradictions. I

don't want to be like someone who struggles for success in the job market. In my workplace, there are many nu qiang ren[1] who give birth very late, like in their 40s. I don't want to become one of them.

In comparison with her career prospects, family well-being was prioritised in conformity with family values. As a result of this, some adjustments had to be made regarding work and family relations when her husband finished his degree in the UK and returned to China. This indicates that people's experience of family life can be significantly conditioned by relational ties with intimate others but also are subject to traditional norms of familism. This 'idealised' version of heteronormative family is deeply rooted in Chinese people's understanding of intimate relationships. Undoubtedly, Xiaobo was not the only participant who claimed that changes (or sacrifices) would be made by women if necessary. A similar account was given by Yufen (31, married, Beijing), who had a postgraduate degree and worked as a high school teacher in Beijing. She articulated the importance of family life, while simultaneously refusing to be a housewife in the long term:

> My family is my priority as we work to make [a] good living. If my family life is harmonious and happy, I'll then put the rest of my heart into work with great effort. However, if conflicts between them happen, I'll certainly return home first. I probably may sacrifice my own career, as he [her husband] is the jia ting zhi zhu [backbone of the family]. I earn far less than my partner, so, I will fully support him [to continue working]. When the children grow older, I will return to [the] workplace again. I believe in traditional gender roles—Nan zi wei da [male-centred] … but I refuse to be a housewife all the time, for instance. I may get rid of it [being a full-time housewife]. I'm a person who combines tradition with modern thoughts, kind of a split [personality].

Both Xiaobo and Yufen were reluctant to pursue career development at the expense of their families' well-being, despite expressing varying degrees of attachment to work. Their attitudes to family and work yielded several rather intriguing and contradictory findings. Although young women in LATs did exercise some degree of strategic agency to

---

[1] The phrase *nu qiang ren* literally means female supermen, and refers to career-oriented professional women who are considered capable of developing work-related skills, while less emphasis is placed on family and housework.

purposefully fulfil their own desires, this agency was not simply a matter of individualistic choice, but remained compromised and conditioned by prescribed social norms in relation to traditional family values (Cook & Dong, 2011; Gregory & Milner, 2009). In this sense, a more conventional way of thinking and practices—refiguring gender roles and reproducing institutionalised heterosexuality—was generated through the idea of the importance of being family-centred and pushing personal development into second place.

One possible explanation for this ambivalence and tension between agency and structure might be attributed to the gendered consequences of social change in China, leading to women facing contradictions, as I argued in Chap. 2. On the one hand, China's rapid changing environment has enabled women to have a greater desire and capacity to enhance their sense of self-worth (Liu, 2008). As Fong (2002) argued, China's one-child policy has empowered urban daughters in terms of negotiating gender norms in ways that benefit them, as they do not have to compete with siblings for parental investment. Although regional disparities and inequalities were identified, opportunities for education and employment along with rising individualism, especially in urban areas, have facilitated singleton daughters' efforts to make individualistic choices and achieve more financial independence than previous generations (Zarafonetis, 2017). This arguably leads many young people to experience greater freedom and autonomy than before in what might be termed building a 'do-it-yourself biography'. On the other hand, these changes do not automatically equate to theories of individualisation, nor is this agency untrammelled, even when the agency can be considered consciously strategic (Jackson & Ho, 2020). The enduring impact of traditions and continuity of social norms surrounding family and gender roles continue to organise Chinese people's understanding and practice of everyday family relationships in the specific cultural and social context of China (Ji, 2017; Kipnis, 2017).

Conclusion

This chapter has been primarily concerned with how a social context that is characterised by the continuing salience of traditions in the collective values and beliefs on familism limits or empowers individuals' experience of agency. In my effort to understand the complexities and intricacies of practices of agency, I used a relational approach and took into account the importance of social and cultural contexts under which individuals make their choices in engaging in non-cohabiting partnerships.

The participants in this study share some structural constraints and relational ties in relationship to their lives, but different amounts and types of agency are exercised due to the balance of economic circumstances, life stages, perceived caring responsibilities and personal career development. Although people, to varying degrees, appreciated the benefits that LAT offered in relation to personal space, extra free time, autonomy from male authority and the traditional division of domestic labour, the dominant institution of heteronormative marriage and family is still considered the most ideal and 'normal' form of intimate relationship in contemporary China.

My data have shown little evidence that individuals have been active agents in ways no longer constrained by traditions. In the same vein, they are not totally imposed on by powerful structural constraints. In fact, people's narratives about their LATs are highly relational. The ways in which people exercise their agency in living a desired co-residential partnership are sometimes impinged upon by their economic conditions and social norms relating to gender roles. In this way, people ended up in LATs as a response to structuring constraints and external institutions. As a result, a sense of vulnerability has led to some (rural) women being left behind to support the family. This form of living arrangement has reinforced gendered family life and reproduced gender inequalities within and beyond the family setting.

Agency also arises from our interactions with others because 'the lives people live continue to be processually and contextually embedded' (Brannen & Nilsen, 2005: 423). In emphasising the relationality of women's LAT practices, during the interviews, their narratives are indicative of the continued importance of family relationships and webs of connections they made with other people in shaping their identities, choices and agency. Even if they are living a slightly different lifestyle, LAT was not seen as an alternative to the social institution of marriage, but was closely bound by family practices, and in particular the perceived needs of their children (Qiu, 2020). In this regard, the relational self as 'study mother' was constructed and evaluated through the ideas surrounding the social institutions of gender norms and family.

Although there was some evidence of strategically using LAT to undo gendered norms among young generations, this is not simply 'a matter of choice' as a result of rising individualism. Moving to a co-residential partnership and living together as a couple with dependent children envisaged at some point in life still seems to be appealing. This appears to be closely relevant to the life stages of people. In the Chinese context, social expectations on 'stable' family life and fertility pressure have placed young women, including those with higher education, at a disadvantaged position in both private and public spheres (Gu, 2021; Qian & Jin, 2018). However, these culturally and socially acceptable norms about family values continue to shape the ways people negotiate and make sense of their personal lives, indicating the practice of relational individualism.

References

Allan, G. (2008). Flexibility, friendship, and family. *Personal Relationships, 15*, 1–16.
Bauman, Z. (2003). *Liquid love: On the frailty of human bonds*. Polity Press.
Beck, U., & Beck-Gernsheim, E. (1995). *The normal chaos of love*. Polity Press.
Beck, U., & Beck-Gernsheim, E. (2002). *Individualization*. Sage.
Borell, K., & Karlsson, S. G. (2003). Reconceptualizing intimacy and ageing: Living apart together. In S. Arber, K. Davidson, & J. Ginn (Eds.), *Gender and ageing: Changing roles and relationships* (pp. 47–62). Open University Press.
Brannen, J., & Nilsen, A. (2005). Individualisation, choice and structure: A discussion of current trends in sociological analysis. *The Sociological Review, 53*(3), 412–428. https://doi.org/10.1111/j.1467-954X.2005.00559.x
Budgeon, S. (2008). Couple culture and the production of singleness. *Sexualities, 11*(3), 301–325.
Burkitt, I. (2016). Relational agency: Relational sociology, agency and interaction. *European Journal of Social Theory, 19*(3), 322–339. https://doi.org/10.1177/1368431015591426
Carter, J. (2017). Why marry? The role of tradition in women's marital aspirations. *Sociological Research Online, 22*(1), 1–14. https://doi.org/10.5153/sro.4125
Carter, J., & Duncan, S. (2018). *Reinventing couples: Tradition, agency and bricolage*. Palgrave Macmillan.
Cook, S., & Dong, X. (2011). Harsh choices: Chinese women's paid work and unpaid care responsibilities under economic reform. *Development and Change, 42*(4), 947–965. https://doi.org/10.1111/j.1467-7660.2011.01721.x
Cronin, A. (2015). Gendering friendship: Couple culture, heteronormativity and the production of gender. *Sociology, 49*(6), 1167–1182.
Davis, D. S., & Friedman, S. (2014). *Wives, husbands, and lovers: Marriage and sexuality in Hong Kong, Taiwan and urban China*. Hong Kong University Press.
Delphy, C., & Leonard, D. (1992). *Familiar exploitation*. Polity Press.

Duncan, S. (2015). Women's agency in living apart together: Constraint, strategy and vulnerability. *The Sociological Review, 63*(3), 589–607. https://doi.org/10.1111/1467-954X.12184

Duncan, S., & Phillips, M. (2011). People who live apart together (LATs): New family form or just a stage? *International Review of Sociology, 21*, 513–532.

Ermisch, J., & Seidler, T. (2009). Living apart together. In M. Brynin & J. Ermisch (Eds.), *Changing relationship* (pp. 45–59). Routledge.

Evertsson, L., & Nyman, C. (2013). On the other side of couplehood: Single women in Sweden exploring life without a partner. *Families, Relationships and Societies, 2*(1), 61–78.

Faircloth, C. (2015). Negotiating intimacy, equality and sexuality in the transition to parenthood. *Sociological Research Online, 20*(4), 144–155.

Fan, C. C., Sun, M., & Zheng, S. (2011). Migration and split households: A comparison of sole, couple, and family migrants in Beijing, China. *Environment and Planning A, 43*(9), 2164–2185. https://doi.org/10.1068/a44128

Fong, V. L. (2002). China's one-child policy and the empowerment of urban daughters. *American Anthropologist, 104*(4), 1098–1109.

Gabb, J. Klett-Davies, M., Fink, J., & Thomae, M. (2013). *Enduring love? Couple relationships in the 21st century.* Survey findings report. The Open University.

Giddens, A. (1984). *The constitution of society: Outline of the theory of structuration.* University of California Press.

Giddens, A. (1991). *Modernity and self-identity: Self and society in the late modern age.* Stanford University Press.

Giddens, A. (1992). *The transformation of intimacy.* Polity Press.

Giddens, A. (2000) 'Preface' to Hakim, C. In *Work-lifestyle choices in the 21st century: Preference theory* (p. vii). Oxford University Press.

Gregory, A., & Milner, S. (2009). Work-life balance: A matter of choice? *Gender, Work and Organization, 16*(1), 1–19.

Gross, N. (2005). The detraditionalization of intimacy reconsidered. *Sociological Theory, 23*(3), 286–311. https://doi.org/10.1111/j.1749-6632.2002.tb02083.x

Gu, X. (2021). You are not young anymore!: Gender, age and the politics of reproduction in post-reform China. *Asian Bioethics Review, 13*(1), 57–76.

Haskey, J. (2005). Living arrangements in contemporary Britain: Having a partner who usually lives elsewhere and Living Apart Together (LAT). *Population Trends, 122*, 35–45.

Hockey, J., Meah, A., & Robinson, V. (2007). *Mundane heterosexualities: From theory to practices.* Palgrave Macmillan.

Holmes, M. (2004a). An equal distance? Individualisation, gender and intimacy in distance relationships. *The Sociological Review, 52*(2), 180–200.

Holmes, M. (2004b). The precariousness of choice in the new sentimental order: A response to Bawin-Legros. *Current Sociology, 52*(2), 251–257. https://doi.org/10.1177/0011392104041811

Holmes, M. (2006). Love lives at a distance: Distance relationships over the life-course. *Sociological Research Online, 11*(3). [Online]. Available at: http://www.socresonline.org.uk/11/3/holmes.html

Holmes, M. (2010). The emotionalization of reflexivity. *Sociology, 44*(1), 139–154.

Inoguchi, T., & Shin, D. C. (2009). The quality of life in Confucian Asia: From physical welfare to subjective well-being. *Social Indicators Research, 92*(2), 183–190.

Jackson, S. (1999). *Heterosexuality in question*. Sage.

Jackson, S. (2010). Materialist feminism, the self and global late modernity: Some consequences for intimacy and sexuality. In A. G. Jónasdóttir, V. Bryson, & K. B. Jones (Eds.), *Sexuality, gender and power: Inter-sectional and transnational perspectives* (pp. 15–29). Routledge.

Jackson, S., & Ho, P. S. Y. (2020). *Women doing intimacy: Gender, family and modernity in Britain and Hong Kong*. Palgrave Macmillan.

Jamieson, L. (1999). Intimacy transformed? *Sociology, 33*(10), 477–494. https://doi.org/10.1080/08858190209528804

Jamieson, L. (2013). Personal relationship, intimacy and the self in a mediated and global digital age. In K. Ortan-Johnson and N. Prior, (Eds.), *Digital sociology: critical perspectives* (pp. 13–33). Basingstoke: Palgrave Macmillian.

Ji, Y. (2017). A mosaic temporality: New dynamics of the gender and marriage system in contemporary urban China. *Temporalités, 26*, 3773. https://doi.org/10.4000/temporalites.3773

Ji, Y., & Yeung, W. J. J. (2014). Heterogeneity in contemporary Chinese marriage. *Journal of Family Issues, 35*(12), 1662–1682. https://doi.org/10.1177/0192513X14538030

Kam, L. Y. (2015). The demand for a "normal life": Marriage and its discontents in contemporary China. In M. McLell & V. Mackie (Eds.), *Routledge handbook of sexuality studies in East Asia* (pp. 77–86). Routledge.

Ketokivi, K. (2012). The intimate couple, family and the relational organization of close relationships. *Sociology, 46*(3), 473–489.

Kipnis, A. (2017). Urbanization and the transformation of kinship practice in Shandong. In G. Santos & S. Harrell (Eds.), *Transforming patriarchy: Chinese families in the twenty-first century* (pp. 113–128). University of Washington Press.

Levin, I. (2004). Living apart together: A new family form. *Current Sociology, 52*(2), 223–240. https://doi.org/10.1177/0011392104041809

Liefbroer, A. C., Poortman, A., & Seltzer, J. A. (2015). Why do intimate partners live apart? Evidence on LAT relationships across Europe. *Demographic Research, 32*(8), 251–286.

Lim, H. J., & Skinner, T. (2012). Culture and motherhood: Findings from a qualitative study of east Asian mothers in Britain. *Families, Relationships and Societies, 1*(3), 327–343.

Liu, F. (2008). Constructing the autonomous middle-class self in today's China: The case of young-adult only-children university students. *Journal of Youth Studies, 11*(2), 193–212.

Luo, C., Yang, X., Li, S., & Feldman, M. W. (2017). Love or bread? What determines subjective wellbeing among left-behind women in rural China? *Gender Issues, 34*(1), 23–43. https://doi.org/10.1007/s12147-016-9171-8

Mason, J. (2004). Personal narratives, relational selves: Residential histories in the living and telling. *The Sociological Review, 52*(2), 162–179. https://doi.org/10.1111/j.1467-954X.2004.00463.x

May, V. (2011). *Sociology of personal life*. Palgrave Macmillan.

McNay, L. (2004). Agency and experience: Gender as a lived relation. *The Sociological Review, 52*(2), 173–190. https://doi.org/10.1111/j.1467-954X.2005.00530.x

Meadows, M. (1997). Exploring the invisible: Listening to mid-life women about heterosexual sex. *Women's Studies International Forum, 20*(1), 145–152.

Morgan, D. (1996). *Family connections: An introduction to family studies*. Cambridge Polity.

Ortner, S. B. (2001). Specifying agency: The comaroffs and their critics. *Interventions, 3*(1), 76–84.

Qian, Y., & Jin, Y. (2018). Women's fertility autonomy in urban China: The role of couple dynamics under the universal two-child policy. *Chinese Sociological Review, 50*(3), 275–309. https://doi.org/10.1080/21620555.2018.1428895

Qiu, S. (2020). Chinese 'study mothers' in living apart together (LAT) relationships: Educational migration, family practices, and gender roles. *Sociological Research Online, 25*(3), 405–420. https://doi.org/10.1177/1360780419871574

Rahman, M., & Jackson, S. (2010). *Gender and sexuality: Sociological approaches*. Polity.

Robinson, V. (2015). Reconceptualising the mundane and the extraordinary: A lens through which to explore transformation within women's everyday footwear practices. *Sociology, 49*(5), 903–918. https://doi.org/10.1177/0038038515591942

Roseneil, S. (2006). On not living with a partner: Unpicking coupledom and cohabitation. *Sociological Research Online, 11*(3), 1–17.

Roseneil, S., & Budgeon, S. (2004). Cultures of intimacy and care beyond 'the family': Personal life and social change in the early 21st century. *Current Sociology, 52*(2), 135–159.

Roseneil, S., & Ketokivi, K. (2016). Relational persons and relational processes: Developing the notion of relationality for the sociology of personal life. *Sociology, 50*(1), 143–159. https://doi.org/10.1177/0038038514561295

Smart, C. (2007). *Personal life: New directions in sociological thinking*. Polity Press.
Smart, C. (2011). Relationality and socio-cultural theories of family life. In R. Jallinoja & E. D. Wildmer (Eds.), *Families and kinship in contemporary Europe: Rules and practices of relatedness* (pp. 13–28). Palgrave Macmillan.
Stoilova, M., Roseneil, S., Carter, J., Duncan, S., & Phillips, M. (2016). Constructions, reconstructions and deconstructions of 'family' amongst people who live apart together (LATs). *The British Journal of Sociology, 68*(1), 78–96.
Twamley, K. (2012). Gender relating among Indian couples in the UK and India: Ideals of equality and realities of inequality. *Sociological Research Online, 17*(4), 103–113.
Upton-Davis, K. (2015). Subverting gendered norms of cohabitation: Living Apart Together for women over 45. *Journal of Gender Studies, 24*(1), 104–116. https://doi.org/10.1080/09589236.2013.861346
Wang, Y. (王跃生). (2013). 中国家庭结构变动分析----基于2010年人口普查资料 [Analysis on the rural family structural changes in China – Based on 2010 census data]. *Social Sciences in China, 12*, 60–77.
Wang, H., & Dong, X. (2010). Childcare provision and women's participation in off-farm employment: Evidence from China's low-income rural areas. In X. Dong & S. Cook (Eds.), *Gender equality and China's economic transformation: Informal employment and care provision* (pp. 228–241). Economic Science Press.
Weeks, M. R. (1989). Virtuous wives and kind mothers: Concepts of women in urban China. *Women's Studies International Forum, 12*(5), 505–518.
Wolf, M. (1985). *Revolution postponed: Women in contemporary China*. Stanford University Press.
Wu, W., Shen, Y., Hu, B., & Du, M. (2020). Non-familial coresidence and life satisfaction: Evidence from China. *Habitat International, 100*, 102188. https://doi.org/10.1016/j.habitatint.2020.102188
Xie, Y. (2013). Gender and family in contemporary China. In *Population Studies Center* (Vol. 13, p. 808).
Xu, Q., Li, J., & Yu, X. (2015). Continuity and change in Chinese marriage and the family: Evidence from the CFPS. *Chinese Sociological Review, 47*(1), 30–56.
Yeung, W. J. J., & Hu, S. (2016). Paradox in marriage values and behavior in contemporary China. *Chinese Journal of Sociology, 2*(3), 447–476. https://doi.org/10.1177/2057150X16659019
Yu, J., & Xie, Y. (2011). The Varying Display of "Gender Display". *Chinese sociological review, 44*(2), 5–30.
Zarafonetis, N. (2017). *Sexuality in a changing China: Young women, sex and intimate relations in the reform period*. Routledge.

CHAPTER 4

Doing Family at a Distance: How Different Are LAT Relationships to 'Conventional' Partnerships?

INTRODUCTION

As I discussed in the previous chapter, some of the reasons for Chinese couples living separately are similar to those in Western contexts, such as job locations. Others are quite different. During my fieldwork in China in 2016, I came across several married women who lived separately from their partner because of their children's education. They were called 'study mothers' (in Mandarin Chinese, *peidu mama*). The term was initially coined by the Chinese media in Singapore to describe women who physically accompany and take care of their children so as to provide them with optimal living and study conditions. This can be achieved in multiple ways; for instance, sending children abroad to receive a Western education accompanied by parent(s), or internal migration to (a low-cost but relatively high-quality) school. Under such circumstances, the household is often split across a country or countries, as the husbands usually stay in the home country or travel to economically developed regions to provide financial support for their family.

The phenomenon of parents (mostly mothers) relocating their residences to accompany their children, both in mental and physical terms, has apparently become a feature in today's China (Huang & Yeoh, 2005). Just two years after my fieldwork, one day when I was reading my interview transcripts, I received a notification from my phone about an upcoming Chinese television drama *Peidu mama* (Always with You). This modern TV series is broadcast in one of the most influential Chinese-language television channels—Zhejiang TV—revolving around the stories of four mothers, with varied social backgrounds, accompanying their high school-aged children in Vancouver to study. The popularity of this TV series certainly reflects a social phenomenon that in contemporary China, under the one-child policy regime (though this was replaced by the two-child policy in 2016), parents usually spare no effort to devote themselves to their only children's education, though this is done by different means (Fong, 2004; Huang & Yeoh, 2005; Shek, 2006). In sociological research, this living arrangement, organised primarily around children's education, has received scant attention (Wang & Lim, 2017). What particularly interests me is the lived experiences of those study mothers during the time of accompanying their children.

In my research, six of 39 participants were mothers of high school-aged children. Therefore, I designed this case-study chapter within the context of the broader book, and within this framework, six Chinese study mothers, whose experiences of accompanying their children while living apart from their partner, were examined. The aim of this chapter is to explore how people within scattered living arrangements 'do' family. By applying Morgan's (1996) 'practices' approach to a non-Western context, I aim to provide empirical evidence of the cultural specificity of family practices in the Chinese context through the lens of study mothers. I also explore how these study mothers negotiate gender roles and construct their identities, as well as the subjective meanings they attach to their experiences in contemporary Chinese society. This is achieved firstly by giving contextual information about these six mothers. This is then followed by a closer examination of how an individual's biographical history affects the ways family is practised and serves as a lens through which the continuity and changes in family life are discussed. I will then look at the diverse reasons underlying couples living apart for children's education and the coping strategies developed by family members, and study mothers in particular. Through looking at their everyday 'doing' of family, the final section in this chapter will investigate how study mothers construct and make sense of their identities during the course of accompanying their children to study. Although it can be seen that moving away from a focus on the role of a wife can be somewhat liberating, I argue that, in being an LAT study mother, for the production of educational mobility, the traditional notion of 'family' is reproduced and practised in an old-fashioned way (for example, providing children with emotional support and preparing their daily meals). This case-study chapter, based on the narratives of six study mothers, provides empirical evidence that social and cultural constructions of gender norms and the ideal of motherhood, as informed by traditional Confucian values, still play key roles in contemporary China (Ji et al., 2017).

The Stories of Six Study Mothers

In comparison with the majority of participants who live apart from their partners owing to different educational and job locations, these six study mothers shared the same reason for living apart from their partners, that is, for the advancement of their children's education, while varying in the ways they perform gender role-related activities to 'do' family. In terms of living arrangements, they all relocated their residences so as to be near to the high school where their children studied, whilst their partner was expected to provide financial support, either by working in their hometown or moving to a more economically developed area.

Demographically, these married women were in their mid-40s and none of them had experienced divorce. They all grew up in the aftermath of the Cultural Revolution (1966–1976) and had experienced profound social and economic changes in their adolescence and adulthood, as China started to experience economic transition to a market economy in 1978. It is worth noting here that they not only vary as a sample in terms of their educational level, family background, occupation and the regions in which they reside, but also in the ways they perform gender role-related activities to 'do' family. As seen in Table 4.1, except for Rosy (46, Beijing), who graduated with a university degree, the rest had graduated from either secondary school or high school. Apart from Qingyan (47, Liaoning) and Guanya (37, Liaoning), who have two children, the rest have only one child aged between 15 and 17 who studied in high school. During the interviews, they talked about their embodied experiences of accompanying their children, in the absence of their husband. For Rosy, accompanying her only son to study overseas played a role in fulfilling gendered expectations of a (qualified) mother and doing parent–child intimacy. Qingyan and Xutong's own biographical story of not being supported by their own parents, combined with the legacy of Confucian culture that emphasises children's interests, were deeply rooted in their everyday

Table 4.1 Mini-biographies of six 'study mothers'

Guanya (37)	As the only child, Guanya was born in a rural family in Liaoning province. She had worked as a part-time teacher in a primary school after she graduated from a secondary school at the age of 17 or 18. Then she had an arranged marriage followed by a patrilocal living arrangement and gave birth to twin sons when she was 21. Guanya was contacted by one of my intermediaries and accompanied her 16-year-old twin sons studying in the town where the key-point high school was located. Her husband stayed at their hometown to run a poultry farm.
Hongli (40)	Hongli and her siblings were born in a peasant family. She took an odd job in a textile mill in her local area after her secondary school graduation. She met her husband, who was an electrician and worked in a different city, on a blind date, and three months later she was married at the age of 22. During the time of accompanying her 18-year-old son to study, she found a part-time job as a cleaner and her husband worked away and came back home normally once a week.
Minzhou (38)	Since Minzhou did not pass the entrance examination of high school, she worked part time in a weaving sack factory. She was introduced at the age of around 20 to her husband and married at 22, and one year later she gave birth to a son. Minzhou and her husband lived together until her husband went to Guangzhou, South China, in 2016. She was a full-time study mother, living with her son and looking after household affairs. She planned to follow her husband to go to Guangzhou, after her son's high school study.
Qingyan (47)	Living in a context of quite significant disadvantage, Qingyan was one of five children in her natal family in Liaoning province. She could not go to a college due to poor financial issues. At that time, she was asked to look after her relative's children and help them with homework. Qingyan was introduced to her husband who was born in a family of seven brothers in Hebei Province, and married within six months after they first met in 1995. Due to her husband's military service in Shanxi Province, she lived alone after marriage and worked as a teacher in a local primary school. She gave birth to a son when she was 28, and then a daughter at the age of 30. For a better life, Qingyan went to Beijing to earn more money, leaving her husband behind to take care of their children. When she was around 41, she came back from Beijing to her hometown and dedicated herself to the education of her children. At the time of our interview, she was a full-time study mother, and her husband was on the kitchen staff in a local school.

(*continued*)

Table 4.1 (continued)

Rosy (46)	Rosy met her husband after gaining her bachelor's degree, and then got married when she was 27. At first, she was doing business with her husband and then had a son in her 30s. In order to give her son a better study environment, they moved from their hometown, Henan Province, to Beijing when her son was about three years old. One year later, she obtained a job in a foreign company, where she has worked for over ten years. She was recruited as my participant, as I overheard her conversation with her friend in a café and knew that she had come back to Beijing for summer vacation. At the time of our interview, Rosy and her son had been in the USA for over two years, while financial support was provided by her husband who remained in Beijing, the capital of China, as the breadwinner.
Xutong (40)	Xutong is the youngest in her natal family. After she graduated from a secondary school, she was introduced to her husband and got married in less than six months. Her husband has been working away from home since their son was about seven or eight years old. At the time of interview, Xutong had accompanied her son for two years during the course of his high school study, while her husband worked in a timber mill and returned to home probably once a month.

family practices. As a result, they pinned their hopes on their children. And Hongli and Minzhou's image as sacrificial mothers was more visible, in comparison with their husbands, through a close examination of everyday food preparation.

Although it is a fairly small sample size, a case-study approach was employed to exclusively interrogate contemporary real-life phenomena at the micro level, both within an individual setting and across settings, so as to represent the subtleties and complexities of an individual's unique experiences in their own right (Baxter & Jack, 2008; Stake, 1995; Yin, 2014). Hockey et al. (2007) used a case-study approach to explore how heterosexuality was practised and reproduced within the sphere of the mundane, through the lens of a participant's biographical life story where agency was engaged in the context of institutional heterosexuality, and their study has partially inspired my choice of method here.

It's important to note that my intention is not to use these study mothers' experiences to represent all Chinese women, as quantitative studies are most likely to do. The primary aim of this chapter is to elucidate the gendered experience of study mothers and how social and cultural constructions of gender and the ideal of motherhood, as informed by traditional Confucian values, shape people's understandings and everyday practices of family in contemporary Chinese society. Therefore, the use of a case-study approach enables me to examine these multiple cases in depth within each setting, but also allows me to illustrate the key themes that are relevant across the sample, with the aim of understanding how these study mothers 'do' family and make sense of themselves. I also examine how Chinese women negotiate gender roles and make sense of their own identities during the course of accompanying and being involved with their children's' education. In doing so, special attention has been given to the context of Chinese social, historical and cultural perspectives.

Continuity in Family Practices

In the field of sociology of the family, Morgan's (1996) theorisation of 'family practices' is very influential in shifting the sociological analysis of 'family' as a structure to understand families as sets of activities that are both significant and unremarkable. In this delineation, 'family' has come to be understood as process-oriented and relational, with a greater emphasis on fluidity, process and the everyday dimensions of 'doing' or 'displaying' family (Finch, 2007). In other words, family is used as a verb and considered to be a changing and culture-dependent social construction that is being done through a set of intimate interactions and everyday 'practices': families are what families do (Smart & Neale, 1999). As such, family members are not only defined by marriage and kinship, as mothers and wives for instance, but are also determined by routines and practices, such as 'doing' mothering. With a focus on active 'doing' through everyday activities, rather than the 'being' of family, this 'practices' approach is useful here in capturing the distinction between the relationships of the families we live with (our relational connections with others) and the families we live by (the ideal) (Gillis, 1996). In this section, I elaborate on how an individual's own biographical experiences were used to help construct their current family life and how family practices themselves are subject to wider social and cultural interpretations, leading to an understanding of their 'doing family' differently.

During the interviews, I noticed that some women often recalled the family they grew up in as a guide to construct how their current family life was practised. In particular, working out how to construct a sense of family and maintain intimacy had become strongly intertwined with an individual's own biographical experience in the past. In some cases, the continuation of doing family was clearly evident when women thought back to their own experiences growing up. This is well exemplified in the experiences of Guanya (37), who did not have a formal job but worked as a substitute teacher at a kindergarten in her hometown in Liaoning. She quit the job due to her (natal) family's heavy farming work and her father's poor physical condition. She repeatedly stressed that 'family is the most important thing for a woman', and this idea was deeply rooted in her heart from a very young age, as she recounted,

> [It's about my] family environment [that made me think in this way]. My parents are in rural areas without being well educated. But my dad gave all his money that he gained to my mom … I thought he showed the greatest trust in my mom … although I am a child of rural parents, my family is harmonious. For example, if my dad would like to do some business which need[ed] more money, my mom would go out to find [people to borrow money] as he felt embarrassed to do this. I think my dad was grateful for having a woman always supporting and encouraging him on his back.

By stressing her 'rural' background throughout the interviews, she seemed to firmly believe that a harmonious family has little (if any) relation to the geographic locations where people were brought up, and by implication, for her, their social background. From her narrative, it was not only because her father had undertaken the role of breadwinner in the family, but her mother had 'properly' performed what a woman, as a wife and mother, should do so that her father could be so happy and they could have a harmonious family (James & Curtis, 2010). This positive praise for her mother served as a reference point in relation to making sense of what a 'good' mother and wife should be like. As she continued, she recounted how her mother passed on her values and skills in relation to being a wife before her marriage:

> My parents are low[ly] educated. But they told me that people must have to know how to *zuo ren* [behave as human beings], even if you don't have literacy skills. I didn't know how to do sewing before I married. My mom then told me that I might be allowed not to do farm work at home, but I had to learn it [how to sew] from her [her mother] before getting married.

From her understanding, rural farming work often requires significant physical labour, which is not a necessary skill that a woman has to learn. However, activities such as sewing, knitting and embroidery are seen as feminine and therefore are expected to be mastered as essential skills by women (Mehra, 1997). In this excerpt, the moral values that Guanya's parents passed down to her illustrate the importance of performing gender 'properly' and thereby doing suitably gendered work in a marital relationship. As a result, the ways that Guanya 'does' family are fundamentally associated with how family life was practised by her own mother. In other words, a strong sense of continuity rather than 'detraditionalisation' in the practices of 'family' has emerged. People cannot easily perform a sense of family in a vacuum, but act according to the social and cultural norms within which they are embedded. Additionally, the scarce amount, character and allocation of resources (such as financial and educational resources) can play a part in 'doing' family. The following excerpt from Guanya reflects her attitudes toward men's engagement with housework when they are reunited, after living apart. As she illustrated,

> I don't expect that men will do many domestic chores. Because I think he's already very tired working outside the home, and cleaning dishes and the house ought to be women's work. [It also includes] taking good care of his parents and children. Because I think the most concerns for men are [their] children and the elderly [parents].

Guanya took it for granted that housework should be women's work and she endorsed the housewife role through her practices. As such, she viewed having mothers to accompany children to study and take care of their daily life as quite 'natural' and normal, even though this comes with some degree of emotional loss, especially at the beginning of a couple's separation.

Reciprocal Family Practices: 'I Hope My Children Can Do Things That I Might Not Have the Chance to Do'

Although acknowledging that family is often practised in patterned ways, it is worth noting that families have increasingly been recognised as dynamic within sociology (Morgan, 1996), because how people understand and do family is culturally specific and contextually dependent. In fact, everyday practices are configured and reconfigured over time (Shove et al., 2012). For my participants, working out how to construct a sense of family has become strongly intertwined with individuals' own biographical experiences in the past. Drawing on three study mothers' past experiences of not being educated, this section will examine their conscious activities of trying to do family differently.

Both Xutong (40) and Minzhou (38) were born in a rural family in Liaoning after the Cultural Revolution, in 1976 and 1978, respectively. To some extent they shared similar life trajectories—both were not the only child in their own natal families. They all gave birth to a single son and accompanied them to study at the time of our interviews, while their husband worked away from home for living. Neither Xutong nor Minzhou had been to high school, but instead stayed at home to do farming work as well as household chores. The reasons they offered regarding the question of 'why not continue studying' were quite similar too. For example, Minzhou explained her schooling experience:

> [People] at that time placed little value on education. My family condition was poor, and my academic performance was also not good. So, it does not matter whether I continued [to study] or not. At that time, most people in my age cohort failing to pass the exam for entering senior high school all worked. Even though you were able to pass the exam and then graduated from high school, the government no longer allocated jobs. There was no difference whether or not you got into a university. As in either case, it was hard to find a job.

Growing up among China's profound social and economic transformation, the dismantling of the socialist job allocation system has led to people, especially women, without substantial education being placed in a disadvantaged position in the labour market (Honig & Hershatter, 1988). Very similarly to Xutong and Minzhou in terms of their experience of growing up, Qingyan (47), along with her five siblings, was also born in a poor peasant family in Liaoning Province. She did not have a stable and permanent job and attributed this to not being given an opportunity to go to a university due to financial issues. As she said,

> [There were] many children in my family. They [her parents] cannot afford us [to do any further education] at the same time. Both my younger sister and I were studying till high school, though we got the admission letters from the university.

However, being a study mother has more to do with her willingness to 'fix' things and provide her children with opportunities to achieve in ways that she could not in her earlier life, even though it may come with a price in terms of married couples having to live apart (Fong, 2004; Huang & Yeoh, 2005). As she articulated,

> I very much admire people who are excellent in studying. The reason that I couldn't go to a university is not because of my intelligence level, instead it's family [financial] conditions … I hope my children can do things that I might not have the chance to do.

In particular, how study mothers arrange family life and make sense of their practices is profoundly shaped by the social prescriptions, economic constraints and cultural values in which they are embedded. With the idea of preventing her children from missing the opportunity of gaining a beneficial education, Qingyan decided to go to Beijing alone in 2006 when her son was seven and her daughter was five, in the hope of earning money. Despite her husband's opposition, Qingyan's agency in relation to resource accumulation was clearly manifested and even increased, as expressed by a 'flexible' family practice in the sense that she has taken a primary role as financial contributor in her family (Morgan, 1996). During the time of working in an estate agency in Beijing, according to Qingyan, her financial condition had greatly improved as her wages were raised from 400–600 yuan (around £44–67 GBP) per month in 2006, to seven or eight thousand yuan (around £781–893 GBP) in 2012.

Nevertheless, she returned to her hometown six years later because her children were about to reach the key stage of their education. In this sense, working practices can also be understood as engaging in family practices; that is, family members reflexively negotiate their gender roles and reproduce relationships through working away (to financially support their children's studies) and coming back (to provide their children with daily care). The rationale behind this appears to relate not only to Qingyan's cultural positioning as a mother and principal caregiver, but also to her biographical experiences of not being supported by her own parents—the agency to 'do' family and mothering in different ways. This further implies that people's parenting ideologies and family practices are not always set in stone but are flexible and intimately reproduced by the changing economy and particular societal context in which people are situated.

Compared to elite and middle-class parents, some working-class, undereducated parents have only limited resources to mobilise and therefore cannot transmit any 'privileges' to their children. However, they firmly believe that pursuing a degree is the 'only' effective path for people, especially those without a 'strong' family background and financial base to promote upward mobility and live a 'different' life. To verify the authenticity of this view, some of the women often recounted their own (unsuccessful) life experiences as an example. Qingyan, for instance, used her so-called 'frustrating life' as a source of enlightenment, to instruct her children:

> If you [her children] study well, you will have a bright future, and your life will not be like mine, running around. I would rather owe you a childhood than an adulthood like mine, as it was much bitterness … I just felt that education, for me like having no [mighty] family background, is a way forward. Otherwise, what else can I choose?

Similarly, Xutong drew on her own experiences of lacking education to enlighten her son:

> If I studied hard, I would not live in the countryside. If our rural children do not get educated, they will remain in rural areas. Education is the only way out if you want to. [If you are] learning well and getting into a good university, you can then find a decent job. If not, you may not even get paid in construction sites, as you cannot do anything without being educated.

The starkly different attitudes toward education between study mothers' own parents and study mothers to their children have to be understood in the Chinese context of a specific social and political environment. For those spending their childhood in the pre-reform era under Mao's extreme socialist collectivism, largely under the legacy of the Cultural Revolution (1966–1976), many people in rural areas placed a low value on academic cultivation.[1] Schooling was often interrupted because of an inability to pay tuition or the family's need for their labour. Due to lack of awareness, knowledge or skills to educate children, people at that time were often 'growing up naturally' with little interference from parents (Liu, 2016: 109). However, the dramatic turnaround in attitudes toward education emerges as a by-product of China's one-child policy (implemented between 1980 and 2015) as well as the mass expansion of Chinese

---

[1] At that time, there was a widely spread discourse in relation to education, defined as 'knowledge is useless'.

higher education in the late 1990s. As a result, the new circumstances, characterised by the child-centred family and fierce competition, have shifted the child-bearing mode from 'growing up naturally' to 'deliberate cultivation and training', which often involves extensive parental care and service (Liu, 2016). Some researchers have noted that investing in children's education has now been regarded as part of a wider strategy of capital accumulation for children (and the family) to achieve a better and higher social-class status (Waters, 2005), especially for those coming from less wealthy areas (Fong, 2004). In line with this argument, my interviews with rural women in this study showed that they have strong awareness of the importance of education and thereby pay excessive attention to their children's schooling experience. Both Xutong and Qingyan's narratives straightforwardly indicate that in present-day Chinese society, being educated with high (tertiary) qualifications is considered as particularly crucial to securing good employment opportunities. Thus, they are consciously determined to do things differently; that is, being a study mother through physically accompanying their children and taking care of their daily lives so that they can fully focus on their study. From their perspective, that is the 'only' method they can offer to help make their children stand out from other people and change their future lives. Therefore, a strong desire for 'doing family' was shown to their children, so as to prevent them from experiencing the 'hard life' caused by not being well educated.

On many occasions, these study mothers, deprived of educational opportunities during the Cultural Revolution themselves, clearly revealed that their children are the only hope to carry out their lost dreams (Fong, 2004). During the interviews, Qingyan repeatedly stressed that her children have the top priority in her heart, and she would do everything for them, even if this meant leaving her husband behind. She claimed, 'I just want to raise and nurture my children. If they are useless and not promising, life would be meaningless for our grown-ups.' It is clear that Qingyan has a high expectation on her children and tied her own life, and even the well-being of the family, closely to her children's future in the long run. As I have demonstrated, family practices are culturally specific and contextually dependent, where the way of 'doing family' is subject to social and cultural constructions of gender around the roles of mothers and fathers. In Confucian culture, individuals are expected to fulfil their duties as parents or children and, for instance, women were considered to be responsible for children's educational attainment and future development (Inoguchi & Shin, 2009; Lim & Skinner, 2012). Accordingly, as a child, being filial to his or her parents is perceived as the basic familial obligation to fulfil. In particular, in the Chinese context, a child seen to be studying hard is considered as one of the most important ways of 'repaying' parents' sacrifices. Nevertheless, to some degree, parents' practices of intimacy, when characterised as devoting themselves to advancing their children's education, have been heightened by conscious calculations concerning how to ensure their children are well educated and so have a bright future (Croll, 2006). As Jamieson (2011: 5.3) argues, 'practices of intimacy are implicated in seeking its success'. In this sense, Chinese study mothers' practices of 'doing family' are partly grounded in traditional views on familial obligation. Therefore, I would suggest that reciprocal family practices are being shaped and often linked to a Confucian ideology of childrearing to ensure parents' security in old age.

Gendered Family Practices: 'I'd Like to More or Less Make It Up to Him'

Chinese parents have a long history of emphasising children's' studies and will do anything they can, even uproot themselves, to provide their children with better study conditions (Fong, 2004; Huang & Yeoh, 2005). The phrase *Meng mu san qian* (literally meaning Mencius' mother moved house three times) is a good illustration of this. It was said that the efforts that her mother had made in relation to her willingness to provide a better learning environment have helped advance the scholarly development of the Chinese sage Mencius (in Chinese, Mengzi; *c*.372–*c*.289 BC).

It is still the case that Chinese parents place greater attachment on their children's success in education just as reflected in the TV series I earlier mentioned. Due to the variety of personal and familial circumstances, parents often try their best to do what they can for their children's well-being and future development, though with different means. Previous research on the geographical splitting of families has predominantly focused on the central role of education in middle-class Asian families, and in framing transnational family strategies in relation to enhancing children's various forms of capital as well as the status of the family (Chee, 2003; Waters, 2015). For example, in order to pass on their advantages and invest in their children's future, Taiwanese parents had dropped their 'parachute' or 'satellite' children into the United States or Canada without the parents, who had returned to their country of origin to accumulate economic capital (Zhou, 1998). Waters (2005) focused on the importance of an overseas education as a strategy to both cultural capital and social reproduction in 'astronaut' families, where families immigrate to Canada and then the head of the household returns to Hong Kong to continue with his occupation. In South Korea, 'kirogi families' that divide themselves between two countries are practised mainly by middle-class families for the purpose of providing their children with Western credentials in response to external changes (Jeong et al., 2014). Due to children's education, the practice of split households reveals gendered patterns: usually the mothers rather than the fathers uproot their lives to accommodate their child, although a few fathers also did so (Lee & Koo, 2006; Waters, 2010). As Morgan (1996: 81) claims, 'it is impossible to write or think about family without also thinking about gender'. Therefore, taking the examples of Rosy (46) and Xutong (40), I will use this section to explore how family practices are mediated with financial resources and shaped by traditional socially constructed gender norms.

Rosy, 46 years old, was the only study mother who had graduated with a university degree. Before becoming a study mother, Rosy worked in an insurance company for over ten years in Beijing, with an annual salary of about 600,000 yuan (about 68,155 in GBP). She migrated to the USA in 2014 for the studies of her 16-year-old son and held a Green Card (for permanent US residency). Her husband has remained in Beijing to run a jewellery business to provide them with continuous financial support. At the time of our interview, she flew back to Beijing for a family reunion. However, residential reallocation was not new for Rosy's family, as she and her husband had once moved together from their hometown in Henan Province to Beijing in 2003 when their son was about three years old. The moving decision was initiated by Rosy: 'It was for [our] children's education. We all know that Henan is a province with a large number of people, but few universities. So [people] faced huge academic pressures', she said with a wry smile.

Owing to China's expansion of higher education during the late 1990s (Wan, 2006), being educated is no longer a taken-for-granted middle-class privilege (Waters, 2005) and the pressure on middle-class families to succeed in the local education system has gradually increased. As such, Chinese children are under huge pressure to study very hard to gain a high score in the National College Entrance Examination (commonly known as 'Gaokao' in Chinese) in order to get into the 'best' universities.

Undoubtedly, the competition is fiercer than ever (Waters, 2005), which is manifested in the number of students taking the Gaokao exam across the years. In 1977, 5.7 million test-takers registered for the exam, the numbers reached a peak of 10.5 million in 2008. According to a recent report from The State Council Information Office (2022), a new high of nearly 12 million students sat the exam in 2022. In Henan Province where Rosy's hukou was registered, one finds the largest number of Gaokao takers, with a total of over 1.2 million people having registered in 2022.

Even though Rosy's son was raised and educated in Beijing, his hukou (household registration) remains in Henan, which means her son was not allowed to attend Gaokao in Beijing. This is mainly because, in China, where people can take Gaokao institutionally depends on where their hukou is. If Rosy's son returns to the registered permanent residence, Henan Province, he would be faced with multiple challenges, such as different learning materials. In order to avoid competition with over a million peers in their hometown, Rosy invested heavily by sending her son abroad accompanied by her, despite the fact that he was reluctant to study overseas at the very beginning. Rosy noted,

> In the very early time, I instilled this idea in him that 'you [her son] are going to study overseas' … his teacher repeatedly stressed this kind of thing [students with non-Beijing hukou need to return to their original registered residence to register for the exam] in all kinds of parents' meetings, he then gradually understood his own situation. We cannot go back to [our] hometown … so the only available option was sending him abroad.

Clearly, such split-family living arrangements derive fundamentally from her son's educational migration. As a response to the local education system, Rosy has the privilege of passing on advantages to her son and withdrawing him from fierce competition for places at top universities. Through this transnational educational migration, her son can access greater educational resources and, by implication, success in a less stressful environment. In this sense, middle-class approaches to childrearing have become more strategic in the current socio-economic context, with parents being increasingly concerned with how to secure and pass on advantages to their children (Irwin & Elley, 2011: 481). With the full support of Rosy's husband, it seems that sending their son abroad for education, in the company of Rosy as a full-time study mother, is an example not simply of an educational strategy pursued by middle-class parents (Gillies,

2005; Reay, 2000), but also of a classed strategy of 'doing' family: it seems that, arguably, only upper-middle-class families can, in reality, 'pull it off'.

Apart from external forces such as the Chinese education system, Rosy's decision to accompany her son to study overseas is also strongly related to her willingness to invest emotionally. It is important to note that at the very beginning Rosy and her husband were struggling to survive and had a difficult time balancing work and family life in Beijing in 2003. Under these circumstances, Rosy sent her son to a local boarding school from kindergarten onwards. After nine years of boarding life (three years of kindergarten and six years of primary school), 'he did form some bad habits', Rosy said, such as thumb-sucking, partly caused by a lack of companionship and a sense of insecurity in his childhood. After apparent deep self-introspection, Rosy claimed that

> Throughout these years, I did feel a sense of guilt for sending him to the boarding school. I owed him … in my heart, I'd like to more or less make it up to him. I'm willing to fix it by accompanying him [during the course of studying abroad].

As Bedford (2004) states, one's guilty experiences are related to things that one does, rather than the way one is. In traditional Confucian culture, taking care of children has commonly been viewed as a woman's responsibility, both practically and educationally. Although recent research has shown a slight transformation in practices of fathering to extend beyond the role of financial provider to a more involved mode of fathering (Choi & Peng, 2016; Wilding, 2018), it is clear that women are still very much expected to put family members' well-being first, while at the same time de-prioritising self-development and putting career development aside, as informed by a distinctively Chinese Confucian collectivism. So, Rosy's sense of maternal guilt was experienced especially when she realised that she could have fulfilled her caring responsibility to her son, but did not do so due to lack of time or effort. Therefore, as a mother, Rosy bore the brunt of the blame for the harm caused by her limited emotional involvement with her son during his childhood when (particularly economic) capital accumulation was more highly prioritised.

Although the decision of being a study mother came at a high price in terms of her established career development (and even marital life) and Rosy was subsequently faced with incomprehension, it enabled her to ultimately fulfil the gendered expectations of a responsible, caring and emotionally engaged mother. As she illustrated,

> Because people view things differently. I enjoyed each other's company during his four years of high school in the USA more than stayed in Beijing making millions. If asking me to choose [between making money and accompanying children] again, I will still choose to be with my son.

In contrast to the traditional roles of authoritarian parents and dutiful children, the willingness and tendency to do 'intensive parenting' of the precious one-and-only child is evident. Compared to her previous parenting belief, Rosy positions herself as 'being on duty' to provide emotional support to help her son escape the fierce competition prevalent throughout the local educational system. From Rosy's perspective, doing motherhood is characterised by child-centred, labour-intensive and emotionally absorbing activities, and may lead to strengthen the practices of mother–child intimacy (Devasahayam & Yeoh, 2007; Hays, 1996). Rosy's mothering practices entail more emotional engagement with 'doing' family life because experience, identity and subjectivity are strongly informed by socially prescribed gender roles in the Chinese context. This further evokes the deep-rooted gendered division of emotional labour in families, making apparent the differential efforts of mothers and fathers (Zhang et al., 2007). Therefore, it is reasonable to argue that gendered family practices, in this regard, are already partially shaped by traditional socially constructed gender norms, and this may, in turn, influence how families headed by women are practised and displayed as an outcome of separation.

Across the data, the gendered family practice is also shown through the concept of *guan* (control, govern, look after, discipline) children with an attempt to prevent children from misbehaving and going astray, or even doing things that only the adults are supposed to do.[2] As shown in the following excerpt, the practices of guan exclusively refer to children's sexual relationships. As Rosy said, 'I don't want to force children to do things that only the adults will do and speak. If he behaves like an adult, he probably will make you a baby [giggling].' Justifications were made by Rosy, as she insisted that physically accompanying her son to study abroad is

---

[2] The *guan* is often used as a verb and literally means 'to control'. In the context of Chinese parenting practices, it is associated with more positive connotation in terms of caring, loving and discipline. See Tobin et al. (1989) for more discussion about Chinese parenting styles.

necessary on the grounds that 'he is just a kid'. From her understanding, children should behave like children, being dependent on and cared for by parents. If her son is independent enough to be able to study abroad alone, she would worry about his personal life and (sexual) relationships.

However, Rosy is not the only mother who expressed concerns over teenage self-discipline when parents are not around. Xutong (40, mother of a 17-year-old son) explained,

> Nowadays [people are] all accompanying their children, except [whose children stay in] school accommodation. Unlike the girls, we [parents] are worried about the boys in general. There are so many *wangba* now.[3] If you are not physically being with them [children], you may not even know where they are. [When you're] accompanying children to study, at least you know that he would eventually come home after school, otherwise, you have no idea where exactly he is if he actually goes to *wangba* ... Parents are all accompanying children to study mainly because of so many temptations in the society. If they [children] have learned to act badly in the absence of parents, then our adult people would have no chance to buy *hou hui yao*.[4]

Being brought up and educated in China, I am fully aware of the importance of the three years' high school study, as it directly affects whether or not people can enter a good university through the Gaokao exam. My research shows that all study mothers, to varying degrees, expect their children to make an effort and fully focus on their study, regardless of Gaokao results. The emphasis on the learning process rather than results has led to some mothers, in particular of the boys, often keeping a close eye on their children's activities that might potentially affect their study. This certainly includes their internet usage activities. According to CNNIC (2016), entertainment applications have been the most important internet applications for young internet users. Indeed, the mass media has reported a series of accidents leading to death, because of fighting occurring in internet cafés due to games being played overnight. Even though there is

---

[3] Wangba (internet café) was seen by many Chinese parents as harmful due to their stereotypical views on the environment of internet cafés, which are often full of smoke with some 'disreputable' youths coming in and out (Sun, 2012). Parents of school-aged teenagers feel a sense of being out of control when faced with online gaming and 'unhealthy' online information, and therefore tend to control children's internet usage.

[4] *Hou hui yao* literally means regret pills. In this context, this slang connotes that there is no going back because it is too late to regret if children were ill-behaved when parents are not around to look after them.

little evidence to support the existence of gender differences in internet addiction and online gaming (Ko et al., 2005), Xutong and other study mothers assumed that boys, rather than girls, were stereotypically more likely to indulge themselves on the Internet, due to a lack of self-discipline and self-control. With this idea in mind, Xutong also acknowledged the necessity of being a study mother in order to *kan haizi* (govern and take care of children) while the fathers are working away to *dagong* (do labour-force work). By her repeatedly highlighting the 'people [that] are all accompanying their children', it is clear that there are some cultural discourses about what people, women in particular, are expected to do, especially if they have children who are being exposed to academic pressures and an 'unhealthy' online environment in a given time period.

Throughout the interviews with study mothers, physically accompanying children day by day facilitated the practices of guan in the name of love. I am aware that the meanings of parental control may be different in China (and other Asian countries) compared to the West, due to their respective cultural differences. The Chinese notion of guan may be seen as 'less of an intrusion upon children's sense of self than in European-American culture', characterised as representing individualism and freedom (Wang et al., 2007: 1593). However, it has long been considered an important feature of child rearing in the Chinese context, interpreted as a symbol of parental love and support (Chao, 1994), which is often associated with better academic performance (Wang et al., 2007). It is clear from my data that the study mothers' narratives of mothering practices, in terms of guan, suggests a gendered division of parenting practices that are already partially shaped by traditional, socially constructed gender norms—*nan zhu wai, nu zhu nei*—with men being in charge of what is outside the home and women the inside (Shek, 2006). Therefore, I would argue that gendered family practices may, in turn, influence how families headed by women are practised and displayed as an outcome of separation.

Everyday Family Practices and Identity Construction

Everyday Practices of Doing Gender: 'His Three Meals a Day Had Me Trapped'

For the sake of children's educational advancement, these six study mothers, to varying degrees, made self-sacrifices in a radical way through uprooting their lives to accommodate their children. Rosy was an exception. She accompanied her son overseas, with the other five remaining in China, and moved from the countryside to a county seat school. Their husbands reunited with family members irregularly due to workloads. It can be very unsettling to move to a new house or leave home, given that one of the meanings of home is 'familiarity' (Scott, 2009: 50). Living in a split household without men, women are often faced with all kinds of challenges and hardships alone in terms of settling in to an unfamiliar environment, dealing with loneliness, caring for children, as well as taking the risk of potential infidelity from partners.

Unsurprisingly, all the study mothers in this research expressed a sense of disappointment and insecurity, to different extents, about what living separately meant for them. This is especially the case for Rosy (46), who had never lived apart from her partners until her only son reached high school. At the time when Rosy and her son flew to the USA, she suffered huge mental pressures and was afraid of the uncertainty that resulted from an unfamiliar living environment and language barriers. As she said,

> As I have had postpartum depression when I gave birth to my son. In the circumstances [of living in a foreign country], it was likely to cause the recurrence of depression. Time difference [between the USA and China] also made me lose sleep.

Dissatisfaction about relocating and living separately from their partners was also manifested in the way women expected to be reunited once circumstances allowed. For example, Minzhou (38) recounted her feelings of helplessness when her husband could only come back home once a year due to work schedules:

> When my son went to school, I stayed at home alone at night. I just constantly checked my mobile phone sending messages to my husband or calling him. But he was busy at work. I felt it very difficult, leaving us alone here. There was nothing that I can rely on, as all responsibilities of taking care of children are fallen on me. Sometimes my mood became worse when he [her son] made me angry … I cried, and tears fell down.

What particularly interests me is, 'Why is it the mothers, not the fathers who often accompany their children to study?' The answers that were frequently given were about the 'only child' and 'food'. This is not only because these women had failed to get credentials themselves and therefore were barely able to provide their children with the necessary academic support. It is more related to their desire for raising the precious 'only child' in the family (Goh, 2011). Due to China's one-child policy, which started in the late 1970s and ended in 2015, Chinese families become child-centred, leading to parents placing greater attachment to their children's well-being and development (Liu, 2022). The sentiment was certainly echoed by Minzhou (38), who grew up in a small town in Liaoning and left school without qualifications. At the time of the interview, she was living with her only son (16 years old), while her husband had been working far away in Guangzhou, South China, for several months:

> We only have this one child. [If I wasn't accompanying him] I would be worried that he might not be able to eat well, and I'd be worried whether he was getting bad and going to the internet café … at least [by accompanying him] I can cook for him here and guarantee the quality of his food. He won't learn bad things and will come back home on time.

During the course of accompanying their children to study, study mothers basically have been performing the caregiving role in a way that organises their daily lives around their children's needs as well as frees them from additional family obligations. In doing so, their daily lives are fundamentally confined to the home setting to provide three homemade meals a day. Along with endless repetition of domestic chores, the experiences of time, for study mothers, are cyclical and fixed in many ways (Scott, 2009). Hongli (40), who found a part-time job during the time of accompanying her children, recounted her daily routine:

> I got up at 5.30 a.m. to prepare his breakfast. At 6.30 a.m. I woke him up and then he ate. I then started working at 7.30 in the morning and came back home to do his lunch at 10.30. He returned from school to have a lunch and then would take a nap. I watched the time and woke him up until he went to school at 1.10 p.m. I continued working from 1.30 to 4.30 p.m. and went home for cooking his dinner. He [was back to eat and] returned to school at 5.30 p.m. and then I cleaned up the house. Sometimes I would go outside for guang chang wu till 7.30 p.m., otherwise I just stayed at home.[5] I picked him up at 9.00 p.m. after school and then boiled the milk

---

[5] *Guang chang wu* (square dancing) is a collective dancing activity practised in public spaces. Although this fitness activity has been criticised for noise pollution (Huang & Mi, 2015; Zhang, 2016), it is popular among *dama* (grannies) who are middle-aged and retired in rural and urban China (Martin & Chen, 2020).

for him. He will continue to study if he wants, and I would read novels or go to sleep around 11 or 12 o'clock.

Similarly, Minzhou's daily routine also largely depends on her son's timetable. She said,

> I prepared breakfast for my son and woke him up at 6.30 in the morning. He went to school at 7 o'clock. Then I cleaned the house before strolling down the streets. At 11 a.m. I got ready to cook his lunch before he came back around 12 noon. He then returned to school at 1 p.m. I would have a nap after he left; otherwise, I went out for groceries. You see, his three meals a day had me trapped [laughter]. Time passed so fast; I had to prepare his dinner at 4 p.m. before he was back at 5 p.m. After he left, I sometimes went to the park for a walk till 7 o'clock and then went back home, watching TV or using my phone. That's it. He'd be back at 9.20 p.m. from school, when I had already prepared him some fruit. He went to sleep around 11 p.m., and so did I.

In the above excerpts, although women's everyday food-related activities seem unremarkable and hardly worth talking about. In fact, some degree of collaboration in order to accommodate other people's timetables was noted (Morgan, 2020). DeVault, in her study *Feeding the Family*, illustrates that cooking as a way of showing care operates as a form of doing gender in which 'a woman conducts herself as recognizably womanly' (1991: 118). Based on the provision of nutritious sustenance and day-to-day accompaniment, this feminine ideal of care constructs an identity for Minzhou (see West & Zimmerman, 1987).

In this sense, moving away from a focus on the role of a wife can be somewhat liberating, as living apart can free women from 'doing his laundry' (Xutong, 40) and 'making his food' (Hongli, 40). On the other hand, the role of mothering was still expected to continue, if not increase, their daily domestic workload. Although there has been a rise in men's participation in housework across the globe to different extents (Altintas & Sullivan, 2016), the continuing dominant gendered discourses still influence how these domestic practices are understood. Women are still 'strongly tied to the traditional connection between food, care, and femininity, including a relationship of obligation and responsibility around food' (Aarseth & Olsen, 2008: 282; see also Parish & Farrer, 2000; Shu et al., 2012).

Negotiating Gender Roles and Identity Construction

According to Jackson (2006), the social institution of gender is often lived out by embodied individuals who 'do gender' through the 'everyday', the routine social practices in a specific context. As social agents, selfhood is relational, and as a result, 'our sense of who we are in relation to others constantly guides our actions and interactions and, conversely, who we are is in part a consequence of our location within gendered, class, racial, and other divisions, and of the social and cultural milieux we inhabit' (Jackson, 2001: 284; see also Jackson, 2011). Through looking at women's everyday activities in LAT relationships, it can be seen that the focus on motherhood, rather than wifehood, is practised by prioritising the well-being of their children ahead of their own personal fulfilment or their spouse, which can in some ways be overwhelming. This is fully manifested with respect to food preparation and distribution as they would prepare nutritious food (Attree, 2005) in the light of their children's preference and eat less (good-quality) food than they provide for them. In this regard, the identity of these study mothers is largely in accordance with the image of 'sacrificial mothers' described by Huang and Yeoh (2005). In their study of 20 middle-class Chinese 'study mothers' in Singapore, they argued that the migration experiences of these women as transient migrants within the transnational households have significantly reinforced their identities as 'mothers', partly because most of the women were confined to the home setting as full-time cleaners and food providers for their children. Therefore, this transnational 'education project' 'hinges crucially on the notion and realisation of the "sacrificial mother"' (Huang & Yeoh, 2005: 391).

Interestingly, my data also found that this 'maternal sacrifice' is reflected in the ways that study mothers negotiate their personal time. I interviewed Hongli (40) in the two-bedroom apartment she was renting with only a few pieces of furniture. When I asked her 'How did you pass time when your son went to school?', she said that she read novels at home, and sometimes went outside for *guang chang wu* (plaza dancing) partly due to having no television at home. She claimed,

> I purposely did not want to have a television. Actually, we have one at our home[town], but I did not bring it with us 'cos I'd be worried it [having TV] would interfere with his [her son's] studies. Accompanying children is the main purpose [of why I am here], and children's study is the most important one.

Even though Hongli acknowledged that having no TV because of her children's study can be boring, these child-centred everyday practices have rarely been questioned but rather are considered as a way of fulfilling mothering responsibilities. In fact, it seems to be a common phenomenon for study mothers to compromise their personal recreational activities during the time when accompanying their children. Through 'maternal sacrifice' manifested with respect to food preparation and personal time arrangements, the image of the 'good' mother is constructed and displayed (Attree, 2005: 235). Ironically, the gendered sacrifice was almost taken for granted, not only by the fathers but by the study mothers themselves. As Rosy recounted, 'My husband could not give up his business, and my son could not stay alone in a foreign country either [without my accompanying him]. So, I choose to go with my son in such a specific and no-way-to-choose situation.' During this process, the involvement of Rosy's husband with his business comes out as a 'non-negotiable fact' to which she has had to adjust her promising career plan and their personal lives.

Similar to Rosy, Minzhou explained,

> I don't think I sacrificed a lot. Actually, everyone in the family do different things for their children, including earning money. Nowadays, all parents *weile haizi er huo* [live for their children] … Life is forcing us to do so [couples living separately], and there's no way to change. I can't ask my husband not to work away from home, [in that case] how could we survive and sustain our life? Likewise, I can't leave my children alone and go together with my husband, as I would regret it for the rest of my life if he [her son] became bad during these three years [of high school]. All parents share the same idea that we can owe anyone except children. No matter you [children] get good or bad marks, parents bear no liability for your academic achievements, because we have already accompanied you and fulfilled our responsibility as parents.

Clearly, the agency of these study mothers in living apart from their partner is relationally constrained and inextricably linked to their children, as I have examined in the previous chapter. In this regard, the traditional gendered division of labour, exemplified in the fact that the fathers are working away from home and the mothers are taking care of children at home, remains powerful in many aspects of contemporary family life and continues to shape the ways that family life should be ideally constructed.

Nevertheless, not all study mothers that I interviewed agreed about the necessity of accompanying their children during the course of their study. This is often related to parents' concerns over their children's lack of independence in general. At the end of the interview, again, Xutong (40) suggested that

> Children could be independent if [we are] not accompanying them. Because of our accompaniment, they would do nothing and had no idea about doing laundry, for instance. Now, high-school children are about seventeen or eighteen. They may have been married and raised a family, if they lived in rural areas. Our children are still being kept under the protection of parents, so, it is useless to accompany them to study.

Peidu (accompanying children to study) is like a double-edged sword. On the one hand, parents feel obligated and necessary to take care of children's daily lives and provide emotional support so that children can fully focus on their studies. On the other hand, parents are aware of negative influences on children's independence. A recent statistic from the National Bureau of Statistics (2019) shows that Chinese high-school students, aged 15–19, were found to have the highest rate in studying time, taking up 8 hours and 2 minutes in a day. This has barely left them much time for leisure and housework. Less explicitly, this comparison between the children of study mothers and those who dropped out of school and remained in the rural areas implies different expectations of children in relation to family obligations. As a response to study-related pressure, Chinese parents (in particular mothers) have naturally taken on the responsibility of caring for their children. As Xutong said, 'I come here for cooking and washing for you [her son]. If he does these things, then what else should I do?' In this sense, her mothering identity was the dominant influence on her practices through which she reclaimed the image of 'good' mothers as supportive, caring and qualified. In so doing, there is an attempt that their children may avoid the same pattern that they had experienced in their own lives in earlier times.

However, when I asked, 'What roles do you think you are undertaking during the course of accompanying your children?', 'A mother', Xutong said, without hesitation. She then claimed,

> Actually, it is not that normal [to always prioritise the role of motherhood], but the reality forces us [the mothers] to do so, and we have to do exactly

in this way. For all study mothers, it is a matter of fact that you can't put your children aside. Because they [children] are very important to you. It's [the] same for all families. Today, there are the only one child in each family. Not only their own parents, but children's grandparents also pay a lot [of] attention to them.

Obviously, Xutong and other study mothers have put their children's education and well-being in first place, given that this is seen as such an important and particular period of their life course. Throughout study mothers' accounts, the gendered division of parenting practices seemed to be accepted as a matter of fact, so that the mothers are seen to be closely involved in and play a more active role in their children's schooling than fathers. As Rosy noted, 'It is a popular phenomenon in China that the husbands involved little with children's education.' At least in my study, the fathers, reported by the study mothers, basically play a dramatically different role in supporting their family members and thus doing family. An interpretation of their gendered practices of family, through which mothering was emphasised, again needs to take into account the specific social, cultural and structural contexts in which people are embedded. One possible implication is that family practices are often intimately bound up with gender practices in which men, as the sole and primary contributors, are responsible for providing continuous financial support by finding jobs that are well paid, whilst being absent from their wife and children's daily lives. These diametrically opposing parenting roles, which men and women have played and continue to play in Chinese society, in turn have reaffirmed the instrumental role of the husband and father in this family living arrangement. During the time of accompanying children, these study mothers found it difficult to find a waged job with flexible working schedules. As a result, women are confined and bound more tightly to the home setting and family chores, which have further deepened the existing gender inequalities in family life and the labour market.

Conclusion

This chapter has paid special attention to the reasons for and family experiences of 'study mothers' during the period of accompanying their children to study in China and, in one case, abroad. The trend of couples living apart driven by educational mobility has to be understood not only as a way of maximising their children's opportunity to accumulate cultural, social and economic capital (Bourdieu, 1986), but also as part of wider family practices in a gendered and rational way. Therefore, this study employs and applies a 'family practices' approach to a non-Western context, given that it provides a more comprehensive understanding by embracing 'both individual and relational behaviour, and habituated routines that may reproduce and sustain pre-existing ways of being together' (Gabb & Fink, 2015:9).

'Doing' family in the form of physically accompanying children in order to provide emotional support and homemade meals every day, not only serves a pragmatic purpose, but also 'performs a symbolic function, with mothers literally constructing a sense of family through their everyday family role' (Gabb, 2008: 91). This set of routine practices has huge implications for reinforcing a dominant ideal of motherhood, and the stereotypical feminine model of caring, 'of serving others'. In my narrative analysis of study mothers' everyday experiences, the role of 'sacrificial mothers' has always been recognised compared to the fathers, based on their day-to-day activities and the efforts they make in relation to their children's well-being in the process of capital accumulation. This kind of taken-for-granted family practice has merged with gender practices whereby women are expected to fulfil their feminine roles as mothers through undertaking caring work and providing emotional support. That is, how people do family is deeply informed by how they perceive their (expected) gender roles. Although the 'traditional' gendered division of labour has been shaken due to women's increased education and participation in the labour market since China's social and economic changes, gendered expectations and the traditional normalised family pattern of women being the primary caregivers remain powerful in contemporary Chinese society (Ji, 2015; Liu, 2014; Zhan & Rhonda, 2003). The traditional forms of family are framed and routinely practised even in the split household (Qiu, 2020). Therefore, this chapter has suggested that family practices play a role in the construction of subjective identities and are inextricably linked to mothering practices; in particular, practices of 'intensive parenting' (Hays, 1996). The underlying ideology, as informed by Confucian values, is to put children's well-being in first place and to prioritise the role of parent compared to any other roles in the family (Choi, 2006).

However, my research stands in sharp contrast to research on LAT relationships in the Western context, which shows that couples living apart could be seen as radical pioneers moving beyond traditional forms of 'the family' and providing a way for women to 'undo' gender and subvert the traditional patriarchal power base at the site of domesticity (Roseneil, 2006; Upton-Davis, 2015). This is in part a recognition that in Chinese families, and even in most Asian families, the ethics of care for children is paramount for mothers, and accordingly, women regard their caregiving role as integral to their identity as mothers. 'Doing' gender in a way that is congruent with cultural and social expectations of gender roles may directly or indirectly contribute to how family is constructed and practised. As Gross (2005) argues, family practices are embedded in both culture and history, in ways that mean the personal and social are inextricably linked (Smart, 2007). Therefore, I would argue that Chinese study mothers' everyday family practices have to be understood alongside their individual biographical histories and wider cultural and social contexts.

However, this could further result in the reproduction of new inequalities at the heart of family practices, in seeing childcare as something that is better performed by 'mothers', and as something that also reinstates care as a feminine activity, as well as reinforcing gender roles and hierarchies. Faircloth (2015) links the concept of intimacy to parenting and examines how the care of children affects the parental couple's intimate relationship. She argues that competing ideologies between 'intensive' mothering and cultural discourses on equal parenting ideology are 'uncomfortable bedfellows'. Although justifications are often given for parents' devotion, some women, for example, are still uprooting themselves at any cost in order to accompany their children and, by implication, to both ensure a better future for their children and protect their own old-age security. Attention to the study mothers' everyday experiences in living apart from their partner due to children's education calls for a greater emphasis on 'gender equality' and intimacy.

Nevertheless, I am aware that this finding may not be universally applicable to all Chinese women, owing to the small sample size. In fact, the results should be taken with caution because they should be understood alongside women's personal biographies and the wider social contexts within which they are embedded. In addition, the current study has only concentrated on women's experiences. Unfortunately, the viewpoints of children while their parents were living separately were not included because they were under 18 and remained at school studying. Far too little research has been done on the role of children in split family living arrangements in the sociology of family and the migration literature. Similarly, men's voices are also missing due to the scope of this study. As people 'do' family in different ways in tackling social, spatial, economic and cultural framework conditions, future studies with a greater focus on children's and husbands' opinions about family life at a distance are therefore suggested.

REFERENCES

Aarseth, H., & Olsen, B. M. (2008). Food and masculinity in dual career couples. *Journal of Gender Studies, 17*(4), 277–287.

Altintas, E., & Sullivan, O. (2016). Fifty years of change updated: Cross-national gender convergence in housework. *Demographic Research, 35*(16), 455–470.

Attree, P. (2005). Low-income mothers, nutrition and health: A systematic review of qualitative evidence. *Maternal and Child Nutrition, 1*(4), 227–240.

Baxter, P., & Jack, S. (2008). Qualitative case study methodology: Study design and implementation for novice researchers. *The Qualitative Report, 13*(4), 544–559.

Bedford, O. A. (2004). The individual experience of guilt and shame in Chinese culture. *Culture & Psychology, 10*(1), 29–52.

Bourdieu, P. (1986). The forms of capital. In J. R. Richardson (Ed.), *Handbook of theory and research for the sociology of education* (pp. 241–258). Greenwood Press.

Chao, R. (1994). Beyond parental control and authoritarian parenting style: Understanding Chinese parenting through the cultural notion of training. *Child Development, 65*, 1111–1119.

Chee, M. (2003). Migrating for the children: Taiwanese American women in transnational families. In N. Piper & M. Roces (Eds.), *Wife or worker? Asian women and migration* (pp. 137–156). Rowman & Littlefield.

Choi, Y. S. (2006). The phenomenon of 'geese-families': Marital separation between geese-fathers and geese-mothers. *Family and Culture, 18*(2), 37–65.

Choi, S. Y., & Peng, Y. (2016). *Masculine compromise: Migration, family, and gender in China*. University of California Press.

CNNIC. (2016). *2015年中国青少年上网行为研究报告 [The 2015 China teenager net behaviour investigation report]* [Online]. Retrieved March 3, 2022, from http://www.cnnic.net.cn/hlwfzyj/hlwxzbg/qsnbg/201608/t20160812_54425.htm

Croll, E. J. (2006). The intergenerational contract in the changing Asian family. *Oxford Development Studies, 34*, 473–491. https://doi.org/10.1080/13600810601045833

De Vault, M. (1991). *Feeding the family: The social organization of caring as gendered work*. University of Chicago Press.

Devasahayam, T., & Yeoh, B. (2007). *Working and mothering in Asia: Images, ideologies and identities*. NUS Press.

Faircloth, C. (2015). Negotiating intimacy, equality and sexuality in the transition to parenthood. *Sociological Research Online*, 20(4), 3. https://doi.org/10.5153/sro.3705
Finch, J. (2007). Displaying families. *Sociology*, 41(1), 65–81.
Fong, V. L. (2004). *Only hope: Coming of age under Chinas one-child policy*. Stanford University Press.
Gabb, J. (2008). *Researching intimacy in families*. Palgrave Macmillan.
Gabb, J., & Fink, J. (2015). *Couple relationships in the 21st century: Research, policy and practice*. Palgrave Macmillan.
Gillies, V. (2005). Raising the 'meritocracy: Parenting and the individualization of social class. *Sociology*, 39(5), 835–853.
Gillis, J. (1996). *A world of their own making*. Harvard University Press.
Goh, E. (2011). *China's one-child policy and multiple caregiving: Raising little suns in Xiamen*. Routledge.
Gross, G. (2005). The detraditionalization of intimacy reconsidered. *Sociological Theory*, 23(3), 286–311.
Hays, S. (1996). *The cultural contradictions of motherhood*. Yale University Press.
Hockey, J., Meah, A., & Robinson, V. (2007). *Mundane heterosexualities: from theory to practices*. Basingstoke: Palgrave Macmillan.
Honig, E., & Hershatter, G. (1988). *Personal voices: Chinese women in the 1980's*. Stanford University Press.
Huang, Y. J., & Mi, L. (2015). *The noisy individual and the silent mass: An survey of the social ecology of contemporary China in square dance*. China Social Sciences Press.
Huang, S., & Yeoh, B. (2005). Transnational families and their children's education: China's 'study mothers' in Singapore. *Global Networks*, 5(4), 379–400.
Inoguchi, T., & Shin, D. C. (2009). The quality of life in Confucian Asia: From physical welfare to subjective well-being. *Social Indicators Research*, 92(2), 183–190.
Irwin, S., & Elley, S. (2011). Concerted cultivation? Parenting values, education and class diversity. *Sociology*, 45(3), 480–495.
Jackson, S. (2001). Why a materialist feminism is (still) possible-and necessary. *Women's Studies International Forum*, 24(3–4), 283–293. https://doi.org/10.1016/S0277-5395(01)00187-X
Jackson, S. (2006). Gender, sexuality and heterosexuality. *Feminist Theory*, 7(1), 105–121. https://doi.org/10.1177/1464700106061462
Jackson, S. (2011). Materialist feminism, the self and global late modernity: Some consequences for intimacy and sexuality. In A. Jonadottir, V. Bryson, & K. Jones (Eds.), *Sexuality, gender and power: Intersectional and transnational perspectives* (pp. 15–29). Routledge.
James, A., & Curtis, P. (2010). Family displays and personal lives. *Sociology*, 44(6), 1163–1180.

Jamieson, L. (2011). Intimacy as a concept: Explaining social change in the context of globalisation or another form of ethnocentricism? *Sociological Research Online, 16*(4), 151–163.

Jeong, Y. J., You, H. K., & Kwon, Y. I. (2014). One family in two countries: Mothers in Korean transnational families. *Ethnic and Racial Studies, 37*(9), 1546–1564.

Ji, Y. (2015). Asian families at the crossroads: A meeting of east, west, tradition, modernity, and gender. *Journal of Marriage and Family, 77*(5), 1031–1038.

Ji, Y., Wu, X., Sun, S., & He, G. (2017). Unequal care, unequal work: Toward a more comprehensive understanding of gender inequality in post-reform urban China. *Sex Roles, 77*(11), 765–778.

Ko, C., Yen, J., Chen, C., Chen, S., & Yen, C. (2005). Gender differences and related factors affecting online gaming addiction among Taiwanese adolescents. *Journal of Nervous and Mental Disease, 193*(4), 273–277.

Lee, Y., & Koo, H. (2006). Wild geese fathers' and a globalised family strategy for education in Korea. *IDPR, 28*(4), 532–553.

Lim, H. J., & Skinner, T. (2012). Culture and motherhood: Findings from a qualitative study of east Asian mothers in Britain. *Families, Relationships and Societies, 1*(3), 327–343.

Liu, J. (2014). Ageing, migration and familial support in rural China. *Geoforum, 51*, 305–312.

Liu, F. (2016). The rise of the "priceless" child in China. *Comparative Education Review, 60*(1), 105–130. https://doi.org/10.1086/684457

Liu, J. (2022). Childhood in urban China: A three-generation portrait. *Current Sociology, 70*(4), 598–617.

Martin, R., & Chen, R. (2020). *The people's dance: The power and politics of Guangchang Wu*. Springer Nature.

Mehra, R. (1997). Women, empowerment, and economic development. *The Annals of the American Academy of Political and Social Science, 554*(1), 136–149.

Morgan, D. (1996). *Family connections: An introduction to family studies*. Cambridge Polity.

Morgan, D. (2020). Family practices in time and space. *Gender, Place & Culture, 27*(5), 733–743.

National Bureau of Statistics (2019). *2018年全国时间利用调查公报 [2018 National Time Use Survey Bulletin]* [Online]. Retrieved March 18, 2019, from http://www.stats.gov.cn/tjsj/zxfb/201901/t20190125_1646796.html

Parish, W., & Farrer, J. (2000). Gender and family. In W. Tang & W. Parish (Eds.), *Chinese urban life under reform: The changing social contract* (pp. 232–272). Cambridge University Press.

Qiu, S. (2020). Chinese 'study mothers' in living apart together (LAT) relationships: Educational migration, family practices, and gender roles. *Sociological Research Online, 25*(3), 405–420. https://doi.org/10.1177/1360780419871574

Reay, D. (2000). A useful extension of Bourdieu's conceptual framework? Emotional capital as a way of understanding mothers' involvement in their children's education? *The Sociological Review, 48*(4), 568–585.

Roseneil, S. (2006). On not living with a partner: Unpicking coupledom and cohabitation. *Sociological Research Online, 11*(3), 111–124. https://doi.org/10.5153/sro.1413

Scott, S. (2009). *Making sense of everyday life.* Polity.

Shek, D. T. L. (2006). Chinese family research: Puzzles, progress, paradigms, and policy implications. *Journal of Family Issues, 27*(3), 275–284.

Shove, E., Pantzar, M., & Watson, M. (2012). *The dynamics of social practice: Everyday life and how it changes.* Sage.

Shu, X., Zhu, Y., & Zhang, Z. (2012). Patriarchy, resources, and specialisation: Marital decision-making power in urban China. *Journal of Family Issues, 34*(7), 885–917.

Smart, C. (2007). *Personal life.* Polity Press.

Smart, C., & Neale, B. (1999). *Family fragments?* Polity Press.

Stake, R. E. (1995). *The art of case study research: Perspectives on practice.* Routledge.

Sun, H. (2012). *Internet policy in China: A field study of Internet Cafes.* Lexington Books.

The State Council Information Office. (2022). *China voices.* [Online] Retrieved June 6, 2022, from http://english.scio.gov.cn/chinavoices/2022-05/31/content_78245753.htm

Tobin, J., Wu, D., & Davidson, D. (1989). *Preschool in three cultures: Japan, China, and the United States.* New Haven, CT: Yale University Press.

Upton-Davis, K. (2015). Subverting gendered norms of cohabitation: Living Apart Together for women over 45. *Journal of Gender Studies, 24*(1), 104–116.

Wan, Y. (2006). Expansion of Chinese higher education since 1998: Its causes and outcomes. *Asia Pacific Education Review, 7*(1), 19–31.

Wang, Y., & Lim, S. S. (2017). Mediating intimacies through mobile communication Chinese migrant mothers' digital 'bridge of magpies'. In R. Andreassen, M. N. Petersen, K. Harrison, M. N. Petersen, & T. Raun (Eds.), *Mediated intimacies: Connectivities, relationalities, proximities* (pp. 159–178). Routledge.

Wang, Q., Pomerantz, E. M., & Chen, H. (2007). The role of parents' control in early adolescents' psychological functioning: A longitudinal investigation in the United States and China. *Child Development, 78*, 1592–1610.

Waters, J. (2005). Transnational family strategies and education in the contemporary Chinese diaspora. *Global Networks, 5*(4), 359–377.

Waters, J. (2010). Becoming a father, missing a wife: Chinese transnational families and the male experience of lone parenting in Canada. *Population, Space, and Place, 16*(1), 63–74.

Waters, J. (2015). Educational imperatives and the compulsion for credentials: Family migration and children's education in East Asia. *Children's Geographies, 13*(3), 280–293.

West, C., & Zimmerman, D. H. (1987). Doing gender. *Gender and Society, 1*(2), 125–151.

Wilding, R. (2018). *Families, intimacy and globalisation: Floating ties.* Palgrave.

Yin, R. (2014). *Case study research: Design and methods.* Sage.

Zhan, H. J., & Rhonda, J. V. (2003). Gender and elder care in China: The influence of filial piety and structural constraints. *Gender & Society, 17*(2), 209–229.

Zhang, Z. S. (2016). Group excitement in the age of individualization—Square-dancing and "Chinese grannies" in sociological perspective. *The Journal of Humanities, 3*, 116–122.

Zhang, Y., Kao, G., & Hannum, E. (2007). Do mothers in rural China practice gender equality in educational aspirations for their children? *Comparative Education Review, 51*(2), 131–157.

Zhou, M. (1998). 'Parachute kids' in Southern California: The educational experience of Chinese children in transnational families. *Educational Policy, 12*(6), 682–704.

CHAPTER 5

Doing Intimacy While Being Apart: Practices of Mobile Intimacy, Emotion and Filial Piety

INTRODUCTION

Traditionally, intimacy is closely related to physical proximity. However, in the increasingly mobile societies in which we live, more people are 'on the move' to seek out new opportunities in employment and relationships, leading to the physical distance between family members becoming greater. Committed couples living apart together (LAT) as a new form of intimate relationships and family living has gained growing scholarly attention. This is well exemplified in the increasing research in commuter marriages (Gerstel & Gross, 1984), weekend couples (Kim, 2012) and dual-career couples in long-distance relationships (Holmes, 2006), and in the focus of this book—LAT relationships (LATs). These changes in families and intimate relationships challenge the conventional assumptions about being a couple, and that intimacy always entails physical proximity and co-presence.

Intimacy, as an important aspect of family life, has been widely recognised as central to understanding family relationships and personal lives (for more extensive work on the conceptualisation of intimacy in family relationships, see Gabb, 2008; Jamieson, 1998, 2011). Although there may be no universal definition of intimacy, it has been widely considered in Western sociology as the qualities of interpersonal relations and the process of building this quality (Jamieson, 2011). It encompasses sexual relations between heterosexual couples in the narrow sense but also extends to parent–child intimacy and friendship, for instance. Giddens (1992) argued that intimacy is built through a dialogue of mutual self-disclosure between equals by talking, sharing inner thoughts and feelings, and listening. Fundamental to this is the importance of intimacy of the self, which is also called 'disclosing intimacy' (Jamieson, 1998). This particular type of intimacy does not, in itself, privilege the physical co-presence of face-to-face relationships (Jamieson, 2013: 18). Existing literature on transnational families shows that people can still sustain a sense of deep knowing and understanding of others, through Information and Communication Technologies (ICTs), when family members are stretched across geographical distances (Kang, 2012; Valentine, 2006; Wilding, 2018). In addition, the rise of digital media coupled with the development of ICTs can blur the boundaries between presence and absence, due in part to its role in creating a sense of constant connection with others (Jamieson, 2013; Wajcman, 2008). Indeed, social relationships do not necessarily cease to exist when members cease being in each other's physical and interactional co-presence (Sigman, 1991: 109). In this sense, self-disclosure is not necessarily confined to territorially fixed designations but can be applied to more individualised and mobile patterns of relating, leading to people experiencing 'mobile intimacy' or 'intimacy at-a-distance' (Elliott & Urry, 2010). Holmes and Wilding (2019: 1) go further, arguing that 'relationships no longer require physical presence in order to be emotionally and socially significant', especially in the context of 'mobile lives' becoming increasingly common (Elliott & Urry, 2010).

Notwithstanding the significance of mutual discourse claimed by Giddens in the formation and maintenance of intimate relationships, Jamieson (2013: 18) demonstrates that it 'may not always be a sufficient way to sustain an intimate relationship'. In practice, there are other practices of intimacy to sustain family bonds and intimate ties, whether they are acts of practical care, physical contact or emotional support (Jamieson, 1998). Drawing on Morgan's concept of 'family practices', Jamieson (2011: 1.2) introduced the idea of 'practices of intimacy', that is, 'practices which enable, generate and sustain a subjective sense of closeness and being attuned and special to each other'. This concept with the emphasis on the 'doing' of intimacy emphasises subjective experience and offers an inclusive perspective to explore the varied ways in which intimacy is developed and experienced. By acknowledging that intimacy can be relational, it also opens the opportunity to look beyond the Western cultures that have a long history of conceptualising the self as autonomous individuals. Practices of intimacy and family practices overlap in cultures that valorise families and intimacy and take it for granted that intimacy is an aspect of family life (Jamieson, 2011: 1.2).

Therefore, this chapter applies the concept of intimacy to the Chinese context and takes a closer look at how people within scattered living arrangements maintain their intimate relationships with their absent partners. I also ask how practices of intimacy are subject to cultural interpretations and social constraints. Through people's range of communication practices, I mainly focus on the use of WeChat with the intent of exploring how ICTs mediate couples' relationships in present-day China. This helps to understand whether Chinese people in LATs de-centre love and long-term monogamous partnerships in the mediated digital age, where people seek out and construct mobile forms of self-identity that are liberated from traditional social expectations (Bauman, 2003; Giddens, 1991). This is then followed by an analysis of emotional aspects of intimacy with considerations of gender. It is also worthy of examination of how practices of family and intimacy intersect with caring (especially for the absent partner's parents) and prescribed gender roles in the specific Chinese context. I also touch on parent–child relationships and intimacy on the grounds that two-parent family parenting relationship remains dominant. Finally, this chapter concludes by highlighting the different ways in which people relating at a distance build, experience and maintain intimacy, while also being informed by the cultural discourses and social institutions of family values and gender norms.

Doing Intimacy in a Mediated Digital Age

Practices of Mobile Intimacy

Throughout the interviews, people shared with me different ways in which they develop intimacy with their partner depending on their life stages and different circumstances. Before moving to a detailed discussion of the use of ICTs in people's everyday lives, which is the focus of this chapter, 'traditional' ways of communication between couples, such as writing letters, are also worthy of attention. In fact, according to my participants, these methods were dominant until the late 1990s when the Internet was just catching on in China (Yang, 2012).

As I demonstrated previously in the chapters, the verbal expression of love and affection (such as saying, 'I love you') was not a common practice among people who were born before China's economic reform. Instead, writing letters was the most popular way to get to know each other and keep in touch, once they had been introduced to their future married spouse. For example, Qingyan (47, married, Liaoning) recalled the time when she and her husband were in the early stage of their relationship. She maintained,

> I was in Hebei [Province] while he was in Shanxi [Province]. We didn't have telephones at that time. If he used a landline phone to speak with me, he had to ring the principal [of my school, because I didn't have a phone]. We communicated mostly through posting letters, like once or twice a week ... [W]e didn't talk much about the future, but our own everyday lives and what had happened around each other. For example, I was teaching [at a primary school] at that time, so I talked a lot about things around teaching, children, and my colleagues. Every time, I might write two or three pages.

Another example comes from Guanya (37, married, Liaoning), who lived quite close to her husband's family and was then introduced to him when she was about 20 years old. She smiled sheepishly when she said during the interview, 'I wrote a letter [to him] only once 'cos I think face-to-face expression can make people feel closer. But writing [about feelings] sometimes has more profound implications than the verbal one.' In her own Guanya's account, her husband was very happy to have received this love letter and he had even taken this opportunity to 'show off' his masculine charm to their twin sons, saying, 'You know, your mother wrote a love letter to me when we were young.' Although acknowledging that face-to-face communication can 'make people feel closer' to each other, it is through the interactions in letters that individuals kept in touch at that particular historical context, and this hand-writing of letters has become their shared memory, as her husband attributed special value to it because of the emotions and self-disclosure that are bound up in it, which are seen as important for developing and maintaining intimate relationships and family bonds (Giddens, 1992).

Nevertheless, writing and posting letters, in affective contexts as an effective way to keep connected between couples, was not frequently mentioned by the younger generation involved in this research. When physical distance prevents co-presence and interaction, the use of social media and communication technologies, as part of the mundane, routinised practices in people's LATs, has changed the practices of intimate relationships by providing an alternative way for communication (Wang, 2016). The growing use of mobile phone and digital media is largely due to the rapid development of the Internet in China (Zhou & Gui, 2017). A recent report published by the CNNIC (2021) shows that the Internet penetration rate reached 71.6% and that rural internet availability has continuously improved to 59.2%. Several researchers have argued that the development of communication technologies has significant importance in maintaining and strengthening connections among geographically dispersed families (Kang, 2012; Zhou & Xiao, 2015). For example, mobile phones, along with their accompanying features, such as in-built cameras, have become an integral part of everyday life to provide a platform for individuals to keep in touch, particularly with others who live in distant regions (Dillon, 2009). In particular, instant messaging applications as the primary mediated communication toolkits have gained much popularity.

In this research, almost all participants reiterated that they often contacted their absent partner by WeChat (in Chinese, Weixin), but with different frequencies involved. They revealed a range of nuanced accounts of how WeChat text and voice messages, and video calls help them rebuild a sense of having linked lives with absent intimate others. For example, Xueyi (25, unmarried) worked as a hotel receptionist in Beijing and her partner worked in North China. During the course of being apart, Xueyi used WeChat to contact him, mostly talking about the trivia of her everyday life: 'like everything that's happened during the day, such as eating, shopping, and details about work'. Another example is from Beibei (28, married, Beijing), whose husband worked away as a military officer:

> We often sent messages through *Weixin*, not phone calls. Because you have to find a private and consistent time [if making a phone call], whereas *Weixin* doesn't need that. For example, I would send him whatever I thought was good to drink or something that was funny. He would reply once he saw it.

It is clear that communication technologies provide new ways for people to do old things to achieve intimacy (Tyler, 2002). In contrast to the kind of disclosure of major aspects of the self, which was seen as central to a 'pure relationship' by Giddens (1992), these 'small talks' about 'what's going on' and phatic communication about 'nothingness' in each other's daily lives have become an indispensable part of people's intimate relationships, especially when people could rarely see each other on a regular basis. In this way, these intensive practices of disclosing intimacy, evident in the ICT-mediated communication among people in a non-cohabiting partnership, are not indicative of the decentring of family life and couple relationships as suggested by the detraditionalisation thesis. In fact, a series of actions of constantly exchanging voice messages, texting, instantly sharing photos and even arguing with each other over trivial things, help develop a sense of deeply knowing that is thought to be fundamental in marking out intimate sexual relationships (Bawin-Legros, 2004; Gabb & Fink, 2015; Jamieson, 2013). This demonstrates that people reflexively work to create their family and 'linked lives' threatened by geographical separation (Qiu, 2022b).

In addition to textual exchanges, a sense of virtual intimacy, which is negotiated by mobile technologies and goes beyond the conventional forms of physical intimacy, may also be experienced through virtual connectivity offered by WeChat video calls. Spending time together digitally, to some degree, enables those geographically distanced to nevertheless take part in family-based activities and maintain a sense of 'presence-in-absence' and 'connected presence' (Jamieson, 2013; Licoppe, 2004; Vetere et al., 2005). For example, Xiaobo (26, married, Beijing), an accountant, would regularly arrange WeChat video calls with her husband who, during the course of interviews, remained in the UK for his PhD study. As she said,

> We have a video chat every week, talking about things that had happened for us during the week, no matter whether they were good or bad. We also shop online together, and sometimes I would pick things for him. Or, we would talk about newly released British or American TV dramas. Normally we would talk for at least one hour, even though there was nothing particularly important to say.

In a similar way, the practice of video calls is also exemplified in the case of Rosy (46, married), who also lived in a transnational family due to her son's education. As she illustrated,

> I actually didn't expect that God would help us via *Weixin*. I seldom send messages to my husband, but he made video calls almost every day while we [Rosy and her son] were in the US.... [H]onestly, we spent much more time together on *Weixin* video calls which were even much longer than our

face-to-face conversations at home [in Beijing]. He called me while he was driving to work in the morning, which coincided with the time when I was off work [in the US]. This is really much better than when we were physically together. [When we were both in Beijing,] I had no idea when he came back home as I was already asleep. We didn't talk very often [when we lived together in Beijing] if there was nothing in particular happening.

The real-time information exchanged through virtual calls, if internet access is available, have increased people's engagement in the lives of absent others and greatly blurred the distinction between 'absence and presence' (Wilding, 2006; Yang, 2014). In practical terms, it also facilitates married individuals who are more likely to have a host of responsibilities with respect to their family and relationship, in discussion during the day (Coyne et al., 2011). When living in a split household, Rosy used WeChat video chats to have regular 'meetings' with her husband discussing 'what furniture should I buy' and thus felt a sense of his presence and 'closeness', which, ironically, she might not have been able otherwise to experience when they were physically together in Beijing. Because the practices of intimacy developed during the time of physical separation had increased her self-reflexivity about her marital relationship, at the end of our interview, Rosy told me that she had started to change and planned to ask her husband out on a date. Under such circumstances, being 'apart' improves or enables being 'together', with the aid of ICTs. Therefore, arguably, these practices of intimacy through communication technologies can be considered as the re-centring rather than de-centring of the committed intimate couple relationship and through which the subjective feeling of another person being present has undergone changes.

Without doubt, practices of intimacy through social media can make contact both quick and convenient. However, it can be problematic due to the fact that they are often 'stripped of these essential communication elements' (Juhasz & Bradford, 2016: 707–708), such as facial expressions, bodily gestures, voice inflection or tone of voice. As a result, misunderstanding or contradictions do occur occasionally, even though people remain constantly in contact through media practice. For example, Yuqing (30, married, Liaoning) talked about her experience of text messaging on WeChat:

> Sometimes when I played jokes via texts or audio messages, misunderstandings would occur if he didn't understand my tone of voice. [The use of]

punctuation I think can even generate contradictory meanings. For example, he might be wondering whether I was unhappy, and I might be thinking why you did this etc. and then conflicts occurred. That's not going to happen when couples are physically together.

In addition, ICTs are not always used by family members, in particular men, for building and maintaining conjugal intimacy between couples. Anli's (41, married) example is a good illustration of this point. Being left at home as a housewife, Anli's husband worked as a truck driver with a tight timetable. Sometimes his workload was quite demanding and could only stay at home for three days a month, whereas during the slow season he might stay for nearly a month. However, when he was home, Anli had hardly experienced a sense of closeness, which she attributed to her husband misusing WeChat, as she complained:

> [When he is away] at least he would call me and talk by *Weixin*, asking me if I have had my dinner. When he was back, I didn't get that feeling. Sometimes we had arguments when he was home, because he seldom talked to me, but very much to others on *Weixin* … Since he is using *Weixin*, he joined a group chat with his former classmates. So, he often went out with them, leaving me alone at home. I had to take care of him every time when he got drunk. So, I do hope he could work away.

My analysis with the emphasis on the 'doing' of intimacy shows that intimate relationships are subjectively experienced, and the ways people engage in practices of mobile intimacy are variously dependent on age, the stage of their relationship and the contexts in which people are embedded. In some cases, young people, and those in the early stages of their relationship, are heavily involved in the digitally mediated process of mutual disclosure through which practices of everyday talks enable them to get to know each other and secure attachment. In other cases, these practices are just not enough if people cannot have a hug when they need it (Xiaobo, 26, married), and 'talking on the phone is not as close as seeing and feeling each other physically' (Minzhou, 38, married). For other people, the ways in which they construct a family and experience conjugal intimacy are not confined to verbal communication and textual discourses, as the younger generations are more likely to be, given that they have usually been together longer than younger couples. For example, having been married for 13 years, Xuanye (39, manager) claimed that they would not keep checking up on each other on a daily basis through mobile phone and WeChat, but his wife would express care by sending him a package of healthcare products during the time he was relocated to work in Tianjin. Even though he didn't ask for it, 'she knows for a long time'. For him, actions speak louder than words. As Qi (2016: 42) argued, intimacy in Chinese society has more to do with actions than words. This resonates with Jamieson's (2011) argument that disclosing intimacy may not necessarily become the key principle of personal life, as self-disclosure may only be appropriate for a particular group. In practice, there are other ways in which people 'do' intimacy and construct their familial relationships.

Potential Risks

Certainly, couples relating at a distance may affect different aspects of their personal lives. Perhaps unsurprisingly, few of them openly talk about the potential influence of living separately on their sexual life as sex matters in China remain largely less liberal than the West in general (Jackson & Ho, 2020). Luckily, during the interview, Hua, a 31-year-old high-school teacher, touched on this:

> I think in real life, the most straightforward influence on couples living separately is on sex. In my inner heart, I do feel that demands are not satisfied, especially when we don't have a child. But I can't do anything about it, sometimes, you know, I simply watch pornographic movies for relief [laughing]. I can't do illegal things, and I have no idea how to resolve this stuff. Because the person is irreplaceable; he's a substantive subject. If you want to solve it, then you have to find replacements. But you know, we're too traditional to go outside to buy that kind of stuff [sex toys?].

Extramarital affairs is another issue that LAT people are frequently worried about during the course of couples living apart. In contemporary China, infidelity is reported as one of the major causes of couple separation (Farrer & Sun, 2003). When the couple lives separately, they are more vulnerable to infidelity (Blumstein & Schwartz, 1983). However, some people in this study firmly asserted that physical distance does not necessarily lead to extramarital affairs. Again, Hua (31, married, Beijing) claimed that 'infidelity may have nothing to do with distance. It can also occur even when couples are physically together'. Mei (34, married, Beijing) expressed a similar attitude and regarded separation as having little consequence for the possibility of having affair. As she said,

> This is and will always be an excuse to say that [couples who are] not physically together will then cause [emotional and physical] infidelity … [T]hat's only a surface phenomenon, they must have other deeply hidden reasons [if people have affairs when they live apart].

Almost all the participants expected sexual fidelity and emotional faithfulness throughout their committed intimate relationship. In a modern couple relationship, sexual exclusivity is seen as one of the fundamental elements of a successful and long-lasting monogamous relationship (Carter, 2012). According to a survey, 95% of the general public in China believe that sex outside the marital relationship was viewed as 'completely' or mostly wrong, and therefore it is destructive to the stability of the family (Zhang et al., 2012). However, recent data show that there has been an upward trend in infidelity in China (Zhang et al., 2021), and by 2015, the infidelity rate reached to 24% (Pan, 2017). The literature has indicated that many opportunities and material foundations under China's rapid urban development and institutional changes in the reform era were created for people to engage in affairs (Luo & Yu, 2022; Xiao, 2011). For example, Luo and Yu (2022) point out that as a result of unbalanced growth in China, rural-to-urban migration offers temporary migrants the opportunities for engaging in undetected sex (also see Zhang et al., 2012). It is also argued that the rising individualism that has emerged in contemporary China leads to changes in attitudes toward sex and marriage (Lo et al., 2010). This often places those being left behind in a vulnerable position. This is exemplified in the case of Shanrui (28, married with a 6-year-old daughter and a new-born baby, Liaoning) whose husband came back home about once every two months as a long-haul trucker. She was conservative about her absent husband's commitment to their marital relationship, especially under the circumstances of knowing very little about her husband's pattern of work:

> During such a long time of separation, to be honest, I really don't know whether he has extramarital affairs or not. Even if it had happened, I would have no way to know as his colleagues are all men and on his side. Although I say that I wouldn't accept it [if he has affairs], it seems like in my deep heart I've acquiesced in [his infidelity]. He said he doesn't have one-night stands, but I still don't believe him.

Shanrui's vulnerability is also shared by Minzhou (38, study mother), whose husband was away for work and could only come back home once a year. She felt a sense of emotional insecurity and therefore worried if her husband had seemed to physically 'desert' her:

> Sometimes his response was lukewarm when we talked on *Weixin*. Then I would wonder if he's having an affair over there. I'm here alone caring for our children. If you [Minzhou's husband] divorce me while the children are going to college, I can't image what my future life would be like.

It is clear that with the widespread usage of mediated communication, people are confronted with endless choices to form a romantic couple relationship. In the Western context, Bauman (2003) demonstrated that traditional life-long monogamous partnerships that once provided solidity have been 'liquified' by the force of social change, consumerism and individualisation. A move away from a fixed residence can also give rise to a fluid and changing family relationship, leading to life-long commitment, monogamous intimate relations being in danger (Hobbs et al., 2017; Holdsworth, 2013). With this growing concern, mobile communication technology has been considered a double-edged sword, because it enables people to connect more easily with others, yet it also facilitates infidelity by allowing deception and the covering up of extra-marital affairs (McDaniel et al., 2017).

Text messages, for instance, have been questioned for having the potential to transform 'ostensibly harmless flirtations into more serious relationships' (Rettie, 2008: 307). As one of my participants, Yuqing (30, married, Liaoning), whose husband is a firefighter in the army, said, 'Although he wasn't able to go away [from the army] freely, I would sometimes worry about whether he [would] send text messages to others [via mobile phones], due to the popularity of social networking platforms.' Indeed, people now have become increasingly networked as individuals in a much-networked society. The use of mobile communication technologies, nevertheless, is not necessarily giving rise to the 'detraditionalisation' of marriage and personal life, which are characterised as uncertain in relation to modern relationships (Beck & Beck-Gernsheim, 2002).

Emotional Intimacy

Emotions are a key element within everyday family life (Morgan, 2011: 110) and often considered crucial for maintaining connected intimate ties and family harmony (Erickson, 2005; Holmes, 2010a). There is evidence that in the context where distance prevents co-present communication and practical care, regardless of the degree to which people have 'chosen' or feel 'compelled', people are more likely to seek more abstract forms of support and connection in order to remain 'close', and emotional support is an indispensable part of sustaining intimate relationships (Finch, 1989; Holmes, 2006, 2010a; Jamieson, 2013). Morgan (2011) suggested that in emphasising how emotions are expressed, the practices approach as a whole has a broader meaning, encompassing not only those practices identified as emotional labour (Hochschild, 1983) or emotional work (Duncombe & Marsden, 1998). It also enables a particular relationship tie to be reaffirmed by enacting a set of emotional practices in relation to others. Therefore, in this section I will pay specific attention to the emotional aspect of intimacy. Although only four men are included in this study, I also look at the intersections of gender and emotions and explore how ways of (un)doing the emotional aspects of intimacy between men and women are imposed and interwoven with the construction and practices of gender and heterosexuality.

In this research, people in LATs often make concerted efforts to maintain intimacy, as relating at a distance, for some people at least, has made things more complicated, especially when it comes to illness. Almost all people had experienced illnesses during the time of couples living apart. Perhaps not surprisingly, very few of them could enlist embodied forms of care from their partner due to distance and other commitments, and under such circumstances, people would often provide other forms of support such as reminding loved ones to take their medicine. This is evident in the case of Zhonglan (24, unmarried, Liaoning), who recalled her experiences of texting her boyfriend that she had diarrhoea after a dinner with her friends. She explicitly expressed how she was pleased to receive her boyfriend's phone calls, with the intent of coming to take care of her, 'even though I knew he wouldn't come [due to job-related distance], but it felt much better to hear him say things like that'. In most cases, however, people told me that they had learnt self-care as they had become 'accustomed' to looking after themselves over the years. Emotional support through talking and listening takes on importance in maintaining couple relationships (Gabb & Fink, 2007; Holmes, 2015).

Previous studies have demonstrated that the emotional work within heterosexual relationships is usually seen as highly gendered in that women, in particular, are viewed as responsible for maintaining relationships and providing emotional support (Duncombe & Marsden, 1993;

Hochschild, 1979). In some cases, my interview data support the idea of the gendering of emotion work. This is evident in the case of Mei (34, married) who worked in Beijing as an engineer, whereas her husband flew off to the USA for work on the first day after they married. She was reflexive about an 'emotionally involved' model of marital relations (Jankowiak & Li, 2017), illustrating that emotional connections are much needed within her family and intimate relations, especially after knowing how this has been 'done' by his husband's family:

> His parents often watch TV together, but without communicating or interacting with each other. Regarding family, their role-playing is child-centred, like he is the father and she is the mother. But they forget the fact that they are husband and wife [to each other]. I wouldn't do that [to my family]. No matter how many children I have, I'll keep reminding myself that we are not only parents but also partners. I might have a higher standard for this and would keep communicating and negotiating with my husband about the importance of keeping emotional communication and family interactions.

Similar to Mei, other female participants in this study also expressed a desire for consciously building and developing emotional connectedness and 'conversational intimacy' (Jankowiak & Li, 2017). They often encouraged their male counterpart to share things that happened around them, including their daily work and work stresses. Nevertheless, the feedback they got was often significantly asymmetrical. Yuqin (30, married), whose partner is a firefighter in the army, recalled that her partner seldom talks about his work pressures as 'he thought men shouldn't say these kinds of things'. Similarly, Linjua (32, unmarried) relayed that her partner said little about his work issues, partly because he did not want his intimate others to be worried about him. Although limited numbers of male participants are included due to the focus of this study, their accounts of the ways they managed emotions have confirmed the gendered division of emotions. In Xuanye's (39, married) account, he provides a fairly typical example of men's unwillingness to participate in the disclosing of self and talking about their difficulties that might be encountered during the time of living apart:

> Basically, I rarely talk about my work with her. This is the difference between men and women [in relation to] facing pressures. Women can mitigate their pressures by talking or crying, but men basically would not. Men hide or hold back [emotions] by themselves … [talking and sharing emotions] might be important, but I'm not good at it.

As Xuanye acknowledged, there are gender differences in the ways people 'do' emotions (Erickson, 2005; Whitehead, 2002). Literature has documented that this contradiction comes from the dominant and entrenched cultural expectations and norms about gender, heterosexuality and marriage, shaping the ways in which men and women should behave emotionally in their intimate relationships (Hochschild, 1983). Given that the traditional male role expectations encourage men to be competitive, for example, rather than disclose vulnerability and personal feelings at an emotional level, fear of making others worried or 'compromising their own masculinity' (van Hoof, 2013: 129) may have driven them to control and withhold their emotions. In this ideology, people need to manage their feelings in line with particular cultural expectations and beliefs about how they think they should be feeling (Elliott & Umberson, 2008; Hochschild, 1983; Lewis, 1978).

Contrary to men's reluctance to talk about work-related stress and vulnerable emotions (anxiety, fear and sadness for instance), the gendered notion of emotionality perceives women as being vocal in articulating their feelings and more emotionally competent and expressive (Illouz, 1997). This might be the result of a taken-for-granted assumption that women are more skilled than men, not only in consoling and comforting others, but also in expressing their own emotions, both facially and bodily (Delphy & Leonard, 1992; Duncombe & Marsden, 1993), or because of the characteristic that love is seen as something feminine (Cancian, 1986). James (1989: 23) holds a similar view, arguing that 'emotional' becomes part of a major cluster of other adjectives by which masculine and feminine are differentiated and through which the emotional–rational divide of female–male is perpetuated (see also Reddy, 2009). Consequently, a gender asymmetry in emotional labour where men are seen to express less and devalue their emotions has emerged.

However, failing to take part emotionally may contribute to a greater source of friction and create varying degrees of difficulty among heterosexual couples, given that the 'institution' of marriage in China is being transformed 'from detached performance of roles, toward a willingness to create bonds of emotional interdependence and empathic mutuality' (Jankowiak & Li, 2017: 156). As a result, contemporary Chinese men's emotional detachment in couple relationships may lead to women's marital dissatisfaction (Chen & Lim, 2012). For example, when distance made other forms of caring impossible, Shanrui (28, married) longed for her husband's emotional support and the feeling of emotional connectedness.

But she obviously was frustrated by the increasingly fewer incoming phone calls from her husband whilst they were apart: 'I'm the one who always takes the initiative to contact him, he never proactively calls me ... I feel like he just doesn't want to talk to me anymore.' Later she told me that she was tired of asking her husband 'how's it going there?' because she always received nothing back from him in return. As a consequence, every time her husband called her, she would ask her daughter to pick up the phone, as she knew 'he must have been missing the girls [rather than me]'.

The case of Wangyang (38) also serves as a good example to illustrate how her husband's emotional detachment in the family caused the 'death' of their relationship. Wangyang is eight years younger than her husband, and they have a nine-year-old son living with her. Although her husband's job had prevented him from providing embodied forms of caring, she said, 'I don't blame you when you work away, but why can't you do something when you're at home?' By leaving childcare and housework completely to Wangyang, her husband did 'nothing' emotionally apart from sending money back to support the family, which made Wangyang think that she was paid for caring for the children, as her husband's income level is three times higher than Wangyang's. The emphasis here is on the type of emotion of what one 'does' and 'feels' rather than what one 'has'. In this regard, the individual's ability to 'do' emotion can shape people's experience of intimacy where emotional action, not merely 'being', has occupied the forefront of the construction of intimacy and family ties. With the demise of emotional connectedness, their marital life, according to Wangyang, is on the brink of divorce, but she still sustains this marital relation in maintaining 'zero communication' with her husband to provide her only son with an 'intact' rather than separated family.

However, the dualist viewing of men as always being emotionally restricted and incompetent is not neatly applicable to all male participants in my sample. In fact, men also 'do' emotion work. Having been physically together with his wife only five years although they have been together for 16 years, Xuanye (39, married) further recounted that

> One day at night, she called me and cried to complain. She was on her period, so she had a bad mood. She felt alone and depressed at night whilst children were not home. [She complained that] she couldn't have a hot meal ready for her when she was back home, even the bed was also cold. Actually, I didn't say that I haven't yet had my food here. At that point, I need to comfort her.

Xuanye's wife's wronged feelings towards his absence of emotional caring and the bodily connection during living apart seem to reflect 'the phenomena of male non-disclosure and gender asymmetry in emotional behaviour' (Duncombe & Marsden, 1993: 229). What might be missing, however, is a more nuanced understanding of the complexity and the ambivalences of emotions that arise and involve here. By saying, 'I need to comfort her', we can see emotional reflexivity (Holmes, 2015) and a sense of the 'emotion work' (Erickson, 2005) that Xuanye would provide to prioritise the comforting of his wife, despite his own feelings. Another example of this can be seen from Qingshu (30, married, Beijing). He and his wife met in the UK where both of them graduated with a postgraduate degree. During the time of our interview, his wife worked as an accountant in the north part of China. He shared the feeling of emotional loneliness he has been suffering:

> Every time when I watched TV or saw my friends who can stay with their partner, I just felt that their lives are happiness. To be honest, I am more emotional than her [his wife]. For me, I like that kind of life—staying together as a couple with children ... I had a strong sense of loneliness when I worked in Shanghai. I went back from work alone and spent all my weekends alone ... we often phoned each other. But still nothing can be changed.

It is clear that Qingshu did feel a degree of vulnerability in an emotional sense due to dual-career locations. In fact, he was not reluctant to say, but explicitly articulated, his emotional reflexivity, which is seen as important in family relationships (Holmes, 2010b; Qiu, 2022a). His feelings about and emotional reliance on his wife are highly relational and imbued with emotion, despite the fact that this non-co-residential partnership would continue if his wife kept pursing her own career development in North China. Under such circumstances, he told me that he had to learn to be accustomed to this living arrangement. In contrast to seeing the expression of emotion as exclusively a female preserve, the common-sense thinking on men's non-disclosure tendencies needs to be carefully examined. As Robinson and Hockey (2011: 149) have suggested, men are capable of reflecting on and showing emotions in certain contexts, but in ways that 'have not been directly comparable with women' in their everyday heterosexual relationships. Likewise, Holmes' (2015) research on heterosexual men in the context of long-distance relationships has supported the idea that men do exercise emotions in different ways and can relate to the feelings of their partners, challenging the stereotypical views of gendered emotionality.

While emotional forms of caring can be moderated by engagement in mediated communication practices, my data indicate how practices of family and intimate relations may sometimes involve not 'doing' emotions, in the sense that people may consciously and reflexively not share unhappy moments with their absent partner. This is exemplified in the case of Lianbao (51, married). At the time of our interview, he had been deployed to work as a manager in Tianjin for over two years. His wife and other family members all stayed in their hometown of Dalian. Although having no other connections and roots in Tianjin, Lianbao mostly shared good news with his wife, as he highlighted:

> For me, I say more if it is good news, but less if not … [I'm] trying not to talk when [I meet with] difficulties. Because it is my own work business. No need to make her worried … After all I am a man coming to this age [who] has already experienced things. I myself can handle these pressures associated with work and others.

Culturally imposed gender expectations have significantly shaped the ways in which people construct and make sense of their family life (Qiu, 2020). The breadwinner's role attached to men informed by the gendered division of labour has been considered as the most fundamental foundation of masculinity identity (Connell, 1995). In post-reform Chinese society, social constructions and practices of hegemonic masculine ideals have predominantly focused on men's capacities to financially support a family while suppressing their emotional feelings (Louie, 2015; Osburg, 2013; Zhang, 2010). Under the circumstance of couples living apart, Lianbo demonstrated his masculinity by not talking or only talking about certain things. From his understanding, managing emotions are of importance in the 'doing' of family. Acts of that kind are not necessarily emotionally detached but may arguably be understood as a way of making an effort, in his own way, to maintain the couple relationship as it is (Gabb & Fink, 2007).

Interestingly, it is not only those who work away (mostly men in this study) but also those being left behind (mostly women) who are engaged in managing their own emotions. For example, Minzhou (40, married) lived with her son in North China while her husband migrated to South China for work and could only come back home once a year:

> I [would] hardly tell him when I was [emotionally] down because he is working alone also having a difficult life there. If I tell him, he'll feel bad too. So, I called him just to check up on him and it [low mood] would go

away then ... [S]ometimes my son made me angry, I wanted to tell him but bit it back. We adult people have to control [our emotions].

Hiding or holding back emotions to place minimal emotional demands upon her husband is performed as part of a wife's responsibility (Finch, 1983). Minzhou is not the only one suggesting that talking about emotional ups and downs appears to be an extra burden on her husband. Similarly, Hongli (40, married) recounted how mobile intimacy during the course of living apart could also be experienced as not communicating with her husband, who worked as an electrician:

> I don't want to mention these trouble things to him. It's useless. He couldn't come back anyway. I know he was also [finding it] not easy working outside [the home]. His work was relatively dangerous with lots of pressures. So, [it is] not necessary to make him worried.

Partly because of deeply 'knowing' her husband, Hongli concealed her loneliness and had no intention of diverting his attention from work. In the context of couples living apart, the practice of familial intimacy here is closely associated with how people 'undo' emotions in a way that controlling or maintaining silence about their own (negative) feelings is performed. Although being left behind at home, some women said that they can easily receive help and talk things through because 'at least relatives and friends live nearby'. This was fundamentally different from their absent partner, who, on most occasions, could not have that support. In this sense, emotions can be 'done' differently as people need to reflexively navigate their emotions in accordance with the contexts in which they are embedded. Not speaking and silences are arguably also crucial in order for relationships to remain intact. As Gabb and Fink (2007: 54) indicate, keeping silent may be used in an attempt at kindness, a deliberate strategy to prevent further distress.

Embodied Practices of Intimacy

Practices of Gift-Giving

According to Jamieson (2011), intimacy is built by practices. When distance prevents people from delivering and receiving embodied and other tactile forms of caring, people have to enact certain behaviours in order to express love and sustain their relationship across space and time (Carter et al., 2016; Holmes, 2010a, 2014; Jamieson, 2013). This led me to move the focus to the practice of gift-giving, in particular among geographically dispersed people. In this way, equal attention has been placed on the practical acts of providing care to other family members as alternative ways of 'doing intimacy' with consideration of the specific cultural and social practice of filial piety. This suggests that prescribed gender roles should be taken into account in order to understand the variety of ways of doing intimacy in a collective sense.

Gift-giving is an important social activity in Chinese culture (Yang, 1994). Informed by the Chinese culture of reciprocity, where people are expected to give gifts and return the favour (Chan et al., 2003; Zhou & Guang, 2007), the practice of giving in affective contexts remains important for the construction of intimacy (Evans, 2008, 2012; Yan, 2016). This practice of buying and giving gifts was highly evident among young participants when they were physically apart and people who were in the early stage of their relationship particularly. For example, Tiantian's (26, unmarried, Beijing) relationship with her boyfriend encountered her parents' opposition due to their unmatched family backgrounds. Although her boyfriend came from the rural community, and did not have a well-paid job in Beijing, Tiantian thought that he valued her, which was expressed in the gifts that she received from her boyfriend. As she said, 'In fact, he doesn't have much money right now, but he bought me an Apple Watch by [his] credit card … I think it's worth cherishing someone who's willing to buy [expensive] stuff for you.'

Gift-giving has been considered as symptomatic of showing love and exclusiveness (Zelizer, 2005). As an engagement gift, Mei (34, married, Beijing) thought to strengthen their emotional bond through buying her husband, whose work needs a lot of travelling, a very expensive world-time watch after they were engaged. She attached special value and commitment to this gift, as she described: 'This watch is important to me. It's the most expensive gift [I've ever bought] so far. I think it means that you [Mei's husband] have gained my recognition.' In this regard, Mei, as the gift-giver, gives not only the gift itself, but also gives part of herself to her husband—the gift-receiver (Mauss, 1990). This evidence based on empirical data is seemingly not in line with Giddens' (1992) finding on the importance of mutually enjoying and deeply knowing as the central aspect of a modern democratic type of relationship, or what he calls 'pure relationship'. The material gifts that integrate various meanings are calculated, not only on the amount of money spent on them, but also on the symbolic meanings that people attach to them, depending on the nature of the relationship with the gift-receiving partner.

More specifically, although people value and often send gifts to loved ones, my data find differences in how people use gifts, for what purposes, what is offered as a gift, and how it is given to show love and affection in familial relationships. These differences are not simply related to personal preference or financial status, but more importantly are conditioned by prescribed gender norms and subject to variations due to context-specific reasons. Throughout the interviews, women seemed to be used to taking the role of 'caregiver' and thinking what living supplies their male partner might need and use in their daily lives. Thus, in reality, they were more likely to shop practically and purchase daily-use items, such as clothes (Jiajia, 23, unmarried), healthcare (Xuanye's wife, 39, married) or skin-care products (Xueyi, 25, unmarried) to their absent male partners. As Linjuan (32, unmarried) said,

> I don't know why [I bought these items]. I just bought it when I saw something suitable for him. Mostly it's about clothes … [H]e never buys me clothes, but normally he would give me handbag or perfume as a gift.

As the above excerpt shows, the absent one (normally the husband) in this study tends to make purchases that allow them to reclaim their masculinity. For example, Lianbao (51, married), working far away as a manager, said that he would buy his wife clothes of good quality, so 'she can better support my work'. Xuanye (39, married) recalled that on special days, he would buy his wife 'things all women want, such as accessories or gold and silver ornaments. No matter what type of women you are, they all like gold and silver ornaments [laughing].' Certainly, the value of the gift people can buy is directly related to their financial situation. The working-away husband's practices of buying 'fine jewellery' reflect their financial choices and implicitly their power and status in the family, as a result of the pattern of gendered family mobility. More importantly, it also shows that men uphold gender stereotypes of women needing to be beautiful, given that women were supposed to support and advance their husband's career after being bought material things to 'look good and beautiful'.

Gifts sometimes are also served as a function of mitigating conflicts and recovering couple intimacy. As shown in my interviews, their male partner, reported by my participants, tends to use gifts to 'break the ice' after quarrels to recover their relationship. This is manifested in Zhonglan's (24, unmarried, Shenyang) story as her boyfriend bought her a pair of sneakers to mitigate their conflicts, 'but it seems to me this makes our quarrels become different in some way, like he's buying me off'. Another example comes from a male participant, Qingshu (30, married), who further explains how he used gifts as an attempt to stabilise the early stage of his love relationship:

> In the early stage of our relationship, [the reason for gift-giving was because] I was afraid that we might split up due to small contradictions. It [gift-giving] was often used [as a way of mitigating conflicts]. I'll also buy her gifts on Valentine's Day and her birthday. If I forgot, she'd be angry, but I'll make it up to her later.

Under some circumstances, giving gifts is out of obligation. In this example, due to his fear of breaking up, Qingshu may have felt obligated to take the lead of buying gifts to secure and solidify his romantic love relationship. According to Nguyen and Munch's (2010) research on people's perceptions of gift-giving in romantic relationships, they found that anxious individuals are more likely to experience a strong urge to use gifts as a means to form affective bonds and secure attachment. Arguably, this suggests that the practices of gift-giving are considered an instrumental way where people use it purposely to maintain an unstable relationship, especially during its initial stages (Joy, 2001).

However, as the nature of Qingshu's relationship shifts and evolves from unstable dating to a long-term marital relationship, his perception of gift-giving between couples has also changed. As he continued illustrating:

> But we are *laofu laoqi* [old couples] now and wouldn't separate easily because of such trivial matters [not often doing gift-giving]. Compared to dating couples at a younger age, I'm concerned more about our future life, including career development, thinking about how to make our family and children's lives better ... because we are now a family with a kid. It's no longer just two individuals, but two sets of families linking together along with responsibilities. It's not going to separate just because of [our romantic relationship being] faded away.

With growing interests in leading a good family life as he and his wife entered a more stable stage of life stage, Qingshu has downplayed the activities of giving gifts in pleasing his wife and showing love but attached a greater importance to fulfil his relational role and responsibility as a father and husband to ensure collective well-being in a family life. In emphasising himself as an omnipotent figure in the family, his familial masculinity is evident in the commitment to making contributions and doing intimacy in accordance with the patriarchal norm of male breadwinning (Wong, 2020; Zhang, 2010). Arguing in a similar way, women participants also experienced a transformation in doing intimacy and making sense of their marital relationship over the life course. For example, having been married for over 20 years, Qingyan (46, married, Liaoning) articulated the common goal she valued to 'live a good life', even at the expense of couples living apart:

> There was [romantic] love at the early stage of our marriage. With the children growing up, our [marital] relationship has upgraded to *qinqing* [familial emotions], with more mutual understanding being involved. [The common goal is] living a better life together.

The ways to 'live a good life' are subject to cultural discourses regarding what a 'family' should be like. As Morgan puts it, 'practices and discourses, the families we live with and the families we live by, are mutually implicated in each other' (Morgan, 2011: 68). In the context of Confucian familism, the gender division of labour dictates women's morally prescribed duties in filial care for elders, spousal care for husbands and motherly care for children, which constitute the functional axis of family life (Kyung-Sup & Min-Young, 2010: 545). As a result, certain forms of practices of intimacy and doing family are valued by people at different stages of the life course.

Practices of Filial Piety

In contrast to the absent one's (often men's) material aspects of giving and doing of intimacy, almost all the women were aware of the importance of caring practice as an indispensable parameter of intimate relationships (Gabb, 2008; Morgan, 2011). In Morgan's (2011) view, caring practices, for the most part informal and unpaid, are embodied practices, where tensions and ambivalence may arise from the intermingling of the physical and emotional labour involved in the caring relationship. In this sense, the emphasis on 'doing', at least in some respects, enables us to explore how inequalities, power and divisions are practically constituted on a daily basis (Morgan, 2020).

When women enter into a heterosexual marriage, providing daily care for (older) family members as part of their gender roles as the daughter-in-law, especially when their male partners were absent from their daily lives, is noticed. For example, Xutong (40, married, Liaoning), living with her children and parents-in-law, makes sense of her caring practices as evidence of doing a family and maintaining couple intimacy:

> We've been married so many years and the feelings that I had when we're just married have already gone. Taking care of parents[-in-law] is more important now.

As Jamieson (2011) suggested, 'just as family practices might fit with and reproduce conventional scripts, so too might practices of intimacy'. In a collectivist culture, such as China, the construction of family is not simply about two individuals, apparent in the traditional Chinese saying that 'When you marry, you don't just marry your spouse, but their whole family' (Xu & Xia, 2014). With a strongly patriarchal and patrilocal family tradition, male heirs and their wives are obligated to provide all-round support for their parents in old age. The norms of patrilocal marriage practice place married women on the filial map of their in-laws (Liu, 2017). In the absence of sons in everyday life, upon marriage, it is the daughter-in-law who performs care (Song et al., 2012). For example, Xinyi (26, married, Beijing), a school teacher, encouraged her husband, a junior doctor, to attend further training in a different city for a year. When they were apart, Xinyi explained,

> I would come over when my father-in-law had problems with technologies, such as downloading apps onto his smartphone or fixing TV cable wires. Sometimes I had to drive my mother-in-law to her mum's home. I have undertaken his [her husband's] role as I have to do more things for his family now [while he is away].

Although family obligation has substantially weakened as a consequence of the individualisation process and China's dramatic changes through economic transitions (Yan, 2010), the ideals of the practice of doing gender roles is still an indispensable part of 'doing' family in contemporary Chinese society. Rooted in traditional gender norms, this has significantly affected the ways in which people build and generate intimacy. Another example can be seen in the case of Anli (41, married, Liaoning) who lived alone at the time of our interview, as her husband worked away as a truck driver and was the sole financial contributor in the family. Every time before her husband went out to work, she would prepare a bag of newly washed clothes for him considering he might be exhausted and lack time to wash. So, when her husband came back home with a bundle of dirty clothes, Anli would wash and get them ready for him again. Although she was freed from childcare labour due to being childless and appreciated the release from 'cooking and cleaning messy house' offered by couples living apart, she was the taken-for-granted family carer for her in-laws. As she revealed,

> He's been working away these years, and it's me taking care of his mother and cooking for her every day … Even though when he was home, he didn't help me do housework. He thought this is woman's business which he shouldn't do.

It is clear that intimacy and inequalities can coexist (Jamieson, 1998) as they remain embedded and persistent even in non-traditional living arrangements as a consequence of gendered family patterns. Social norms surrounding gender division of labour and the feminised notion of care work have contributed directly and indirectly to the ways in which family is socially constructed and culturally practised. In accordance with filial obligations, 'doing' the role of a virtuous wife and filial daughter-in-law as part of their gender roles is fundamental to a woman's construction and maintenance of a stable and harmonious marriage relationship. By this, I would argue that the practice of family and doing intimacy is culturally mediated by perceived practices of filial piety, considering the institutionalised family obligation remains prevalent and continues to shape the overwhelming majority of people's personal lives in China (Qi, 2015).

Parent–Child Intimacy

Many participants often talked about their children growing up, if they had them, when reflecting on the potential influences of the absent partner on family life. Since the implementation of China's one-child policy in the late 1970s, an intact family, which includes two parents with one child, has been seen as good for familial stability, until the recent universal two-child policy implemented in 2016. The lack of one parent in family life, no matter whether temporary or permanent, is inadvisable and regarded as harmful by society, especially for the well-being of children (Settles et al., 2013). Although parent–child intimacy is not the focus, either in this chapter or in this book overall, due to a lack in the sample of children, many married participants often have been concerned with the impact of the departure of a parent on everyday family life. As it is a common phenomenon that women in this study often live with their children as a consequence of couples living apart, I am therefore interested in how the absent fathers care for children and do parenting at a distance. In the context of the limited male participants included in this study, I attempt to examine the strategies that people used in their reactions to such family life.

Although women (and men, to different extents) value the autonomy and freedom offered by LATs, in general they did not see any potential advantages for their children as a result of couples living apart. For example, some male participants in my sample seemed to be anxious about their daughters not being brave but too 'feminine'. Xuanye (39, married), father of an 11-year-old daughter, thought that his daughter had a timid personality and was not brave enough. He ascribed his daughter's 'personality weaknesses' to the 'lack of a father figure in her everyday life':

> Now the positive influence of fathering, such as determination and courage, was too little [for her]. Her [his daughter's] life was surrounded by women only, such as her aunties, nanna, and grandma. Even though she's in school, her PE teacher is a woman as well.

In contrast, some mothers of teenage boys, in particular, expressed concerns over the lack of a 'father–son talk' about 'men's stuff'. Therefore, Guanya (37, married) had to teach her son sex education by herself, considering that teachers, especially in rural schools, are often ashamed of and give little emphasis to teaching the subject (Aresu, 2009; Zhang et al., 2007). In an LAT family, where the father is often absent and can hardly 'do' fathering on a daily basis, concerns regarding parent–child intimacy have arisen. For example, Wangyang (38, married) worried about whether her son was behaving in a 'masculine enough' way, due to his father being missing from their everyday family life. It seemingly suggests that the presence of a father figure and embodied practices are central to masculinity construction and parent–child intimacy (Louie, 2015). Again, this is shown in the case of Xuanye (39, married), who told me a poignant story that happened in 2006, and in his words, made a 'deep impression' on him. Due to work commitment, he had been working away in Ningbo, a port city in eastern China, since 2000. He left childcare completely to his wife and visited family members every two or three months. One time when he returned to his home in Dalian and asked his two-year-old daughter to say 'baba' (dad), she did so. However, when his niece called him uncle, his little girl followed her and thoughtlessly said 'uncle' as well. Xuanye was shocked to hear this and related the following to me:

> She [Xuanye's daughter] had no memories of me, and treated me like other ordinary people. I knew this wasn't right. It was an irresponsible attitude towards her life. Then I discussed it with my wife, and finally I decided to give up my career and terminated cooperation with my partnerships in Ningbo. Then, I went back to Dalian [his hometown].

In addition, a series of incidental intimacies, such as a few words of praise or sitting together at a table, are often seen as a way of 'doing' fatherhood and showing an appropriate masculinity (Wilding, 2018). Recent years have seen an increasing demand for greater parental (and paternal in particular) involvement in the contemporary Chinese parenting culture (Li, 2020). The idea of how to do parenting has become particularly important, especially when one parent is absent from children's everyday lives. In order to build an image of a responsible and caring father, Xuanye reunited with his family members, although he went back to Ningbo again about four years later for reasons of providing greater financial security for his family. It could be argued that men do express feelings and men's emotional attachment and a breadwinner role can coexist (Dermott, 2003). Recent literature suggests that intimate fathering cannot be viewed through the same lens as intimate mothering, because men and women have access to different cultural resources and often perform a different work–family role (Dermott, 2003). With the existence of the domestic division of labour between mothers and fathers being clear cut, and men's capacity to financially support the family taken as a display of their masculinity and, more broadly, to 'do' family, men's capacity to perform hands-on care is often limited (Zang, 2011).

Due to the child-centred family pattern being a product of China's one-child policy, family members, albeit it through different means, sought to invest heavily in their relationships with their only child. This is evident in the case of Lianbao (51, married) who works for a company as a manager, living far away from home due to work demands. He said that he would continue financially to support his daughter—25 years old—who had a paid job in their hometown, Dalian, as the below extract shows:

> Every time she calls me, she must have run out of money. I will support her financially if she wants to buy expensive items, have a beauty spa, or take beauty injections. Normally, she will negotiate or ask me if it costs over 5000 yuan [around 620 in GBP]. In most cases, I approved it because I wasn't around, with few opportunities to take care of her. If I'm [financially] capable of supporting her, I will allow her to beautify herself, as girls all love being beautiful. This can also be seen as a way to make up for [the time I've been away from] her.

It is possible to indicate that parents in LATs do value their relationship with children and try to make efforts in different ways to make up for their absence. Similarly, Hua (31, married) and her husband were also living apart as dual-career couples, and their story provides an illustrative example of how they creatively construct a 'normal' family at distance. Living with in-laws to provide childcare on a daily basis, Hua worked in Beijing as a high-school teacher, while her husband served in the army in South China. Being aware of the social phenomenon of *sang ou shi jiaoyu* (widowed parenting), where one parent is severely absent from parenting while leaving the education of children entirely to the other parent (mostly mothers), Hua has come up with 'solutions'. In order to create a male character in her son's everyday life, she moved to a traditional intergenerational co-residence living arrangement. In this way, the role of father was temporarily replaced by another male family member, that is, the children's grandfather. As she explained,

> I often assign tasks to my father-in-law. He needs to raise my son as much as he raised his son, doing everything that a boy should do. Because I literally don't know what it was like growing up as a man, isn't it? So, I was very happy when I saw my father-in-law take my son to climb trees and perform somersaults.

As the interview continued, she demonstrated that compared to the notion of an absent father, she was even more concerned about the 'hands-off image of a father' who was physically present but did not 'really' engage in the children's lives. As Hua explained, 'A father is not just simply a title, instead it means a constant companion. In doing so, he can then become a qualified father.' In this regard, Hua's understanding of family and the notion of fatherhood is in line with Morgan's (1996) idea of the importance of 'doing' in the construction of family and parenting. Instead of 'being' there as a father, she recognised the importance of 'doing' fathering in a way beyond physical proximity in developing father–child intimacy. Due to her husband's work schedule, he can only reunite with family members during the period of his annual leave. Under such circumstance of a father being absent, Hua often sends *xiao shipin* (short videos) by WeChat, which normally last less than a minute, to her husband. As she claimed,

> Occasionally, *Weixin* video chats are not enough to 'quench his thirst'. I'll take some xiao shipin and send them to him. He asked me to take more as well, as he really misses our son. Then he can save and watch them over and over again. This [way of sending short videos] is perhaps more meaningful than having video chats.

Although distance prevents her husband 'doing' fathering in a physical term, the evidence from Hua's narrative suggests that the practices of mobile communication devices can enrich the way of doing fatherhood. Kang's (2012) research examines how Chinese young migrants in London use internet tools to maintain long-distance intimacy with their ageing parents in China. Similarly, Zhou and Gui's (2017) study on Chinese family intergenerational interactions suggests that new media, such as WeChat, play an in-between role in facilitating a 'distant but close' family relationship between parents and children. At the time of our interview, Hua's husband had been away for over five months. It seems that temporarily 'seeing' their young son through video chats could not effectively lessen the father's deep and emotional thoughts when being physically apart from him. This is because of the feature of video chats that all the aural and visual information will end once one of the parties hangs up the phone. By repeatedly watching short videos about his son's mundane everyday practices sent by Hua, he was able to understand that his son was recently 'learning to talk', although he was far away from his family. Accordingly, he would read parenting books delivered by Hua in order to have a better understanding of children's growth. It is through the mediated communication practices that the absent father could 'do' fathering, such as virtually taking part in children's development, and building up knowledge about what had happened to his son every single day.

Due to time limits, children were not included in this study because they remained at school studying during the time of my fieldwork in China. Therefore, there was limited knowledge in relation to their opinions on their parents living separately and how this family living arrangement may influence their perceptions of intimate relationships and family life. These questions could be another future direction for research to engage in.

Conclusion

In this chapter, I have examined the practices of intimacy in the context of geographically distant couples in China. My analysis provides subtleties and nuanced understandings of the various ways people in LATs create, negotiate and reproduce familial ties, through a set of practices of mobile intimacy, emotion and embodied practices of caring. When distance prevents co-presence, the communication technologies have become an integral part of people's everyday lives, and the practice of intimacy is largely restricted to verbal/textual self-disclosure and virtual activities within the context of family separation. My analysis shows that practices of everyday talks and sharing day-to-day types of feelings between separated couples play a role in generating and maintaining a sense of subjective closeness. In this way, people make efforts and act as 'networked individualism' (Rainie & Wellman, 2012) to build relational connections with intimate others, which contests the idea of the breakdown or decentring of family life. I suggest that changes in doing intimacy at a distance do not always, or inevitably, individualise and alienate people from others or sets of conventions and relational ties. Instead, and importantly, this transformation can enable people to adopt a variety of creative approaches to maintaining and enhancing committed heterosexual relationships of love, care and support, challenging claims that the breakdown of relationships has become a late-modern norm. While by no means exclusively, young people are far more likely to disclose intimacy through mediated communication. This is partly due to their extensive digital experience and the early stage in their relationships. Although disclosing intimacy can be mediated digitally, it remains problematic if physical touch and embodied forms of support, for some people, are a primary way of expressing a sense of intimacy and being a 'family' (Gabb & Fink, 2007).

Another dimension of family living that this chapter is concerned with is emotion. Within the context of family relationships, emotional work is performed in various ways. Although gendered stereotypes that have associated men with emotional reticence have been found in this study, this did not mean anything in terms of the depth of feelings experienced in their relationships. While much of the studies on the family practices approach emphasise 'doing', this research provides new insight on how acts of not doing can be articulated as a way of doing family. Both men and women seek and provide emotional support to each other while at the same time consciously 'undo' emotions. This blurs the ways in which emotions are (expected to be) experienced and expressed. It could be argued that practices of hiding and managing emotions can also be seen as important as sharing emotions.

In the split households as a result of the gendered pattern of migration in China, family practices often operate in a way that involves gendered care for family members. Couples living apart does not necessarily mean that women can avoid the obligations of care. Instead, doing gender in conformity with the social expectations of gender roles in the provision of family care has greatly contributed to the stability of the normative forms of 'family' and conjugal intimacy. However, this finding is contrary to previous studies that have suggested changes in the patterns of parent care practices, where women have increased capacity to provide practical, financial and emotional support for their natal family and even refuse to provide old-age support for their in-laws (Liu, 2017). In addition, this chapter also paid attention to the practice of gift-giving as a way of showing love and affection in a familial context. However, gender differences in what to give, when to give and why to give are varied and subject to specific cultural and social contexts. Although it is seen as instrumental, men's practices of giving certain types of gifts are intertwined with their practices of gender and masculinity construction.

Despite very few male participants included in this study, their narratives about practices of parent–child intimacy at a distance have still proved useful and therefore are included in this chapter. When faced with the missing 'father figure' in the family, mothers sometimes have to reflectively work out how to rebuild a family environment where their (male) children can construct a sense of masculinity, as they perceived it. My analysis also shows that Chinese fathers are actively finding ways to engage in children's daily lives, although they are geographically apart, which supports the evidence from previous studies that Chinese fathers are more engaged and involved with their children (Li, 2020; Li & Lamb, 2013). Through the examination of the 'doing' of intimacy among people in non-conventional partnerships, this research discussed various ways in which people reflexively construct and make sense of their intimate relationships and family lives, and argued that people generate and sustain intimacy in ways that are shaped by gender norms and the cultural practices and social conventions of 'family' in China.

References

Aresu, A. (2009). Sex education in modern and contemporary China: Interrupted debates across the last century. *International Journal of Educational Development, 29*(5), 532–541.

Bauman, Z. (2003). *Liquid love: On the frailty of human bonds.* Polity Press.

Bawin-Legros, B. (2004). Intimacy and the new sentimental order. *Current Sociology, 52*(2), 241–250. https://doi.org/10.1177/0011392104041810

Beck, U., & Beck-Gernsheim, E. (2002). *Individualization.* Sage.

Blumstein, P., & Schwartz, P. (1983). *American couples: Money, work, sex.* William Morrow.

Cancian, F. (1986). The feminization of love. *Signs, 11*(4), 692–709.

Carter, J. (2012). What is commitment? Women's accounts of intimate attachment. *Families, Relationships and Societies, 1*(2), 137–153. https://doi.org/10.1332/204674312X645484

Carter, J., Duncan, S., Stoilova, M., & Phillips, M. (2016). Sex, love and security: Accounts of distance and commitment in living apart together relationships. *Sociology, 50*(3), 576–593.

Chan, A. K., Denton, L. T., & Tsang, A. (2003). The art of gift giving in China. *Business Horizons, 46*(4), 47–52.

Chen, J. Y. Y., & Lim, S. L. (2012). Factors impacting marital satisfaction among urban mainland Chinese women: A qualitative study. *Asia Pacific Journal of Counselling and Psychotherapy, 3*(2), 149–160.

CNNIC. (2021). *The 48th China Internet Development Statistical Report* [Online]. Retrieved March 10, 2022, from https://www.cnnic.com.cn/IDR/ReportDownloads/

Connell, R. W. (1995). *Masculinities.* University of California Press.

Coyne, S. M., Stockdale, L., Busby, D., Iverson, B., & Grant, D. M. (2011). "I luv u:)!": A descriptive study of the media use of individuals in romantic relationships. *Family Relations, 60*(2), 150–162.

Delphy, C., & Leonard, D. (1992). *Familiar exploitation.* Polity Press.

Dermott, E. (2003). The 'intimate father': Defining paternal involvement. *Sociological Research Online, 8*(4), 28–38.

Dillon, M. (2009). *Contemporary China: An introduction.* Routledge.

Duncombe, J., & Marsden, D. (1993). Love and intimacy: The gender division of emotion and emotion work. *Sociology, 27*(2), 221–241. https://doi.org/10.1007/978-1-4614-4508-1_4

Duncombe, J., & Marsden, D. (1998). "Stepford wives" and "hollow men"? Doing emotion work, doing gender and "authenticity" in intimate heterosexual relationships. In G. Bendelow & S. J. Williams (Eds.), *Emotions in social life: Critical themes and contemporary issues* (pp. 211–227). Routledge.

Elliott, S., & Umberson, D. (2008). The performance of desire: Gender and sexual negotiation in long-term marriages. *Journal of Marriage and Family, 70*(2), 391–406.

Elliott, A., & Urry, J. (2010). *Mobile lives*. Routledge.

Erickson, R. (2005). Why emotion work matters: Sex, gender, and the division of household labor. *Journal of Marriage and Family, 67*, 337–351.

Evans, H. (2008). *The subject of gender: Daughters and mothers in urban China*. Rowman and Littlefield Publishers.

Evans, H. (2012). The intimate individual: Perspectives from the mother-daughter relationship in Urban China. In A. Kipnis (Ed.), *Chinese modernity and the individual psyche* (pp. 119–147). Palgrave.

Farrer, J., & Sun, Z. (2003). Extramarital love in Shanghai. *The China Journal, 50*, 1–36.

Finch, J. (1983). *Married to the job: Wives' incorporation in men's work*. George Allen and Unwin.

Finch, J. (1989). *Family obligations and social change*. Polity Press.

Gabb, J. (2008). *Researching intimacy in families*. Palgrave Macmillan.

Gabb, J., & Fink, J. (2007). *Couple relationships in the 21st century*. Palgrave Macmillan. https://doi.org/10.1007/98-3-319-59698-3

Gabb, J., & Fink, J. (2015). Telling moments and everyday experience: Multiple methods research on couple relationships and personal lives. *Sociology, 49*(5), 970–987.

Gerstel, N., & Gross, H. (1984). *Commuter marriage: A study of work and family*. Guildford Press.

Giddens, A. (1991). *Modernity and self-identity*. Polity Press.

Giddens, A. (1992). *The transformation of intimacy*. Polity Press.

Hobbs, M., Owen, S., & Gerber, L. (2017). Liquid love? Dating apps, sex, relationships and the digital transformation of intimacy. *Journal of Sociology, 53*(2), 271–284.

Hochschild, A. (1979). Emotion work, feeling rules, and social structure. *American Journal of Sociology, 85*(3), 551–575.

Hochschild, A. (1983). *The managed heart: Commercialization of human feeling*. University of California Press.

Holdsworth, C. (2013). *Family and intimate mobilities*. Palgrave Macmillan.

Holmes, M. (2006). Love lives at a distance: Distance relationships over the life-course. *Sociological Research Online, 11*(3), 70–80.

Holmes, M. (2010a). Intimacy, distance relationships and emotional care. *Recherches Sociologiques et Anthropologiques, 41*(1), 105–123.

Holmes, M. (2010b). The emotionalization of reflexivity. *Sociology, 44*(1), 139–154. https://doi.org/10.1177/0038038509351616

Holmes, M. (2014). *Distant relationships: Intimacy and emotions amongst academics and their partners in dual locations*. Palgrave Macmillan.

Holmes, M. (2015). Men's emotions: Heteromasculinity, emotional reflexivity, and intimate relationships. *Men and Masculinities, 18*(2), 176–192. https://doi.org/10.1177/1097184X14557494

Holmes, M., & Wilding, R. (2019). Intimacies at a distance: An introduction. *Emotion, Space and Society, 32*, 1–4. https://doi.org/10.1016/j.emospa.2019.100590

Illouz, E. (1997). *Consuming the romantic utopia*. University of California Press.

Jackson, S., & Ho, P. S. Y. (2020). *Women doing intimacy*. Palgrave Macmillan.

James, N. (1989). Emotional labour: Skill and work in the social regulation of feelings. *The Sociological Review, 37*(1), 15–42.

Jamieson, L. (1998). *Intimacy: Personal relationships in modern societies*. Polity Press.

Jamieson, L. (2011). Intimacy as a concept: Explaining social change in the context of globalisation or another form of ethnocentricism? *Sociological Research Online, 16*(4), 151–163.

Jamieson, L. (2013). Personal relationships, intimacy and the self in a mediated and global digital age. In K. Orton-Johnson & N. Prior (Eds.), *Digital sociology: Critical perspectives* (pp. 13–33). Palgrave Macmillan.

Jankowiak, W., & Li, X. (2017). Emergent conjugal love, mutual affection, and female marital power. In G. Santos & S. Harrell (Eds.), *Transforming patriarchy: Chinese families in the twenty-first century* (pp. 146–162). University of Washington Press.

Joy, A. (2001). Gift giving in Hong Kong and the continuum of social ties. *Journal of Consumer Research, 28*(2), 239–256.

Juhasz, A., & Bradford, K. (2016). Mobile phone use in romantic relationships. *Marriage and Family Review, 52*(8), 707–721.

Kang, T. (2012). Gendered media, changing intimacy: Internet-mediated transnational communication in the family sphere. *Media Culture Society, 34*(2), 146–161.

Kim, Y. (2012). Ethnographer location and the politics of translation: Researching one's own group in a host country. *Qualitative Research, 12*(2), 131–146.

Kyung-Sup, C., & Min-Young, S. (2010). The stranded individualizer under compressed modernity: South Korean women in individualization without individualism. *British Journal of Sociology, 61*(3), 539–564. https://doi.org/10.1111/j.1468-4446.2010.01325.x

Lewis, R. (1978). Emotional intimacy among men. *Journal of Social Issues, 34*(1), 108–121.

Li, X. (2020). Fathers' involvement in Chinese societies: Increasing presence, uneven progress. *Child Development Perspectives, 14*(3), 150–156.

Li, X., & Lamb, M. E. (2013). Fathers in Chinese culture: From stern disciplinarians to involved parents. In D. W. Shwalb, B. J. Shwalb, & M. E. Lamb (Eds.), *Fathers in cultural context* (pp. 15–41). Taylor & Francis Group.

Licoppe, C. (2004). 'Connected' presence: The emergence of a new repertoire for managing social relationships in a changing communication technoscape. *Environment and Planning D: Society and Space, 22*(1), 135–156.

Liu, J. (2017). Intimacy and intergenerational relations in rural China. *Sociology, 51*(5), 1034–1049. https://doi.org/10.1177/0038038516639505

Lo, V. H., So, C. Y., & Zhang, G. (2010). The influence of individualism and collectivism on internet pornography exposure, sexual attitudes, and sexual behavior among college students. *Chinese Journal of Communication, 3*(1), 10–27.

Louie, K. (2015). *Chinese masculinities in a globalizing world*. Routledge. https://doi.org/10.4324/9781315884646

Luo, W., & Yu, J. (2022). Sexual infidelity among the married in China. *Chinese Journal of Sociology, 8*(3), 374–397. Online First. https://doi.org/10.1177/2057150X221108574

Mauss, M. (1990 [1925]). *The gift: The form and reason for exchange in archaic societies* (trans. W.D. Halls). Routledge.

McDaniel, B. T., Drouin, M., & Cravens, J. D. (2017). Do you have anything to hide? Infidelity-related behaviors on social media sites and marital satisfaction. *Computers in Human Behavior, 66*, 88–95.

Morgan, D. (1996). *Family connections: An introduction to family studies*. Polity Press.

Morgan, D. (2011). *Rethinking family practices*. Palgrave Macmillan.

Morgan, D. (2020). Family practices in time and space. *Gender, Place & Culture, 27*(5), 733–743. https://doi.org/10.1080/0966369X.2018.1541870

Nguyen, H., & Munch, J. (2010). Romantic gift giving as chore or pleasure: The effects of attachment orientations on gift giving perceptions. *Journal of Business Research, 64*, 113–118.

Osburg, J. (2013). *Anxious wealth: Money and morality among China's new rich*. Stanford University Press.

Pan, S. [潘绥铭]. (2017). *2000–2015 年中国人的'全性'. [The Chinese Sexuality, 2000–2015]*. 1908 Press (in Chinese).

Qi, X. (2015). Filial obligation in contemporary China: Evolution of the culture-system. *Journal for the Theory of Social Behaviour, 45*(1), 141–161. https://doi.org/10.1111/jtsb.12052

Qi, X. (2016). Family bond and family obligation: Continuity and transformation. *Journal of Sociology, 52*(1), 39–52.

Qiu, S. (2020). Chinese 'study mothers' in living apart together (LAT) relationships: Educational migration, family practices, and gender roles. *Sociological Research Online, 25*(3), 405–420.

Qiu, S. (2022a). Family practices in non-cohabiting intimate relationships in China: Doing mobile intimacy, emotion and intergenerational caring practices. *Families, Relationships and Societies, 11*(2), 175–191. https://doi.org/10.1332/204674321X16468493162777

Qiu, S. (2022b). Negotiating intimacy and family at distance: Living apart together relationships in China. In S. Quaid, C. Hugman, & A. Wilcock (Eds.), *Negotiating families and personal lives in the 21st century* (pp. 77–92). Routledge. https://doi.org/10.4324/9781003039433

Rainie, L., & Wellman, B. (2012). *Networked: The new social operating system*. MIT Press.

Reddy, W. M. (2009). Historical research on the self and emotions. *Emotion Review, 1*(4), 302–315.

Rettie, R. (2008). Mobile phones as network capital: Facilitating connections. *Mobilities, 3*(2), 291–311.

Robinson, V., & Hockey, J. (2011). *Masculinities in transition*. Palgrave Macmillan.

Settles, B. H., Sheng, X., Zang, Y., & Zhao, J. (2013). The one-child policy and its impact on Chinese families. In K. Chan (Ed.), *International handbook of Chinese families* (pp. 627–646). Springer.

Sigman, S. (1991). Handling the discontinuous aspects of continuing social relationships: Towards research of the persistence of social forms. *Communication Theory, 1*, 106–127.

Song, L., Li, S., & Feldman, M. W. (2012). Out-migration of young adults and gender division of intergenerational support in rural China. *Research on Aging, 34*(4), 399–424. https://doi.org/10.1177/0164027511436321

Tyler, T. R. (2002). Is the Internet changing social life? It seems the more things change, the more they stay the same. *Journal of Social Issues, 58*(1), 195–205.

Valentine, G. (2006). Globalizing intimacy: The role of information and communication technologies in maintaining and creating relationships. *Women's Studies Quarterly, 34*(1/2), 365–393.

van Hoof, J. (2013). *Modern couples? Continuity of change in heterosexual relationships*. Routledge.

Vetere, F., Gibbs, M., Kjeldskov, J., Howard, S., Pedell, S., Mecoles, K., & Mueller, F. (2005). Mediating intimacy: Designing technologies to support strong-tie relationships. In *Conference on human factors in computing systems association for computing machinery*.

Wajcman, J. (2008). Life in the fast lane? Towards a sociology of technology and time. *British Journal of Sociology, 59*, 59–77.

Wang, X. (2016). *Social media in industrial China*. UCL Press.

Whitehead, S. M. (2002). *Men and masculinities*. Polity.
Wilding, R. (2006). Virtual intimacies? Families communicating across transnational contexts. *Global Networks, 6*(2), 125–142.
Wilding, R. (2018). *Families, intimacy and globalization: Floating ties*. Palgrave Macmillan.
Wong, M. (2020). *Everyday masculinities in 21st-century China: The making of able-responsible men*. Hong Kong University Press.
Xiao, S. (2011). The "second-wife" phenomenon and the relational construction of class-coded masculinities in contemporary China. *Men and Masculinities, 14*(5), 607–627.
Xu, A., & Xia, Y. (2014). The changes in mainland Chinese families during the social transition: A critical analysis. *Journal of Comparative Family Studies, 45*(1), 31–53.
Yan, Y. (2010). The Chinese path to individualization. *British Journal of Sociology, 61*(3), 489–512.
Yan, Y. (2016). Intergenerational intimacy and descending familism in rural North China. *American Anthropologist, 118*(2), 244–257.
Yang, M. M. (1994). *Gifts, favors, and banquets: The art of social relationships in China*. Cornell University Press.
Yang, G. (2012). A Chinese Internet? History, practice, and globalization. *Chinese Journal of Communication, 5*(1), 49–54.
Yang, H.-C. (2014). Young people's friendship and love relationships and technology: New practices of intimacy and rethinking feminism. *Asian Journal of Women's Studies, 20*(1), 93–124. https://doi.org/10.1080/12259276.2014.11666174
Zang, X. (2011). Family and marriage. In X. Zhang (Ed.), *Understanding Chinese society* (pp. 35–48). Sage.
Zelizer, V. A. (2005). *The purchase of intimacy*. Princeton University Press.
Zhang, L. (2010). *In search of paradise: Middle class living in a Chinese Metropolis*. Cornell University Press.
Zhang, L., Li, X., & Shah, I. H. (2007). Where do Chinese adolescents obtain knowledge of sex? Implications for sex education in China. *Health Education, 107*(4), 351–363.
Zhang, N., Parish, W. L., Huang, Y., & Pan, S. (2012). Sexual infidelity in China: Prevalence and gender specific correlates. *Archives of Sexual Behavior, 41*(4), 861–873.
Zhang, Y., Wang, X., & Pan, S. (2021). Prevalence and patterns of extramarital sex among Chinese men and women: 2000–2015. *Journal of Sex Research, 58*(1), 41–50.
Zhou, C., & Guang, H. (2007). Gift giving culture in China and its cultural values. *Intercultural Communication Studies, 16*(2), 81–93.

Zhou, B., & Gui, S. (2017). WeChat and distant family intergenerational communication in China: A study of online content sharing on WeChat. In K. Xue & M. Yu (Eds.), *New media and Chinese society. Communication, culture and change in Asia* (Vol. 5, pp. 185–206). Springer. https://doi.org/10.1007/978-981-10-6710-5_11

Zhou, B., & Xiao, M. (2015). Locative social media engagement and intergenerational relationships in China. In L. Hjorth & O. Khoo (Eds.), *The Routledge handbook of new media in Asia* (pp. 219–228). Routledge.

CHAPTER 6

Conclusion

This research has paid specific attention to the living apart together (LAT) relationship in the context of contemporary China. With a focus on the intersection of tradition and detraditionalisation of intimate lives, the cultural legacy of Confucianism, and rising individualism, the central aim of this study has been to examine how this group of people living outside the conventional family make sense of, negotiate and reproduce family life and maintain intimacy across physical distance. Literature on transformations of intimacy, individualisation, relationality, family practices and intimacy have fundamentally framed this research focus. Considering that LAT relationships (LATs) have not been systematically researched in China, I drew on contemporary sociological and feminist studies to expand my perspective on the lived experiences of Chinese women in LATs. This first in-depth qualitative research makes an original contribution to the literature on family life and intimate relationships by providing new empirical evidence of the cultural specificity of family practices and intimacy in the context of an ever-shifting Chinese society.

My data on 39 LAT people (including only four men) provide rich and detailed accounts of how Chinese people reflexively negotiate gender roles and construct family lives under the context of contemporary Chinese society. In order to investigate whether and to what extent China has undergone the detraditionalisation of family life, this book has extensively discussed relational practices of agency in living a desired co-residential partnership, everyday practices of 'doing' family and identity construction, and the strategies that people have employed to maintain intimacy when relating at distance. These three themes were chosen and examined as the interview data confirmed the salience of these aspects of everyday practices among LAT people. In addition to my personal curiosity about people's experiences of living in diverse family forms, my focus on mundane and everyday family life is deeply inspired by Hockey et al. (2007) and Lefebvre's (1991) work. As Lefebvre (1991: 97) maintains, everyday life is 'profoundly related to all activities, and encompasses them with all their differences and their conflicts; it is their meeting place, their bond and their common ground'. Rather than viewing these aspects as a concrete entity, they are closely related, and all play a role in the construction of family lives as circumstances change.

Despite the small number of people involved, placing their subjective narratives in their wider social and cultural context helps to unpack how women at different life stages negotiate the changing patterns of personal life. Participants' accounts of their personal relationships and family lives indicate little evidence of the detraditionalisation of family life, despite the fact that younger generations do have more freedom and become individualised, compared with their parents' generation, at least in some aspects of their personal life. Compared to people who were born under Mao's era (1949–1976), the post-reform (1978 onwards) generation of young people, under China's one-child policy in particular, tend to be exposed to the Western culture of individualisation and embrace more individualised lifestyles according to their own choice, while a long-term monogamous marital partnership remains of paramount concern for all, including young participants in my study. When Chinese young people make decisions regarding their own intimate relationships, the collective family is still being taken into account, demonstrating the remnants of Confucian values on family life. This reflects that the long-standing Confucian patriarchal tradition (even if in some ways weakened) and institutional arrangements are seen to go hand in hand with the rise and influence of Western individualism and detraditionalisation. People can hardly make sense of changes in their intimate lives without considerations of the web of relationships and local context in which they are embedded. In this regard, relationships are not experienced and sustained merely on the basis of mutual satisfaction, as suggested by Giddens (1992). The ways in which people organise and construct their everyday family lives are highly relational (Smart, 2007) and, in some cases, bear the imprints of Confucian thinking, in the sense that practices deemed traditional may be reinvented and made use of under modern conditions.

Through a closer examination of the motivations and reasons underlying people's LATs, agency was discussed in Chap. 3. I have examined how far women exercise purposive agency and to what extent their agency was relationally and emotionally constrained. Chinese society has a long tradition of holding the core values of familism. However, the coexistence of the growth of individualism and the processes of modernisation and detraditionalisation has served as a good illustration of how agency can be defined as a relational practice. In my effort to understand the complexities and intricacies of people's practices of agency in their LATs, I took into account of the importance of relational bonds and the specific social and cultural context under which individuals make their choices in living their family lives. People's narratives about their LATs and the ways in which they respond to changes are highly relational and contextual. When LAT is chosen as a negative-preference response to external structuring constraints, a sense of vulnerability to limited financial resources and caring responsibilities emerged, leading to some women being left behind to support the family. In this sense, family life is essentially shaped and constructed surrounding the gendered family roles and maintained through gender inequalities. As such, family contributions are perceived in a gendered way as reflected in this study. In emphasising the relationality of women's LAT practices, people invest enormously in undertaking gendered roles as mothers, daughters and spouses. Although some young women in this study do exercise a certain amount of purposive and agentic agency in living apart so as to sustain personal autonomy while keeping couple intimacy, the 'conventional' ideas of living a 'normative' family life with intimate others and prescribed gender roles continue to shape the ways people negotiate and make sense of their personal lives. Despite the fact that women in my study indicated varying degrees of freedom and autonomy offered by LAT, it should be acknowledged that none of them intended to use LAT as a strategy for 'undoing' gender (Upton-Davis, 2015), or an alternative way to do coupledom (Levin, 2004). In China, moving to a co-residential partnership and living together as a couple with dependent children envisaged at some point in life still seem to be appealing.

By shining a spotlight on those whose agency in living a coresidential partnership was relationally constrained by existing caring obligations to their children, such as the study mothers, I specifically explored the split household driven by children's education in Chap. 4. By applying Morgan's (1996, 2011) 'practices' approach to the non-Western context, I asked how the gendered experiences of Chinese 'study mothers' has impacted upon their everyday practices of 'doing' family and identity construction. As Jackson (2006, 2013) argues in relation to dimensions of gender and heterosexuality, practices and discourse (of what it means to be a 'good' or 'proper' mother) are 'mutually implicated', as everyday practices are themselves implicated in discourses (for instance through the examples used to support an understanding of a 'good' family in popular culture (Morgan, 2011: 68–69)).

For a woman, being a full-time study mother, even when it is at the cost of living separately from her partner and established career development, has been considered as a way to privilege 'motherhood' over 'wifehood', as part of 'womanhood'. This kind of taken-for-granted gendered family practice has merged with gender practices, whereby women are still expected to fulfil their feminine roles as mothers in an old-fashioned way (such as providing children with emotional support and preparing their daily meals), despite the fact that they may also suffer emotional loss themselves during the time of accompanying their children to study. The fathers, in this study, are often expected to provide continuous financial support as a way of 'doing' family while being absent from their wife and children in their daily lives. These dramatically opposite parenting roles reinforce and entrench the existing traditional gendered division of labour and gender hierarchy in contemporary Chinese society. Based on my participants' narratives of the everyday 'doing' of family, I have argued how family is culturally constructed and practised in order to reclaim conventional forms of family and gender norms in Chinese social, historical and cultural contexts. Family practices in the multi-locale household setting can take place in many different forms of living arrangements and people's practices of intimacy are often implicated with practices of gender, class and social norms.

Another central issue that this book has been concerned with is the ways people experience family mobilities and how people develop and maintain intimacy in the mediated digital age. In Chap. 5, I draw on Jamieson's (1999, 2011) concept of practices of intimacy and take a step forward to examine the practices of information and communication technologies (ICTs) through which mobile intimacy has been shaped and rebuilt. It is undoubted that communication technology changes the way people communicate and the practices of mobile intimacy through texting, and audio and video activities have blurred the distinction between presence and absence. However, my data show little evidence of the decentring of monogamous partnerships driven by social and technological change, tearing apart family and intimate relationships. Instead, discussion of practices of intimacy across distance has seen physical intimacy transformed into other forms of intimacy in which people make efforts and act as networked agents to enhance existing relations in the affective context.

It was evident from participants' narratives that practical doing and giving by exchanging gifts were also appreciated and seen as a way of expressing love and exclusiveness. This finding resonates with those of Jamieson (1999, 2011) and Gabb (2008) but is in contradiction with Giddens (1992) who placed greater emphasis on 'knowing' and regarded mutual self-disclosure as at the heart of forming a democratic type of intimate relationship. More importantly, as I have earlier argued that family practices are conditioned by and fit with social and cultural norms, so too might practices of intimacy. Given the specific Chinese social and cultural context where filial piety (*xiao*) has been seen as central to Confucian family values, women, as wives and daughters-in-law, are expected not only to take care of their own conjugal family but also the extended family, especially when men are working away from home. Zhang's (2016) research on young Chinese mothers' negotiations of familial obligations found out the importance of not only being filial to the elderly parents, but also displaying xiao, in the maintenance of (intergenerational) familial relationships. By interviewing women (married, in particular) in LATs, my research confirmed the importance of being filial to the elderly. However, I would argue that women's practice of familial obligations and taking care of the elderly were also highly valued and appreciated by their husbands, and were seen as important in the maintenance of heterosexual marital intimacy. A sense of obligation to elderly parents and these practices of intergenerational care are closely implicated with practices of conjugal intimacy and gender roles. Arguably, intimacy can be related to the 'doing' of gender, and 'doing' family according to gender roles, as well as practices of filial piety in China.

In addition, emotional aspects of support and caring were also given important emphasis by LAT people in the construction of intimacy. When distance prevents embodied forms of caring, both men and women in my sample valued verbal forms of emotional support provided by the absent partner, with women giving more but receiving less from their male counterpart. This gendered emotionality, despite being evidenced by the small sample size of the male participants in this research, can be seen to generate contradictions between couples and become a greater source of unhappiness among heterosexual couples. However, my data challenge the traditional conception of gendered emotionality, as men in the study do exercise emotion and can be reflexive about their feelings to their partner. In fact, both men and women seek and provide emotional support to each other while at the same time consciously 'undo' emotions. This is because practices of hiding and managing emotions are also seen by LAT people as a way of caring and doing intimacy.

Through looking at the subtleties and nuances of Chinese women's experiences of LATs, the data, on the whole, have shown that the participants were quite conservative in their attitudes with regard to marriage and family relations, and thereby there was little evidence throughout my interviews to support the view that people in LATs tend to deprioritise love and commitment, leading to detraditionalisation of marriage as an institution. In addition, my data provide little evidence to support the idea that China has undergone the same (if much debated) transformation as in Western societies, inherent in the theory of individualisation and the assumed, attendant transformation of intimacy, in particular. Under the lingering patriarchal family system and what could be seen as, in some ways at least, the revival of Confucianism, people's lifestyles are still expected to conform to traditional prescribed gender roles and adhere to social norms, whilst simultaneously finding a way to assert their own desires and individualised choices.

Noticeably, it should be borne in mind that, in the context of this book, data were collected in two research sites in China (Beijing and Liaoning Province). Therefore, this research cannot provide a full picture of people in LATs in China. The findings of this study are drawn from in-depth face-to-face interviews that I conducted with 35 women and 4 men who, during the time of my fieldwork, were in LATs. Although my sample, on the whole, can be seen as diverse in terms of age, educational level and social background, far less variation within generations and geographic locations was noted. The majority of the participants I recruited in Beijing were well-educated (young) people with relatively well-paid jobs. In contrast, in Liaoning Province, the majority of participants were born into working-class families and said that they had no choice but to leave one person at home to take care of other family members, whereas their partner (normally the male) worked away to earn money. However, though differences could still be seen between those women who were brought up in wealthy families in Liaoning and lived separately from their partners and other groups, the lack of a more extensive intra-regional differences in my sample meant that the findings of this research do not therefore represent a wider population, albeit the participants had multiple occupations and varied in age. With the large geographical variations in China, as a vast country, one possibility for future study could be to pay special attention to the variations between urban and rural locations so as to gain a wider picture of people's experiences and perceptions of intimate relationships.

Holmes (2004) used joint interviews to study dual-career couples in distance relationships, which she found useful to understand changes for couple relationships. However, this research did not use this method due to the fact that partners were away for different reasons during the course of my fieldwork in China. Therefore, the ways in which men 'do' family and maintain intimacy across distance remain indiscernible. Future study would be benefited by including a wider group of men's voices and investigating specifically how masculinity informs their everyday family practices and the meaning they attached to intimacy. Joint interviews in future work could also provide a new perspective in understanding how individuals present themselves as couples during the knowledge co-construction process.

Unfortunately, the viewpoints of children while their parents were living separately were not included because they were under 18 and remained at school studying. Therefore, future research with a greater focus on children is suggested to explore the implications that parents' LATs have placed on their perceptions of love, marriage and family relationships. Lastly, older people's attitudes toward LATs could also be a productive focus, given the fact that there is a growing number of Chinese 'floating grandparents' who migrate with their adult children to the city in order to provide childcare (Qi, 2018).

References

Gabb, J. (2008). *Researching intimacy in families*. Palgrave Macmillan.
Giddens, A. (1992). *The transformation of intimacy*. Polity Press.
Hockey, J., Meanh, A., & Robinson, V. (2007). *Mundane heterosexualities: From theory to practices*. Palgrave Macmillan.

Holmes, M. (2004). An equal distance? Individualisation, gender and intimacy in distance relationships. *The Sociological Review, 52*(2), 180–200. https://doi.org/10.1111/j.1467-954x.2004.00464.x

Jackson, S. (2006). Gender, sexuality and heterosexuality: The complexity (and limits) of heteronormativity. *Feminist Theory, 7*(1), 105–121.

Jackson, S. (2013). Sexuality, heterosexuality and gender hierarchy. In C. Ingraham (Ed.), *Thinking straight: The power, the promise, and the paradox of heterosexuality* (pp. 15–37). Routledge.

Jamieson, L. (1999). Intimacy transformed? *Sociology, 33*(10), 477–494. https://doi.org/10.1080/08858190209528804

Jamieson, L. (2011). Intimacy as a concept: Explaining social change in the context of globalisation or another form of ethnocentricism? *Sociological Research Online, 16*(4), 151–163.

Lefebvre, H. (1991). *Critique of everyday life, Volume 1: Introduction* (translated by J. Moore). Verso.

Levin, I. (2004). Living Apart Together: A new family form. *Current Sociology, 52*(2), 223–240.

Morgan, D. (1996). *Family connections: An introduction to family studies.* Polity Press.

Morgan, D. (2011). *Rethinking family practices.* Palgrave Macmillan.

Qi, X. (2018). Floating grandparents: Rethinking family obligation and intergenerational support. *International Sociology, 33*(6), 761–777. https://doi.org/10.1177/0268580918792777

Smart, C. (2007). *Personal life: New directions in sociological thinking.* Polity.

Upton-Davis, K. (2015). Subverting gendered norms of cohabitation: Living Apart Together for women over 45. *Journal of Gender Studies, 24*(1), 104–116.

Zhang, Y. (2016). Practising and displaying xiao—Young mothers' negotiations of obligations to elders. *Journal of Chinese sociology, 3*(1), 1–20.

Appendices

178 APPENDICES

Table A.1 List of the socio-demographics of 39 participants

	Name	Age	Education level	Marital status	No. of children	Occupation	Site of fieldwork	Method of recruitment
1	An	23	MA	Unmarried	N/A	Graduate student	Beijing	WeChat
2	Nan	24	MA	Unmarried	N/A	Village cadre	Beijing	WeChat
3	Mei	34	BA	Married	N/A	Engineer	Beijing	WeChat
4	Huangzhe	25	College	Unmarried	N/A	Education agent	Beijing	WeChat
5	Xiajie	27	MA	Unmarried	N/A	HR	Beijing	WeChat
6	Yunyue	24	MA	Unmarried	N/A	Graduate student	Beijing	Intermediary—friend A
7	Xiaobo	26	MA	Married	N/A	Accountant	Beijing	WeChat
8	Maixi	30	BA	Married	N/A	Fast food manager	Beijing	Snowballing (from Yunyue)
9	Qingshu	30	MA	Married	F-2 years	Self-employed	Beijing	WeChat
10	Xueyi	25	College	Unmarried	N/A	Hotel receptionist	Beijing	Met by chance
11	Bingyu	29	BA	Married	N/A	Teacher	Beijing	WeChat
12	Rosy	46	BA	Married	M-16 years	Study mother	Beijing	Met by chance
13	Hua	31	MA	Married	M-2 years	High-school teacher	Beijing	Intermediary—high-school teacher
14	Yufen	32	MA	Married	F-6 years, F-3 years	High-school teacher	Beijing	Intermediary—high-school teacher
15	Jieyu	45	Primary school	Married	F-21 years, F-15 years	Hotel cleaner	Beijing	Met by chance
16	Tiantian	26	BA	Unmarried	N/A	Travel agent	Beijing	Intermediary—friend B
17	Lianbao	51	College	Married	F-25 years	Vice manager	Beijing	Intermediary—old sister
18	Linjuan	32	BA	Unmarried	N/A	Accountant	Beijing	Intermediary—old sister
19	Xuanye	39	BA	Married	F-11 years	Vice manager	Beijing	Intermediary—old sister
20	Jiangling	47	Primary school	Married	M-24 years, F-20 years	Maternity matron	Beijing	Snowballed (from Rosy's colleague)

21	Xinyi	27	BA	Married	N/A	Primary school teacher	Beijing	WeChat
22	Jiajia	23	MA	Unmarried	N/A	Graduate student	Beijing	WeChat
23	Zhuli	25	BA	Unmarried	N/A	Self-employed	Beijing	Intermediary—Friend C
24	Beibei	28	BA	Married	N/A	Public servant	Beijing	Snowballed (from Zhuli)
25	Zhonglan	24	BA	Unmarried	N/A	Graduate student	Liaoning	WeChat
26	Yuqing	30	BA	Married	N/A	Education agent	Liaoning	WeChat
27	Liangjing	45	BA	Married	M-17 years	Self-employed	Liaoning	Intermediary—my father
28	Pingping	45	Middle school	Married	F-17 years	In-house tailor	Liaoning	Intermediary—my relatives
29	Anli	41	Middle school	Married	N/A	Housewife	Liaoning	Intermediary—my relatives
30	Yafang	51	Middle school	Married	F-28 years	Housewife	Liaoning	Intermediary—my relatives
31	Hongli	40	Middle school	Married	M-18 years	Study mother (with a part-time job)	Liaoning	Intermediary—community director
32	Wangyang	38	High school	Married	M-9 years	Electricity fee collector	Liaoning	Intermediary—my father
33	Wanglei	56	College	Married	M-32 years	Retired	Liaoning	Intermediary—my relatives
34	Guanya	37	Middle school	Married	M-16 years M-16 years	Study mother	Liaoning	Intermediary—community director
35	Qiangyan	46	High school	Married	M-17 years F-15 years	Study mother	Liaoning	Intermediary—community director
36	Shanrui	28	Middle school	Married	F-6 years F-12 months	Housewife	Liaoning	Intermediary—my relatives
37	Minzhou	38	Middle school	Married	M-16 years	Study mother	Liaoning	Intermediary—community director
38	Xutong	40	Middle school	Married	M-17 years	Study mother	Liaoning	Intermediary—community director
39	Zhaowen	52	Primary school	Married	F-29 years	Nursing worker	Liaoning	Intermediary—community director

Index

A
Agency, 32
　relational, 75
Autonomy, 2, 8, 12, 13, 18, 33, 43, 45, 49, 65–67, 71, 73, 75, 78, 84, 85, 87, 90, 91, 155, 171

C
Child-centred, 156
Chinese
　context, 36
　society, 1
Cohabitation, 5, 10–12, 31, 46, 68, 87
Communication technologies, 135
Confucian values, 9, 99, 101, 123

D
Delayed marriage, 48–53
Detraditionalisation of family life, 169
Diversity, 1

Divorce, 4
Doing family, 102
Duncan, S., 11

E
Education, 1
Educational migration, 111
Elderly parents, 9, 173
Embodied Practices, 148–154
Emotion, 13, 16, 23, 75, 131–161, 174
Emotional work, 159
Equality, 33
Extramarital
　affairs, 46

F
Familism, 40
Family, 23
Family life, 169
Family practices, 2, 21, 23, 32, 34, 35, 41, 53, 54, 78, 79, 83, 86, 91,

98, 101–124, 132, 153, 160, 169, 173, 175
Feminist, 13
Filial obligation, 41
Filial piety, 9, 23, 36, 40, 43, 131–161, 173
Food, 101
Friendship, 11, 12, 76, 84, 85, 132

G
Gender inequalities, 23
Gender roles, 2
Gift giving, 149
Guanxi, 17

H
Hegemonic ideas, 85
Heteronormative family, 89
Heterosexuality, 90
Heterosexual marriage, 153
Heterosexual relations, 77
Homosexuality, 50

I
Identity, 6, 17, 19, 20, 38, 67, 71, 73, 75, 79, 81, 113, 115–122, 124, 133, 147, 170
In-depth interviews, 8, 14
Individualism, 3, 11, 23, 31, 32, 36, 39–41, 45, 47, 53, 65, 66, 78, 79, 85–91, 115, 140, 159, 170, 171
Infidelity, 116
Insider, 15
Intergenerational care, 173
Intergenerational co-residence, 48
Intimacy, 2, 5, 7, 9, 13–16, 19, 21, 23, 31–54, 65, 68, 81–83, 85, 99, 102, 109, 113, 124, 131–161, 169–175
Intimate
  lives, 31
  relationships, 1–5, 8–10, 13, 17, 20, 24, 31–35, 37, 40, 42, 44, 45, 54, 65–68, 76, 83–86, 89, 91, 102, 124, 131–138, 140–144, 147, 152, 156, 159, 161, 169–171, 173, 175

K
Kinship, 32

L
Labour
  force, 16
  market, 38
Life course, 69
Living apart together (LAT), 1–3, 8, 13, 22, 65, 77, 131, 169
Love, 11

M
Marital
  practices, 43
  seperation, 5
  status, 5
Marriage, 39
masculinity, 147
Mate selection, 43
Migrant workers, 6, 70
Migration, 160
Mobile intimacy, 131–161, 172
Mobile phone, 135
Modernisation, 37
Modernity, 32
Motherhood, 79

O

Obligation
  caring, 72
One-child policy, 36

P

Parental involvement, 45
Parent-Child Intimacy, 154–159
Parents
  elderly, 9
Partnership
  coresidential, 171
  heterosexual, 76
Patriarchal family, 174
Patrilineal families, 50
Patrilocal family, 1
Personal network, 17
Positionality, 19–21
Power dynamics, 16, 19–21, 23
Practices of intimacy, 34
Pure relationship, 11, 33, 36, 83, 149

R

Rapport, 15
Reflexivity, 19–21
Relational bonds, 171

Relationality, 66–69, 91, 169
Romantic love, 33
Rural-to-urban, 1

S

Self-reflexivity, 76
Snowball sampling, 17
Status hypergamy, 51
Structure, 66
Study mothers, 23, 97, 104, 109, 115
Subjectivity, 113

T

Traditional family, 78
Transformation of intimacy, 2, 42, 54, 169
Transnational family, 109

V

Vulnerability, 71, 72

W

WeChat, 16, 133, 135

Milton Keynes UK
Ingram Content Group UK Ltd.
UKHW022324141123
432578UK00005B/180